Understanding Dialogue

Linguistic interaction between two people is the fundamental form of communication, yet almost all research in language use focuses on isolated speakers and listeners. In this innovative work, Pickering and Garrod extend the scope of psycholinguistics beyond individuals by introducing communication as a social activity. Drawing on psychological, linguistic, philosophical and sociological research, they expand their theory that alignment across individuals is the basis of communication, through the model of a 'shared workspace account'. In this workspace, interlocutors are actors who jointly manipulate and control the interaction and develop similar representations of both language and social context, in order to achieve communicative success. The book also explores dialogue within groups, technologies and the role of culture more generally. Providing a new understanding of cognitive representation, this trailblazing work will be highly influential in the fields of linguistics, psychology and cognitive science.

MARTIN PICKERING is Professor of the Psychology of Language and Communication at the University of Edinburgh. He served as editor of the *Journal of Memory and Language*, was recipient of the Experimental Psychology Society mid-career award, and is a Fellow of the Royal Society of Edinburgh.

SIMON GARROD is Professor of Cognitive Psychology at the University of Glasgow. He was awarded the Distinguished Scientific Contribution Award by the Society for Text and Discourse. Between 1989 and 1999 he was also Deputy Director of the ESRC Human Communication Research Centre. He is a Fellow of the Royal Society of Edinburgh.

T0381686

Understanding Dialogue

Language Use and Social Interaction

Martin J. Pickering

University of Edinburgh

Simon Garrod

University of Glasgow

CAMBRIDGE
UNIVERSITY PRESS

CAMBRIDGE
UNIVERSITY PRESS

University Printing House, Cambridge CB2 8BS, United Kingdom

One Liberty Plaza, 20th Floor, New York, NY 10006, USA

477 Williamstown Road, Port Melbourne, VIC 3207, Australia

314–321, 3rd Floor, Plot 3, Splendor Forum, Jasola District Centre,
New Delhi – 110025, India

79 Anson Road, #06–04/06, Singapore 079906

Cambridge University Press is part of the University of Cambridge.

It furthers the University's mission by disseminating knowledge in the pursuit of
education, learning, and research at the highest international levels of excellence.

www.cambridge.org
Information on this title: www.cambridge.org/9781108473613
DOI: 10.1017/9781108610728

© Martin J. Pickering and Simon Garrod 2021

First published 2021

A catalogue record for this publication is available from the British Library.

ISBN 978-1-108-47361-3 Hardback
ISBN 978-1-108-46193-1 Paperback

Cambridge University Press has no responsibility for the persistence or accuracy
of URLs for external or third-party internet websites referred to in this publication
and does not guarantee that any content on such websites is, or will remain,
accurate or appropriate.

Contents

Part IV   Extending the Shared Workspace Framework

Figures

Tables

Glossary

Alignment. Two individuals are aligned at a given level of representation to the extent that they have the same representation as each other. Alignment has two dimensions (Figure 6.1). First, linguistic alignment involves alignment of linguistic representations, and dialogue model alignment involves alignment of situation models and dialogue game models. Second, focal alignment is short-term and relates to individual steps in the process of alignment, and global alignment is long-term and takes place over the dialogue as a whole (see Section 6.1).

Collective. In a multi-party dialogue, a collective is a group of individuals who play a single conversational role (see Figure 10.2).

Commentary. A commentary is a contribution that has a commentary function. The commentary function is to indicate meta-representations of alignment or misalignment in order to manage subsequent contributions.

A **positive commentary** indicates high confidence in alignment – that is, that the addressee meta-represents alignment. So when the speaker utters *I met John yesterday*, the commentary *uh-huh* indicates that the addressee believes he has the same representation as the speaker, for example with respect to the reference of *John*. The speaker therefore can continue as planned.

A **negative commentary** indicates low confidence in alignment – that is, that the addressee meta-represents misalignment. The commentary *eh?* indicates that the addressee believes that he does not have the same representation as the speaker. In this case, the speaker has to identify the likely misalignment and attempt to repair.

Comparator. A comparator compares a prediction of an action or associated internal state with an actual action or associated internal state and feeds back the comparison to the system that can produce a subsequent action. In our terminology, a monitor is a comparator for language.

Control. There are several types of control of action (including language) relevant to our account.

Closed-loop control is when feedback from the outcome of an action is used to correct that action.

Distributed control is when all agents in a cooperative joint activity exert some control over the activity.

Individual control is when a single agent exerts control over the agent's own actions.

Pseudo-closed-loop control is when the discrepancy between the predicted and actual action is used to modify the action accordingly. It occurs when an agent uses a forward model in monitoring and repair.

Conversational roles. These are the roles that can be distinguished in multi-party dialogue (see Figure 10.3). Dialogue games involve two **players**: the **initiator** (who performs the first move) and the **respondent** (who can complete the game or become the initiator for an embedded game). The **active audience** can play subsequent games but cannot complete the current game. The players and the active audience are the **contributors** – they contribute to the success of the dialogue. The **passive audience** cannot contribute to the dialogue but is taken into account by the players. **Overhearers** also cannot contribute and are not taken into account by the players.

Cooperative joint activity. A kind of joint activity that involves cooperation. See Section 2.1 for extensive discussion.

Depiction is using iconic signs in communication. Such signs may be gestures or sounds that mimic actions and other events.

Designer. The producer of a monologue (such as the writer). The **audience** of a monologue plays an equivalent role to the **passive audience** in a dialogue (see conversational roles).

Dialogue game is how interlocutors interact to achieve their joint goal in the dialogue. For example, an information-seeking game is when one interlocutor interacts with her partner to elicit information and the partner responds accordingly. One interlocutor carries out the initiation move in the game and the other carries out the response move. Initiation moves in dialogue games sometimes correspond to individual speech acts (e.g. the initiation move in an information-seeking game will often correspond to an interrogative speech act).

Dialogue game model is the part of the dialogue planner which enables an interlocutor to keep track of where both interlocutors are in a dialogue game.

Dialogue routine is when interlocutors use the same linguistic expression to refer to the same thing in a particular dialogue (though sometimes the routine will of course persist). See Section 7.1.4.

Forward modelling.

Forward models are mappings from an action command to its predicted outcomes. They have two forms: (1) the forward action model that maps the action command to the representations that lead to the action, and (2) the forward perception model that maps from the representations that lead to the action to the perceptual representation of the action.

Inverse models are the converse mappings, from the perceptual representation to the representations that lead to the action, and from those representations to the action command. In motor control systems, forward and inverse models are typically paired.

An efference copy is a copy of the action command that is used for modelling the action. It provides the input to the forward models.

Implementer. The mechanisms that produces actions and interprets them.

The joint action implementer does so as part of cooperative joint activities.

The dialogue implementer does so as part of dialogue. It makes use of the mechanisms involved in processing language and refers to representations of semantics, syntax and phonology.

Individual activity. Any activity performed by one individual.

Joint activity. Any activity performed by two (or more) individuals.

Joint affordance. A joint affordance is the behaviour in a cooperative joint activity that is enabled by an object or event in that activity. For example, the instrumentation in a large plane jointly affords flying by the pilot and co-pilot, and the sign *John* jointly affords interpretation as part of a dialogue (e.g. the interlocutors treat it as a reference to a particular John).

Joint attention. A and B jointly attend to an entity if they both attend to it (i.e. it is in parallel attention) and the entity is manifest.

Joint intention is when both actors of a cooperative joint activity intend to do something together even when each does not intend to do it alone.

Joint manipulation occurs when both actors manipulate an object as part of a cooperative joint activity. A and B jointly manipulate a buffet if they help each other to sample it; they do not do so if they simply select their own dishes.

Manifest. In a cooperative joint activity involving A and B, an entity is manifest if A is confident that both A and B attend to it and B is confident that A and B attend to it. Entities in the shared workspace are typically (but not necessarily) manifest.

Meta-representation of alignment. An interlocutor meta-represents alignment of X if she is confident that she has the same representation of X as her partner. When this is the case, she **m-tags** her representation of X.

Minimal dyadic conversation. Two interlocutors having a face-to-face, informal conversation.

Monadic cognitive science. Cognitive science in which the constructs are defined with respect to an individual person's mind.

Monitor. A monitor compares a prediction of an utterance or associated internal state (e.g. its semantics, syntax, or phonology) with an actual utterance or associated internal state and feeds back the comparison to the language production system.

    Self-monitoring occurs when an individual monitors her own utterance or associated internal state. (It can use either closed-loop or pseudo-closed-loop control.)

    Other-monitoring occurs when an individual monitors her partner's utterance. (It uses closed-loop control.)

    Joint monitoring occurs when an individual monitors a joint utterance – that is, a combination of her own and her partner's contributions to a dialogue. (It uses closed-loop control.)

Monologue is a form of communication in which the communicator cannot receive any response from the audience. It involves two roles: the **designer** and the **audience**.

Parallel attention. *A* and *B* attend to an entity in parallel if they both attend to it.

Planner. The mechanisms that plans actions and interprets those plans.

    The joint action planner does so as part of cooperative joint activities.

    The dialogue planner does so as part of dialogue. It makes use of the mechanisms involved in processing dialogue games and situation models.

Prediction-by-association is prediction based on associations between events. For example, if *A* has previously observed that X precedes Y, then when *A* sees X, *A* predicts Y.

Prediction-by-simulation is prediction based on simulating another's action. For example, when *A* is attempting to shake hands with *B*, *A* can predict *B*'s upcoming hand position by imagining preparing her own hand movements and treating them as *B*'s movements (though potentially adjusting for differences between *A* and *B*). When *A* is listening to *B*, *A* can predict *B*'s utterance by imagining preparing her own utterance and treating it as *B*'s utterance.

Production and action command. An **action command** emanates from an action planner and initiates two processes. One process produces the behaviour and the other process produces the predicted perception of the behaviour. See Section 3.1. A **production command** is the linguistic equivalent of an action command. The production implementer converts the production command into a series of linguistic representations (semantics, syntax and phonology). The production command also instigates processes leading to a predicted percept of the utterance being produced. See Section 5.2.

Props are entities that are involved in a cooperative joint activity. Props need not be 'static' objects, but can also be changing aspects of the environment. For example, the band music constitutes a prop for tango dancers. See also Section 11.1.

Reference is when a linguistic expression is used to correspond to a particular entity. The entity can exist in the world, but it also can be represented in a person's mind.

Representational parity is equivalence between the representations involved in (for example) language production and language comprehension.

Salience is the state or quality of an item that makes it stands out from its neighbours.

Shared workspace. In a cooperative joint activity involving A and B, the shared workspace contains entities that are in A and B's parallel attention.

Simulation is the process by which a perceiver represents another entity's performance of an action in the same way that she would represent her own performance of that action. Typically, this is assumed to involve the conversion of a perceptual representation into an action-based representation.

Situation model is a bounded (i.e. limited) representation that captures key elements of a situation under discussion. See Section 6.1.1.

Steps. The dialogue planner makes use of steps – that is, sequential components of the plan. See Section 9.1.

Synchrony. Two individual are in synchrony when they construct and modify representations in time with each other. This can lead to synchronized activity as well as synchronized mental states.

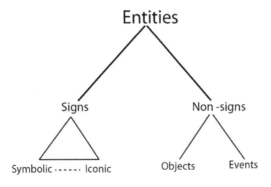

Status of entities in the shared workspace

Preface to *Understanding Dialogue: Language Use and Social Interaction* (Pickering & Garrod)

Individual people read books and prepare speeches on their own, but they can do so only because they have learned what they need to do and have practised extensively. In contrast, pairs of people find dialogue quite natural and largely straightforward, at least once they have mastered the language itself. We have always tried to understand how people use language, but rather more recently we realized that it is not enough to understand how they comprehend and produce monologue. We therefore had to address the challenge of dialogue.

There is of course a vast amount of research on how language is used in interaction – in all types of dialogue from casual conversation to formal exchanges in political or institutional contexts. Such research is conducted by linguists, sociologists, anthropologists, historians and literary theorists, and of course by some psychologists. But the great majority of this work is not concerned with what goes on in people's minds. In contrast, cognitive psychologists and neuroscientists do focus on the mind, but specifically on the individual mind engaged in monologue. There is little research on the cognitive mechanisms underlying interactive language.

To study such mechanisms, we need to do three things. First, we need to situate interlocutors within a system. It is not enough to study what each interlocutor does. We also need to understand how each interlocutor's contributions affect the other interlocutor and influence their subsequent contributions – that is, how the interlocutors jointly control the progress of the dialogue. Second, we must appreciate what is different about using language in dialogue – for example, a speaker has to be able to prepare an utterance and simultaneously comprehend an acknowledgement or query by their addressee. And third, we need to develop a theory of moment-by-moment processing. Dialogue is extremely fast and exquisitely timed, and we need to understand mechanisms that work in the order of tens or hundreds of milliseconds. This book addresses the first two concerns and takes a more preliminary approach to the third – so that an extensive programme of experimental work can use the largely chronometric methods of the cognitive sciences to understand the mechanisms of dialogue.

In the past, we have both focused extensively on isolated language processing, like almost all researchers trained as psycholinguists. And we stress that
we remain interested in monologue, partly because it is an extremely important
form of language use, but primarily because we eventually aim to understand
language use in all its diversity. To some extent, we initially regarded dialogue
as a new challenge. Simon Garrod was concerned with reference resolution in
text comprehension and decided to ask how interlocutors manage to co-refer in
the 'maze game', whereas Martin Pickering applied the method of priming
from language production to see how interlocutors repeat each other's syntactic structures. We both realized that alignment was key to dialogue – as a result
of interaction, interlocutors construct similar representations to each other and
therefore understand each other. We developed alignment in our paper,
'Toward a Mechanistic Theory of Dialogue', which is the theoretical starting
point that led to this book.

However, alignment cannot fully explain how dialogue works – for
example, why interlocutors can time their contributions so well in relation to
each other. We therefore turned to theories of joint action and in particular to
the use of prediction. In recent psycholinguistics, prediction has a central role,
but the focus is on predicting the next word in monologue, primarily to allow
slightly faster processing. In dialogue, prediction is far more fundamental –
interlocutors could not respond to their partners (or indeed interrupt them)
almost instantaneously without predicting what they were going to say and
when. We wrote a paper, 'An Integrated Theory of Language Production and
Comprehension', which argued how comprehenders use their production
systems to make predictions, as part of a general theory of joint action. It
developed our approach but did not focus on dialogue itself.

This book began as an attempt to integrate the theory of prediction and joint
action with the theory of alignment. But in doing so, we realized that a new
framework was needed, one that regarded dialogue as a cooperative joint
activity within a system that is controlled by both interlocutors. We argue that
the interlocutors 'post' their contributions to what we call a shared workspace –
an aspect of reality that contains the words and objects that the interlocutors
use as part of the cooperative joint activity of dialogue. They perceive, predict
and monitor the contents of this workspace and are engaged in a system
involving the interlocutors and the workspace itself, with the dialogue involving constant loops between these components. In this way, dialogue can lead to
communicative success or failure. It should be possible to understand how
dialogue takes place and what mechanisms interlocutors use to support it.

Our proposals are primarily concerned with face-to-face dyadic interaction –
which we regard as the basic form of language use. But ultimately, we wish to
understand more complex interactions (as well as monologue). Towards the
end of the book, we consider multi-party dialogue, dialogue in which the

interlocutors are remote from each other and dialogue that is modified by technology. The book was completed before coronavirus struck, but we are writing the preface at a time when everyone's lives have been greatly affected by it. Like most people, we rapidly started using videoconferencing technologies, and it has become clear that our framework is very well suited to understanding their effects – for example, a shared document is a prop that typically enhances the shared workspace. Clearly, exploring the effects of such technologies in terms of the shared workspace framework is a potential application of our work.

In one sense, this book has been long in the making – the ideas that we developed go back about twenty years, when we began to construct our approach to dialogue. Over this long period, we have presented aspects of our work to many audiences and wish to thank a large number of people who have helped us to develop our ideas. But we have written the book over the last few years, and from during that time, we particularly thank Dale Barr, Larry Barsalou, Holly Branigan, Ruth Corps, Nic Fay, Chiara Gambi, Oliver Garrod, Rob Hartsuiker, Lauren Hadley, Peter Pickering, Natalie Sebanz, and members of the Edinburgh Psycholinguistics Coffee Group and the Glasgow CSCAN seminar group.

We dedicate this book to Martin's family Elizabeth, Clara, Harry and Amelia, and to Simon's wife Irene and grandchildren Albi, Archie, Faye, Flynn and Joey.

21 July 2020

1   The Challenge of Dialogue

Let's start with an extract from a dialogue in which two players work together using a computerized maze game (Garrod & Anderson, 1987). In this extract, one player A is trying to describe her position to her partner B who is viewing the same maze on a computer screen in another room.[1]

Example 1.1

1———**B:** ... Tell me where you are?
2———**A:** Ehm : Oh God (*laughs*)
3———**B:** (*laughs*)
4———**A:** Right : two along from the bottom one up:
5———**B:** Two along from the bottom, which side?
6———**A:** The left : going from left to right in the second box.
7———**B:** You're in the second box.
8———**A:** One up :(*1 sec.*) I take it we've got identical mazes?
9———**B:** Yeah well : right, starting from the left, you're one along:
10———**A:** Uh-huh:
11———**B:** and one up?
12———**A:** Yeah, and I'm trying to get to ...

Up to (7), it is clear that A and B have different understandings of A's location. But after A's concerned question in (8), they start to appreciate and address their confusion. And by (12), they appear to have the same understanding of A's location and to use the same language to describe that location. We say that they have started to become *aligned*, both with respect to the understanding of the situation and with respect to their use of language to describe that situation.

Alignment is the extent to which individuals represent things in the same way as each other. We argue that alignment is fundamental to communicative

---

[1] Here, : refers to a brief pause, *1 sec.* to a longer pause. Overlapping speech is not annotated. Throughout the book, A is treated as female and B as male.

success. For an interaction to be successful, the interlocutors represent relevant aspects of the world (such as the maze position) in the same way as each other. To do this, we argue that they also represent relevant aspects of the language (such as the meaning of *one along*) in the same way. They also seek to be as efficient as possible – not using unnecessary words, not leaving long pauses and not having to repair mistake after mistake.

In everyday dialogue, interlocutors constantly make rapid, short contributions, so that they share the workload. In our example, both interlocutors have to process language extremely rapidly and efficiently, a situation which is quite typical in dialogue. Without appreciable delay, they interpret each other's utterances, complete them, repeat their choices of expressions, and realize when it is their turn to speak and when to stay silent. Many of these decisions clearly take no more than a few hundred milliseconds. It is the aim of this book to explain how people can routinely engage in successful dialogue using mechanisms of the sort that are basic to human cognition.

Now imagine the maze game dialogue as though one interlocutor were contributing without the other. If so, *A* would say:

> 2———**A**: Ehm : Oh God (*laughs*)
> 4———**A**: Right : two along from the bottom one up:
> 6———**A**: The left : going from left to right in the second box.
> 8———**A**: One up :(*1 sec.*) I take it we've got identical mazes?
> 10———**A**: Uh-huh:
> 12———**A**: Yeah, and I'm trying to get to ...

This of course makes no sense. An overhearer could not fully determine what *A* is trying to convey, and a researcher could not explicate the processes that underlie *A*'s utterances. Why does *A* describe a position in the maze (4 or 6)? What is the relevance of *One up* (8) or *Uh-huh* (10)? Why does *A* produce the extended query in (8)? Why does *A* produce a disfluency in (2) and a pause in (8) but no pauses elsewhere?

B's contributions would be equally unintelligible and uninterpretable on their own.

> 1———**B**: ... Tell me where you are?
> 3———**B**: (*laughs*)
> 5———**B**: Two along from the bottom, which side?
> 7———**B**: You're in the second box.
> 9———**B**: Yeah well : right, starting from the left, you're one along:
> 11———**B**: and one up?

Why does *B* use the rather odd construction *Two along from the bottom, which side?* or the words *two* and *along* (5)? Similarly we cannot interpret why *B* laughs (3) or, perhaps more interestingly, why *B* splits a complete utterance over two contributions (9 and 11).

In this format, we cannot appeal to the fact that *A* has used these expressions immediately before. In order to understand what the interlocutors are saying, we have to consider what they both say, so that we can determine the interdependencies between the contributions. This means that we cannot adequately understand the underlying cognitive mechanisms – how they select words and grammatical constructions, plan contributions and speak in a reasonably fluent and intelligible manner – without analysing both interlocutors at the same time.

1.1   Individuals in the Dialogue System

Dialogue is a form of joint activity. In the most general sense, a joint activity is simply an activity in which two (or more) individuals contribute. But dialogue involves a much more precise notion. The individuals have to commit to taking part in the dialogue, and they have to interact to work towards a common goal with their contributions affecting their partner's contributions. The individuals are therefore tightly linked as part of a system. To understand dialogue, we need to understand both the structure of the system and the roles of the individuals-within-the-system.

Specifically, we interpret dialogue as a *cooperative joint activity*, in which the individuals are committed to the activity, respond to the intentions and actions of each other, and support the activity to ensure its success (notably, by compensating for a partner's mistakes in order to keep the activity on track). This notion is derived from Bratman's (1992) notion of shared cooperative activity, which occurs when duettists sing, workmen build something together or footballers perform a move together. But we extend it to include joint activities with a competitive component (e.g. chess players cooperate on following the rules but compete to win). Hence we can include rational arguments as well as friendly conversations, because the interlocutors are still committed to promoting the success of the dialogue. They do so by exerting distributed control over the progress of the dialogue, for example by providing feedback to their partners when necessary. Underlying the interlocutors' behaviour is what Bratman (1992) calls a joint intention – an intention to perform the activity as a whole, even though each individual does not intend to perform it alone.

Cooperative joint activities are a major challenge for cognitive science. Almost always, it analyses thought and behaviour in the individual – how individuals perceive, remember or reason, or indeed how they use language. Even when cognitive science concerns itself with social cognition, the focus is on how one individual represents and processes socially relevant information. In other words, the constructs are defined with respect to an individual – what happens in one person's mind. And a theory cannot make claims about the relationship between two minds – for example, whether those minds are aligned. We refer to this dominant approach as *monadic* cognitive science. Our book goes beyond monadic cognitive science and treats the dyad rather than the monad as the basic unit of analysis.

1.2   The Shared Workspace Framework

Imagine two individuals preparing to construct a piece of flat-packed furniture. They take the relevant pieces from the boxes and lay them out on a rug between them. For example, they might separate different types of screws into piles, keeping them apart from the hinges and the handles, and then lay out the parts of the drawer – the component they have to construct first. At this point, they plan to join up the front with one side of the drawer (with one individual holding the pieces of wood while the other screws them together), and they have to select the right screws to do so. They therefore both focus on some of the pieces in front of them – those pieces that are in their upcoming action. They then perform this cooperative joint action by manipulating just these pieces, and they do so in what we call a *shared workspace*.

The shared workspace is highly restricted in scope. It contains what is relevant for the here-and-now – in other words, the pieces needed for the current action (e.g. the wood and screws), not for potential future actions (e.g. not the back of the drawer). And it is the physical basis of alignment – that is, it contains the objects that the individuals represent. These contents are typically manifest to both individuals – that is, they both attend to its contents, and both assume that their partner does so too. However, these contents do not have to be manifest to both individuals (or indeed to either). For example, the individual holding the wood might believe that the individual holding the screws is aware of the wood (i.e. the wood is manifest), but the individual holding the screws might not believe that the individual holding the wood is aware of the screws (i.e. the screws are not manifest).

But it contains more than just objects. It also contains events, typically the individuals' behaviours that contribute to the cooperative joint activity. Moreover, the individuals communicate about construction, for example discussing who will hold the pieces of wood, or indicating which screw to use. Such communicative acts change the contents of the shared workspace for two reasons. They lead to some objects (or perhaps events) entering the workspace at the expense of others. But in addition, the workspace now contains the communicative acts themselves – whether it is the utterance *Use the largest screws* or a pointing gesture towards those screws. These acts are likely to be manifest to both individuals, as they are likely to assume that they both attend to the words in a communicative context. Each individual can add objects and events, communicative acts, or their combination to the workspace, and can manipulate them or combine them with their partner's contributions.

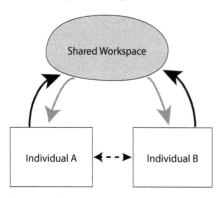

Figure 1.1 The shared workspace framework for cooperative joint activities.

Our framework involves a system in which two individuals interact via the shared workspace (see Figure 1.1). They can both manipulate the contents of the shared workspace (via the upward black arrows) according to need, either one after the other or both at the same time. And they can monitor or predict any aspects of the workspace (via the downward grey arrows) in order to assess the progress of the joint activity and determine its likelihood of success. These arrows therefore capture information flowing in both directions between the workspace and each individual. The individuals therefore link up to the shared workspace as a system. We can (monadically) analyse the individuals-within-the-system, for example considering the nature of their private cognitive representations that they use in interaction (e.g. the linguistic representations underlying an utterance). But we can also (non-monadically) analyse the system as a whole, for example considering the relationships between each individual's representations and the relationships between each individual's behaviour.

1.3   Alignment via Interaction

We assume that alignment underlies many successful cooperative joint activities, and that it corresponds to a well-functioning shared workspace. But alignment is a relationship between the individuals' cognitive representations, and does not relate to the workspace directly. In Figure 1.1, alignment is illustrated using the dashed horizontal arrow between the individuals. Unlike the other arrows, it does not illustrate information flow (as the individuals' representations are private). The information goes via the shared workspace, but its effects are (often) to promote alignment. The investigation of alignment (e.g. determining what leads to individuals having similar representations) is not monadic, because alignment can be understood only by comparing different individuals.

Our focus is on alignment as a consequence of interaction. Interlocutors communicate with each other and as a result tend to develop many similar representations, both with respect to language and to their broader understanding of the topic under discussion. For example, if *A* calls someone a chef, then *B* is likely to use the word *chef* as well, perhaps pronounce it similarly and refer to the same person. If *A* then uses an unusual grammatical construction (e.g. *the chef that's smiling*), then (as we shall see) *B* often uses that construction in a subsequent utterance (e.g. *the waiter that's surly* instead of the more common *the surly waiter*). Interlocutors are typically unaware of such alignment.

We argue that alignment is a consequence of parity (equivalence) between representations used in production and comprehension. When the upward arrows reflect language they correspond to production, and when the downward arrows reflect language they correspond to comprehension. When information flows up from one interlocutor to the shared workspace and then down to the other interlocutor, it leads to alignment.

Alignment does not merely relate to language and its interpretation but rather to models of the situation under discussion. Our furniture builders have models of the physical basis of the action – in this case, the drawer under construction. In successful cooperative joint activity, their models are aligned with each other, and also correspond closely to the contents of the shared workspace. We propose that they continue constructing, and continue discussing their construction, and as a result align on a more extensive situation model, which incorporates representations corresponding to the current shared workspace and aspects of the history of the interaction.

Each interlocutor also has their own representations for planning and carrying out the dialogue, but these are joint representations in the sense that they take into account the part played by the interlocutor. So when *A* answers *The left* to *B*'s question *Two along from the bottom, which side?*, *A* represents something like 'Two along from the bottom on the left'. The representation takes into account both *B*'s and *A*'s contributions. It is a (perhaps imperfect) model of the situation under discussion – and *A* and *B* are aligned in this respect if they have the same model as each other. In addition, their representations (such as their models of the maze) reflect the contents of the shared workspace (such as the configuration of the maze).

The combination of a need to develop extensive situation models and a limited capacity shared workspace means that interlocutors attempt to align efficiently. For example, they try to align on succinct referring expressions with fixed interpretations – which we call *routines*. More generally, they attempt to say just enough to communicate efficiently. In addition, they attempt to time their contributions to the shared workspace optimally, so that they can access and act on those contributions when they need to – without

exceeding the capacity of the workspace. But it is also possible to enhance the shared workspace by highlighting aspects of it to the interlocutors, for example by having a physical whiteboard that represents some aspects of shared workspace or by technologies such as social media.

1.4   Organization of the Book

The book is organized into four main parts. Part I presents the shared workspace framework. We introduce it in relation to cooperative joint activities in general (Chapters 2 and 3) and establish the general properties of the framework, which we then interpret in relation to dialogue (Chapters 4 and 5). We describe the dyadic system itself and the way that the joint actors control the system.

Part II contains two chapters that are concerned with the interlocutors. Chapter 6 presents the theory of interactive alignment and primarily focuses on the alignment of linguistic representations underlying the utterances that each speaker contributes to the dialogue. Such representations enable interlocutors to formulate phrases, words or gestures that move the dialogue forward. Chapter 7 is concerned with the alignment of non-linguistic representations which we call dialogue models. These models capture two important aspects of a dialogue: the situation model that represents what is being discussed and the dialogue game model that represents the conversational moves by the interlocutors (e.g. information-probing).

Part III explains how interlocutors use the shared workspace to achieve alignment of cognitive representations. The shared workspace offers a limited window on that part of the world that joint actors can manipulate and observe. Because it is severely limited in scope, they need to use it as efficiently as possible. Chapter 8 describes how interlocutors put just enough information into the shared workspace to achieve alignment and distribute the information between them as efficiently as possible. Chapter 9 discusses how interlocutors time their contributions to fit in with each other's contributions fluently. By saying just enough and in good time, interlocutors optimize the interactive alignment process.

Part IV extends the shared workspace framework beyond the 'minimal dyad'. Chapter 10 considers multi-party conversation in relation to conversational roles (such as game players, audiences and collectives), with respect to both alignment and control. It then applies the framework to restricted dialogue and, importantly, to monologue. Chapter 11 relates the framework to culture, and considers both cultural institutions (such as conventional activities) and cultural artefacts – that is, technologies that can enhance (and change) communication such as illustrations, writing and electronic devices.

Part I

The Shared Workspace Framework

2 A Systems Analysis of Joint Activity

As we have noted, the cognitive sciences have focused on individual rather than joint activities. Specifically, there has been little concern with the mental representations and processes that take place within individuals as they participate in joint activities, with the relationship between these individual processes or with their relationship to the joint activity as a whole. This is the case both for joint activity in general and for dialogue in particular. In this chapter, we therefore develop a systems analysis for joint activity. In Chapter 4, we turn specifically to dialogue.

It should be apparent that joint activity needs to be analysed as a whole. Consider the example of two individuals constructing a piece of flat-pack furniture (see Figure 2.1). In this figure, the woman is holding two components (pieces of wood) in place while the man is using a screwdriver to screw them together. Clearly the activity would fail if one of them were performing their part of the activity but the other were not, and an analysis of the activity makes sense only if we consider both individuals. Moreover, an analysis of one individual makes no sense unless it is interpreted in the context of the other. For example, the man can reasonably formulate the goal of connecting the pieces together because the woman is holding them in place, and decide to hold the screwdriver at a particular height because that is the height that is compatible with how the woman is holding the components. Similarly, the woman's activity makes sense only because she knows that the man is in a position to use the screwdriver.

To take a different example, if we wish to interpret a game of chess, we cannot fully understand either player's moves considered on their own. For example, Black might move her king in response to White's check; it would not be possible to understand Black's move and to assess Black's reasoning without knowing White's position as well as Black's. Even a positional move such as castling has long-term consequences for the game as a whole.

In such activities, these conclusions seem fairly obvious – no one would presumably attempt to understand an individual's role without taking into account the other individual's role. But the monadic focus of cognitive science suggests that researchers might develop accounts of individual activity and hope

Figure 2.1 Two people constructing a piece of flat-pack furniture.

that they can somehow be applied, without essential modification, to individuals taking part in joint activity. In fact, we argue that the study of language use also has a monadic focus: psycholinguists have (to the extent that they think about dialogue at all) often assumed that what is known about individual language use can be 'slotted into' a study of dialogue. We do not believe this is the right approach for dialogue in particular or joint activity more generally. Therefore our focus in this chapter is to understand joint activity in a way that always pays attention both to the individuals' activity and to their role within the system. As is standard in cognitive science, the understanding of the individuals remains central, but their individual cognitive processes and actions must also be interpreted as part of the system. Before discussing the nature of systems, we need to consider joint activities more generally.

2.1   Cooperative Joint Activities

We begin by informally illustrating key characteristics and dimensions of what we call *cooperative joint activities* (see Table 2.1). These activities differ in many ways, but in all cases the participants realize that they are part of the activity (and presumably believe that their partners realize they are part of the activity as well).[1] Moreover, they share the goal of taking part in the joint activity and have agreement on what constitutes success. This is obviously the case in cooperative activities such as constructing furniture, but is also the case in some competitive activities. For example, chess players compete to win the game, but cooperate by both taking part in the game (and in this case, success means playing the game to its completion).

Activities involving more than one person in which these properties do not hold are not cooperative joint activities (and we do not dwell on their

---

[1] They may also believe that their partner believes they are part of the activity (and so on). We ignore such complexities for current purposes.

Table 2.1 *Examples of cooperative joint activities*

Shaking hands. This is a symmetric joint activity —that is, the participants perform the same action at the same time. It has a well-defined goal and a clear conventional structure. It is likely to be successful (assuming both parties wish to shake hands) because they can slightly modify their individual actions as appropriate, for example speeding up slightly, which they do on the basis of their perception of their partner's behaviour.

Playing (singles) tennis. This is a serial joint activity when considered in terms of the strokes. That is, the players perform strokes one after the other, though obviously both of them can move at the same time. A player's stroke depends on the outcome of the partner's previous stroke (i.e. speed, position, and spin of the ball) and on the partner's current and predicted position. It is a well-defined competitive activity (i.e. each player wishes to win and knows the conditions involved in winning, such as the rules and scoring system).

Jointly constructing a piece of flat-pack furniture. This has a well-defined joint goal (correctly constructing the furniture in a reasonable time). It involves communication as well as physical activity and is collaborative (i.e. both succeed under the same conditions). The participants' roles may be fixed (one directs and one constructs) or vary (each takes turns to hold the pieces or use a screwdriver), and can involve serial or parallel activity. At a given time, the participants are normally performing different activities.

Dancing a tango. This is closely coupled, in the sense that each partner's action can only be successful if it is appropriately timed and executed with respect the other's action. It is also a fully parallel joint activity, in that both partners are acting all the time, and therefore constantly developing their actions in accord with each other.

Moving a heavy table. In this parallel activity, the precise distribution of effort is critical – both partners need to apply particular forces at exactly the right moment with respect to each other. They can perform the same activity (e.g. lift) or can perform complementary activities (e.g. push vs pull) – that is, different activities that fit together in the joint action as a whole.

Playing a game of chess. This is a loosely coupled joint activity, limited to making sure that each partner plays by the rules (e.g. taking turns, surrendering captured pieces). Both players have the same role.

Nurse assisting surgeon in operation. This is an asymmetric and parallel joint activity, with a clear director. The surgeon directs the nurse, for example to hand over the appropriate implement at the right moment. The roles do not change throughout the operation.

Pilot and co-pilot flying a passenger plane. This is an asymmetric and parallel joint activity, in which one participant controls the aircraft at a given time, and the other plays a supporting role (e.g. monitoring the altimeter or warning lights). The pilot is globally in charge, thus defining who controls the aircraft, but the co-pilot takes temporary control when authorized to do so.

interpretation). For instance, two people might walk in step with each other, without either of them realizing that they are doing so. This situation is quite different from a straightforward case of joint activity when two soldiers are marching. Alternatively, two workers might be directed to perform different aspects of a task (e.g. mending the aerial vs tuning the TV) so that both are necessary for success (a working TV) without realizing that another worker is involved, and therefore without sharing the goal of joint participation. In a rather different example, young children often play side-by-side without interacting.[2]

In other words, participants in a cooperative joint activity are committed to playing their part in the activity. They are also committed to accepting the rules of that activity. For example, chess players must be committed to abiding by the rules (e.g. not moving the knight like a bishop or moving twice in a row). In such cooperative joint activities with an element of competition, participants might cheat, but the activity breaks down if they do it publicly (unless there is some renegotiation to allow leeway in what is allowed). If they cheat privately (therefore 'getting away with it'), then they are still committed to the activity in the relevant sense (e.g. assuming that other participants will typically obey the rules). Many cooperative joint activities are of this kind, and include most competitive sports, as well as haggling in a market.

Even in purely cooperative joint activities, participants can fail to act as expected, for example by loafing instead of working. Again, they are still committed to the activity in our sense, but also there is a degree of competition. Of course, if other participants do not accept the behaviour of the loafer, or if everyone loafs, the joint activity breaks down. But if a breakdown does not occur, then the participants remain committed, in a way that does not occur when two people are contributing to a joint activity without realizing that they are taking part in such an activity. In sum, our concern is with joint activities that we define as requiring joint commitment to the activity. This includes a belief that their partner is also committed to the activity.

Our definition of cooperative joint activity relates to what Bratman (1992) calls *shared cooperative activity* (SCA). He provides examples such as singing a duet together, painting a house together, taking a trip together, building something together or performing a cooperative move together in basketball. Bratman's intuition is that readers realize what makes something an SCA but do not know how to define it, and he attempts to provide such a definition. SCA involves commitment to the joint activity, mutual responsiveness (with participants responding to the intentions and actions of each other), and a

---

[2] See for example Kail and Cavaunaugh (2007).

Table 2.2 *Properties of different cooperative joint activities*

Activity/property	Fully cooperative	Locally symmetric	Globally symmetric	Sequential	Time critical
Shaking hands/ moving piano	√	√	√	X	√
Playing tennis	X	X	√	√	√
Constructing furniture together	√	X	√	X	X
Dancing a tango	√	X	X	X	√
Nurse helping surgeon	√	X	X	√	?
Playing chess	X	X	√	√	X
Pilot/co-pilot flying together	√	X	X	X	X

commitment to mutually supporting the activity to ensure its success (e.g. compensating for a partner's mistakes in order to keep the activity on track).

Like Bratman (1992), we assume that cooperative joint actors have collective intentions of the form 'I intend that we do something' – that is, when an individual intends that a group acts in a certain way (see Schweikard & Schmid, 2013).[3] But unlike Bratman, we do not require the activity as a whole to be cooperative (i.e. to be *fully cooperative*). Instead, we are interested in activities with a cooperative component. Such activities are, however, within the spirit of Bratman's enterprise. He considers chess, an activity that is not an SCA because it is competitive, but argues that it is 'cooperative down to a certain level'. Essentially, by following the rules of chess, the players are acting in a shared and cooperative manner. (This is unlike many activities that are not SCAs even though they have some characteristics in common with them, such as when house painters try to use different colours, or when duettists will not help their partners because they wish to see them stumble.) We regard chess as a cooperative joint activity from the perspective of a commitment to rule-following and to the successful completion of the game. Importantly, dialogue is an example of such an activity (see Chapter 4).

Now let us consider other characteristics that vary across the cooperative joint activities in Table 2.1 (see Table 2.2). Our concern is not with all dimensions over which the activities may vary, but is rather to explicate those properties that are relevant for cognition. For example, we care about whether participants act

---

[3] We adopt one approach to collective intentionality; see Tuomela and Miller (1988) and Searle (1990) for prominent alternative accounts. Note that we refer to *joint intentions* rather than *we-intentions*.

concurrently (i.e. in parallel) or not, because this affects whether they have to process two components of the activity at once or not. But we are less concerned about the power relationships between the participants or how familiar they are with each other. Such differences might be highly relevant to situating forms of activity within societies or institutions (see Chapter 11), but their effects on the cognitive processes underlying joint activity are indirect (e.g. they might affect participants' roles, such as leader and follower).

Consider symmetry – whether both participants play similar roles or not. Such symmetry can be local or global. In locally symmetric activities, the participants do the same thing – at an appropriate level of description, and within a margin of error – at the same time. So piano movers can of course hold the piano slightly differently, but they are performing the same acts of lifting and moving. In shaking hands, each partner moves their hand up and down at the same time (though they might differ in tightness of grip). But in both cases, the participants are locally symmetric with respect to the critical aspects of the joint activity. In locally asymmetric activities, this is not the case. Often, they may not be able to do the same thing, as in dancing a tango, where the moves tend to be comple-mentary and the two partners ('male' and 'female') have different sets of permissible moves (e.g. support vs being supported). Serial activities are neces-sarily asymmetric, as only one participant can act at a given time (e.g. chess).

Local symmetry contrasts with global symmetry, which occurs when both partners play (essentially) the same role in the activity as a whole. In globally symmetric activities, participants follow the same rules, have the same goal, and (importantly) have equivalent control over the local structure – though of course some activities may be globally symmetric in some respects but not others. In chess the two players are globally symmetric (except in relation to who moves first), but they are locally asymmetric as at any given time one player may move and the other may not. In contrast, two people constructing flat-pack furniture may globally play similar roles (they can each do all components of the activity) but at each individual step decide who will hold the two pieces steady and who will screw them together (and control turn-taking by saying *finished*). Other joint activities are globally asymmetric, as in tango dancing ('male' vs 'female' dancers) or surgery (when the nurse only acts in response to the surgeon's command).

Next, cooperative joint activities can involve concurrent or sequential con-tributions. Clearly local symmetry requires concurrency as both participants are acting at the same time, but local asymmetry is compatible with both participants acting at the same time (e.g. tango dancing) or one participant doing nothing (e.g. chess).

Finally, cooperative joint activities can be more or less time-critical (though in Table 2.2 we treat this as a dichotomy), and they vary with respect to how important it is for the partner to respond immediately. In chess, each move takes many seconds or minutes (or even days in correspondence chess), and the structure of the activity is unaffected by response time. But in tennis, a late return leads to a lost point. In surgery, the nurse sometimes has to respond immediately to the surgeon's request, but sometimes a delay is acceptable. The extent to which concurrent activities are time-critical can also vary. Dancing a tango, playing a duet, and shaking hands simply do not work if the participants are not synchronized (i.e. within tens or hundreds of milliseconds). But furniture construction is often not time-critical (e.g. one partner can hold the pieces together until the other is ready to use the screwdriver).

Why do particular activities fit into Table 2.2 where they do? For example, why are some activities locally symmetric, why are some time-critical and why do some admit extensive concurrency but not others? There are two parts to this explanation. Some differences can be explained without referring to participants' limitations, and are due to social/institutional factors or ones relating to the relevant physical environment. A game based on chess but which had both players moving at once (e.g. by writing their moves down and revealing them at the same time) would simply be a different game, and so the sequentiality of chess is enshrined in the rules. In tennis, sequentiality (of strokes) occurs both because the players must stay on their own side of the court (a social/institutional factor) and because the ball cannot be on both sides at once (a physical factor).

Other differences are at least partly due to participants' limitations and their responses to those limitations. Some limitations are due to physical constraints, for example that people have only two hands and can lift objects of only a certain weight. But others are at least partly due to cognitive constraints. For example, the pilot of a passenger plane has a co-pilot acting concurrently, in part because an individual pilot cannot monitor all the flight instruments included in the cockpit sufficiently reliably (see Hutchins, 1995). By selecting a particular scalpel, a nurse can save the surgeon time and cognitive effort that can be better employed deciding on planning an incision. In Chapter 4, we shall see the importance of interlocutors' cognitive (and perceptual) limitations on dialogue.

Note that all our examples in Table 2.2 involve cooperative joint activities that are defined by the goal. For example, the joint goal of shaking hands is of course for the individuals to shake hands, and the joint goal of playing chess or tennis is to play the game to its conclusion (and within that joint goal, each player has the individual goal of being the winner). But many joint activities are more open-ended. For example, two people visiting a museum together may engage in a series of joint activities, and those activities may not be pre-defined.[4]

---

[4] In practice, the individuals will often negotiate the series of joint activities, typically while those activities are taking place. Such negotiation of course involves dialogue (see Chapter 4).

We note that many experiments involve artificially constructed cooperative joint activities, which could be fitted in to Table 2.2. For example, Knoblich and Jordan (2003) had dyads work together to control the position of a circle over a moving target, with one pressing a button to accelerate the circle and the other pressing a button to slow it down. The experiment demonstrated the importance of receiving feedback about a partner's actions for developing a fluent joint action. Similarly, Skewes et al. (2015) had dyads perform a joint aiming task in which they were asked to synchronize mouse clicks. When the task was sufficiently difficult, the partner with the harder task became less adaptive and served as the leader. In such tasks, participants are aware that they have a joint goal and realize that its success depends on how coordinated their individual actions are. Clearly the activity depends on the task defined by the experimenter (i.e. the experimenter defines the rules of the activity), and is used by the experimenter to understand cognitive representations (and how each individual's representation is related to the other's).

These experimental examples help us construct an analysis of cooperative joint activity. They are also informative about constraints on individual cognitive representations, perhaps relating to how quickly they can be constructed or the extent to which they become similar across the individuals. For example, we might consider the extent to which participants can do the same thing at the same time (i.e. act concurrently and with local symmetry). At this point, it becomes clear that we need an account of both the actors' individual cognitive representations and of the system in which the actors perform.

2.2   Systems within Cognitive Science

In a system, the functions of the parts cannot be fully understood except in relation to the system as a whole. In her analysis of cognitive systems, Wilson (2002) states that 'for a set of things to be considered a system in the formal sense, these things must be not merely *aggregate*, a collection of elements that stand in some relation to one another (spatial, temporal or any other relation). The elements must in addition have properties that are affected by their participation in the system. Thus, the various parts of an automobile can be considered as a system because the action of the spark plugs affects the behaviour of the pistons, the pistons affect the drive shaft, and so on' (p. 630, her italics). Similarly, the components of an individual's mind (or brain) have to be understood in relation to each other. For example, perceptual and memory mechanisms influence each other in particular and regular ways (though they may also get external inputs from the environment). In addition, many systems have some degree of persistence – that is, they are relatively stable. For example, individuals' minds (or brains) constitute a stable (in Wilson's terms, obligate) system because their organization (e.g. with respect to perceptual systems or working memory) does not vary over time.[5]

As Wilson (2002) argues, individual minds do not usefully constitute a system with the environment as whole, because the system would change every time the individual's environment changed (and we cannot have a theory about the environment as a whole). This is therefore not stable. In contrast, we can consider tightly interacting dyads as a system: we have already noted that collaborating individuals systematically affect each other and their interaction cannot be understood by considering them in isolation. The individuals can of course come and go in a way that parts of an automobile or perceptual and memory mechanisms cannot. In fact, many systems allow components to be inserted or removed – for example, a system consisting of a CD player and a CD. The appropriate level of systems analysis addresses the relationship between any CD player and whichever CD happens to have been inserted, with the assumption that the critical properties of any individual CD and any individual CD player do not differ from any other one.

So what do we mean by being stable? Clearly, any system that involves two individuals, or indeed one individual and an aspect of the environment such as a computer or other machine, can be split up (unlike the mind). Indeed, the specific pair of individuals might never re-form. However, different interactions between individuals (or individual and machine) will have similar structure – and as researchers, we can make generalizations about such interactions. Such generalizations require a systems analysis, and the system is *recurrently stable*.

In cooperative joint activities, both individuals are aware that they are both performing the activity and are therefore both part of the system. They therefore accept certain commitments (i.e. playing their role) and assume that their partner does too. Moreover, all such activities have a lifetime – a beginning, a middle and an ending – with the individuals coming together and eventually splitting apart. For recurrently stable activities, the same or different individuals can subsequently come together again, and it is possible to apply the same systems analysis to the new dyad. Note that one or both individuals may need to indicate when the joint activity is to begin, or indeed to propose a particular joint activity. Similarly, they may need to indicate when the activity is over.

Two further properties of a system are the extent to which it is self-sufficient and what we shall call the tightness of coupling. Systems can be closed and hence self-sufficient, in that the only input to each individual comes from the

---

[5] They may of course develop over an individual's lifetime. But such development is systematic and orderly, and contrasts with the external environment which can change dramatically and repeatedly as the individual moves around. In other words, an individual's mind may not be entirely stable, but it is far more stable than the individual's environment.

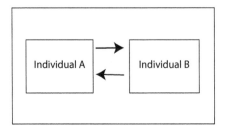

Figure 2.2 A simple model of a closed dyadic system for cognitive science.

action of the other individual. In Figure 2.2, we represent a closed system because the only input to individual *B* comes from individual *A* and vice versa.

The arrows in Figure 2.2 constitute a loop – it is possible to go from individual *A* to individual *B* to individual A and so on. In other words, the loop reflects the effect of each individual on the other. For example, we can represent chess in terms of Figure 2.2, with individual *A* corresponding to White and individual *B* to Black. The upper arrow in Figure 2.2 represents a move by White and Black's perception of White's move; the lower arrow represents a move by Black and White's perception of Black's move. The loop continues until the game is over. The tightness of the loop (with respect to time) depends on the speed of the game. In lightning chess, each move (and hence step in the loop) may take less than 10 s; in correspondence chess, it may take days.

In a dyadic cognitive system, every behaviour by one individual might affect the other individual and produce a response in tens or hundreds of milliseconds. But some joint activities can involve a much 'looser' loop (as for example when exchanging letters by post). However, loops do not simply differ with respect to timing. They also differ with respect to the amount of information that is cycling. For example, interaction between competing sprinters is very limited (you might speed up immediately if you see a competitor overtake you), in contrast to interaction between tango dancers. Understanding such properties of the loop is central to understanding many joint activities.

Of course, chess is a sequential activity in which the moves alternate. More specifically, White moves and Black perceives that move, then Black moves and White perceives that move. There is no concurrent activity. So Figure 2.2 represents chess adequately. But other joint activities (e.g. jointly carrying a piano) involve concurrent behaviours and perception by both individuals. Figure 2.1 does not capture such situations so well. For example, it cannot capture the fact that each individual may perceive the ongoing joint activity (e.g. that the pair of lifters are not in sync).

In Figure 2.2, the arrows represent behaviours that are produced by the individual at the blunt end and perceived by the individual at the sharp end (the arrowhead). But in many forms of cooperative joint activity, the participants can be affected by factors that are not due to either of them. These effects are caused by *props* that are integral to the activity. For example, the joint action of attaching two components of flat-pack furniture may fail because one component is faulty. Similarly, the chess players' moves are affected by the position of all the pieces on the board. Note that props need not be 'static' objects, but can also be changing aspects of the environment. For example, the band music constitutes a prop for the tango dancers. Figure 2.2 cannot capture the role of props.

The simple (sender-receiver) model is conceivably adequate for some sequential activities that involve discrete contributions. It would be possible to incorporate monitoring into this model (with feedback flowing in the opposite direction from each arrow). But it is inadequate for cooperative joint activity in general, for two main reasons. First, the props (e.g. the chess board and pieces) are not represented. The only way to include them is to have arrows from the environment to each individual – a representation that does not straightforwardly capture the fact that the relevant environment is (usually) common to both individuals. Second, both individuals can contribute concurrently during many forms of cooperative joint activity (see Table 2.1). It is then obviously impossible to interpret the interaction as involving *A* making a contribution, *B* interpreting that contribution, *A* making a new contribution, and so on. So we cannot make use of Figure 2.2 as a way of capturing what happens in cooperative joint activities and we therefore abandon it later in the chapter.

2.3   The Individual-within-the-System

We are concerned with individuals as well as the relationships between individuals in a system. Specifically, we are concerned with cognitive representations, which are internal to each individual. For our purposes, such representations are components of mental organization at a level of abstraction appropriate for cognition (e.g. relating in some way to memory, reasoning or language). We use representation loosely to cover both 'declarative' components and processes that can act over those components. Some representations may be concerned with purely internal mechanisms (e.g. a plan to move an arm), but others are models of external reality, with which they share relational structure (Craik, 1943/1967).[6]

---

[6] Craik (1943/1967) put it thus: 'My hypothesis then is that thought models or parallels reality, that its essential feature is not "the mind", "self", "sense data" nor "propositions" but symbolism, and that this symbolism is largely of the same kind as that which is familiar to us in mechanical devices which aid thought and calculation. ... If the organism carries a "small-scale model" of

The focus on individuals' representations is standard in cognitive science (and therefore we can in principle relate these representations to neural implementation, for example). Our approach therefore contrasts with the area of social psychology that is concerned with interpersonal and group behaviour. It also contrasts with research into 'collective cognition', which for example shows the benefits or otherwise of collective problem solving (Hargadon & Bechky, 2006), collective memory (Roediger & Abel, 2015), or the 'wisdom of the crowd' (Galton, 1907). In such studies, the interest is not with the individuals' cognitive representations, but rather with some aspect of group performance.[7] In contrast, we are concerned with individual cognitive representations that are likely to be as intricate as the representations that individuals use when operating alone.

But at the same time, our concern is not with the representations in isolated individuals but rather with the representations in individuals-in-relation-to-a-system. Most cognitive science focuses on isolated individuals – it implicitly or explicitly concerns itself with representations in one individual and not with the relationship between representations. Such monadic cognitive science may be appropriate when no system is involved, as when individuals are perceiving or remembering stimuli (e.g. in most traditional perception and memory experiments), even if those stimuli refer to other people (as in much social cognition). But we argue that it is inappropriate for the study of cooperative joint activity, including dialogue.

In our systems-based approach, we can study the relationship between representations in different individuals. For example, we ask whether two individuals construct similar or related representations to each other, or determine whether we can distinguish a 'leader' and a 'follower' on the basis of the timing or complexity of their representations. Analysis that makes reference to two individuals' representations and their relationship is not possible in monadic cognitive science, because only one individual is studied at a time.

Just as different forms of cooperative joint activity have different properties, so the representations of the individual participants have different properties with respect to each other. Their representations for a cooperative joint activity

---

external reality and of its own possible actions within its head, it is able to try various alternatives, conclude which is the best of them, react to future situations before they arise, utilize the knowledge of past events in dealing with the present and future, and in every way to react in a much fuller, safer and more competent manner to the emergencies which face it' (p. 57).

[7] Note that our primary concern is with the effects of closed-loop interaction within a dyad, under conditions where we may assume quite complex representations in each individual. This contrasts with collective cognition, where the focus is on the aggregate and where the interest is often in how quite simple behaviours at the level of the individual lead to complex and often counter-intuitive aggregate behaviours (e.g. better or worse performance than individuals in isolation, or apparently rational individual behaviour that leads to group irrationality).

will of course generally mirror the activity itself (including its relevant context). For example, if the activity is symmetric and concurrent (so that both participants are doing the same thing at the same time), their mental representations will tend to involve the same elements and processes, with those processes acting on the elements at the same time. If two people jointly lift a piano, they construct similar motor plans to each other and then enact them simultaneously (within some margins of error). In an asymmetric joint activity (e.g. a pilot and a co-pilot flying a plane), some of the representations are different (because the cognitive processes involved in controlling the plane's movement and those involved in monitoring the dials are different), but other representations, for example with respect to the goal of the activity or with respect to the rules of turn-taking, may be similar. In sum, we focus on individual (cognitive) representations, but consider them with respect to a pair of individuals – something that would not be the case in the type of analysis that occurs in monadic cognitive science.

So our proposal is to interpret cooperative joint activity using a systems analysis. More specifically, we distinguish between an analysis of the structure of the system, which focuses on the system as a whole, and analysis of the individuals as parts of that system. This second aspect of the analysis is concerned with individual representations, but importantly those representations are interpreted with respect to the rest of the system (both its structure and the representations of the other individuals). From our perspective, this second aspect is central. It is described in terms of (individual) cognitive representations, but it allows analysis that relates to other individuals' representations (e.g. with respect to their similarity). So in summary, we seek to understand both the individual-within-the-system and the system as whole, in order to investigate the cognitively rich system that underlies cooperative joint activity.

2.4   Distributed Control for Joint Activities

2.4.1   Control of Individual Behaviour

When someone constructs a piece of flat-pack furniture, she needs to establish an overall goal (e.g. to build a desk) and a set of sub-goals (e.g. to connect the legs to the base, to connect the base to the back, to construct the drawer). She also has to formulate a plan of action to achieve the goal and sub-goals, taking into account the available components. This plan specifies the processes involved in implementing (i.e. executing) the action of achieving the goal and sub-goals. These processes include drilling holes for the screws and therefore specify the motor programs involved in positioning the drill with respect to the drawer. These implemented actions produce physical consequences, for example screws in their correct locations. In any task, we can distinguish the plan (to achieve the goal and sub-goals), the mechanisms involved in implementing the plan, and the physical consequences themselves that are the result of plan implementation (see Miller et al., 1960).

The plan can be inflexible (i.e. ballistic), for example specifying an unchangeable order of sub-goals (e.g. drawer first). If so, the furniture builder would have to implement the plan exactly, or the goal would not be achieved. But this inflexible implementation will fail if there is any problem with achieving a sub-goal. For example, she might have to stop constructing the drawer because the cordless drill ran out of power before the sub-goal is achieved. It does not make sense for her to stand around doing nothing; instead, she can manually connect the legs to the base while waiting for the drill to recharge. But to do this, she needs to attend to the process of achieving the sub-goal. Specifically, she has to monitor what she is doing and identify problems, and then she has to be able to change behaviour while it is taking place. She therefore needs a *control* mechanism that is separate from the mechanisms that *implement* the plan and actually build the furniture.

More generally, a mechanism of control provides a means for modifying behaviour. This mechanism makes use of feedback, either about the behaviour itself or about the process (the plan and its implementation) that leads to the behaviour. Specifically, the feedback provides evidence about whether everything is working as expected, and is the consequence of monitoring. If there is a problem, either the plan or its implementation can be modified and the behaviour can be changed. We therefore assume a split between the implementation of the behaviour and a mechanism that monitors this process. The monitor compares some aspect of the implementation or the behaviour with the intended implementation or behaviour. This intention is a consequence of the plan and is a representation of the relevant goal or sub-goal (e.g. the structure of the drawer or the trajectory of the drill). The representation can be regarded as an 'ideal model' (i.e. of what should happen), and the process that leads to behaviour modification is the comparison (or monitoring) of the outcome of the behaviour and this 'ideal model'.

2.4.2   Control at Different Layers

In a complex task such as building flat-pack furniture, a problem might occur at the level of planning (e.g. if the builder chooses the wrong order of sub-goals), at the level of implementation (e.g. if the drill runs out of charge), or at the level of physical consequences (e.g. if a screw goes in at the wrong angle and prevents the drawer closing). So control can be applied at any of these layers to help deal with the problem. For example, the furniture builder can monitor the plan, implementation or physical consequences and act on the output of any of these. If she (i.e. her monitor) notices that an aspect of the plan is not being fulfilled, she can revise it by reordering the sub-goals (i.e. to achieve the goal a different way) or change the goal (e.g. not include the drawer). Her changes have consequences for implementation (i.e. when she uses the drill) and physical consequences (i.e. when the holes are made). If she notices that the implementation is failing (as in the case of the drill), she can revise the implementation (e.g. recharge the drill). If she notices a problem with the physical consequences (the shape of a hole), she can redirect the drill (which changes the implementation and the physical consequences). Note that she can monitor many different aspects of the task, from small sub-goals (e.g. one screw does not fit properly into the drawer) to the task as a whole (the desk wobbles). Moreover, the plan, implementation and physical consequences are all linked together, though a specific act of monitoring is directed at one of these layers.

Notice that this description involves what is called *closed-loop control*, whereby the control mechanism monitors the process (i.e. the plan, implementation, and physical consequences) and lets the output of the monitor feed back into the process so that it can be changed appropriately.[8] However, closed-loop control may also work in a rather different way from the way we have described. The control mechanism can provide a prediction of the process (again, the plans, implementation, or physical consequences), and then the monitor compares these predictions with the actual process. The difference (error) between prediction and process provides the feedback that allows the process to be changed. This is sometimes called *pseudo-closed-loop control* (Grush, 2004).

Importantly, the 'loop' in closed-loop control can vary in many ways – informally, it can be 'tight' or 'loose'. One dimension of course relates to timing, which might differ for different aspects of the activity. For example the furniture builder might very rapidly notice that a hole is at the wrong angle and send feedback to change the angle of the drilling within a few hundred milliseconds. But she might take longer to notice that the drill is losing power (because it is still going too fast for her to notice), or she might not decide to stop drilling immediately she detects the problem. In fact, an understanding of how such feedback loops work is central to the explanation of human behaviour.

---

[8] Such control contrasts with *open-loop control*, in which there is no feedback (and therefore any control of the process is determined before the process begins), and so the process is ballistic. It should be clear that human behaviour (such as furniture-building) cannot in general be explained by open-loop control.

2.4.3   Distributed Control for Joint Activities

Now let us consider the situation in which two people collaboratively construct a piece of flat-pack furniture. Because the task is collaborative, they have (essentially) the same goal – to construct the furniture correctly. They may well have the same hierarchy of sub-goals; but if they do not, the individual sub-plans associated with these sub-goals must mesh together in such a way as to support the overall plan of building the furniture (see Bratman, 1992). In other words, what one participant plans to do should not get in the way of what the other plans to do at any level and those individual sub-plans should support each other. The participants may differ with respect to how aspects of the plan are executed. For example, one person might be in charge of the drill and would therefore plan at a specific moment how to use the drill (e.g. to make a hole now). The two furniture builders would also make different contributions to implementation (e.g. one would operate the drill, and the other would hold the wood up). They would therefore produce different physical consequences (e.g. the person operating the drill would produce the holes in the wood).

Such joint activities are therefore complex and change dynamically. It is in general impossible for an individual to stick to a pre-formed plan unless she can be entirely confident about the relevant aspects of her partner's performance – for instance, whether she drills a hole in time for him to insert the screw. This means that control is especially necessary for joint activities. Specifically, both partners must be able to use closed-loop control, so that they can use the feedback from their own and their partner's performance to direct subsequent activity. In fact, it must be possible to monitor your own performance and the performance of your partner, and determine whether they are appropriate, not merely on their own, but with respect to each other. If either an individual aspect of performance (e.g. I can't operate the drill or you can't lift the wood), or a joint aspect of performance (e.g. you are holding the wood too high for my drill) is problematic, then you must modify your plan or its execution, or indicate that I need to modify my plan or its execution (or both).

Importantly control can be performed by both individuals – perhaps at the same time, or at different times during the joint activity. This means that the control of the activity (in this case, building the furniture) is *distributed* across the individuals. It would in theory be possible to have a 'servant' who acted solely on instruction from the 'master' and did not perform any monitoring, so that control was located entirely in the 'master'. But in most joint activities, both individuals exercise some degree of control.

The lowest level of any activity (whether individual or joint) is the behaviour and its physical consequences. But these consequences do not

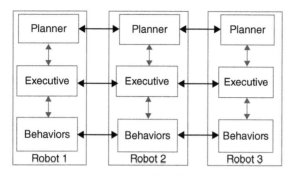

Figure 2.3 Layered multi-robot architecture (based on Simmons et al., 2002). Each robot has three layers that can interact with each other and can communicate with the equivalent layer in the other robots.

merely consist of effects on the physical world (e.g. a hole in the wood) but also effects on the individuals' behaviours (e.g. their hand positions). And in joint activities with no props, the physical consequences consist entirely in behaviour and relate to the effects of each individual's activity on the other (and of course themselves). In Table 2.1, shaking hands and dancing a tango are examples of such activities.

To understand distributed control and its relationship to planning, implementation and behaviour, let us briefly consider how roboticists have addressed the question of coordinating robot performance, so that each robot can perform different parts of a single task efficiently (i.e. without extensive overlap in their efforts). For example, Simmons et al. (2002) describe how three autonomous robots with different capacities (an overhead crane, a mobile manipulator, and a roving eye) can coordinate to assemble large-scale structures that require both heavy lifting and dexterous manipulation (see Figure 2.3). They treat each robot as an autonomous agent (in our terms, an individual), involving a planning layer, an executive layer (which corresponds to our layer of implementation), and a behavioural layer. It should be clear that this analysis includes individuals with structured representations (the three layers and the vertical connections within each robot) and a system (the horizontal connections between the layers).

Interaction (as indicated by the horizontal connections) can take place at each of the layers, leading to coordinated activities. At the behavioural layer, coordination is the result of sensor/effector feedback loops – the way that one robot responds to another's behaviour on a moment-by-moment basis. At the executive (implementation) layer, the tasks can be coordinated so that they occur at the right time or location with respect to each other, and the robots can monitor each other's progress (and initiate modifications if necessary).

(Our use of *implementation* avoids ambiguity about the word *executive*, as modern psychologists tend to regard executive control as very high level; e.g. Baddeley, 1996.) Finally, coordination at the planning layer allows them to jointly construct novel plans that are appropriate for each of them, and can, for example, negotiate their roles (e.g. whether each robot should take charge of particular sub-tasks).

Simmons et al. (2002) focus on the interaction of three robots with very different capabilities. In contrast, our concern is with two individuals who have (roughly) the same cognitive and behaviour abilities. (A robotic analogy might be two driverless cars in a convoy.) More fundamentally, people cannot directly interact at the plan or implementation layers, because these layers involve representations that can be observed or inferred only as a consequence of behaviours – they do not have wireless connections that could communicate planning or implementation.

So now let us return to the flat-pack furniture builders. An example of interaction at the behavioural layer is when one individual holds a screw at a particular height and the other tightens the screw at the same height. In robotic terms, the feedback would relate to sensors and effectors. Interaction at the implementational layer occurs when one individual starts to hand over a component and the other then reaches over and grasps it. This involves the two individuals linking the way in which they implement their arm movements. Interaction at the planning layer occurs when they establish the precise order in which they are going to combine components of the furniture (most likely using language to do so). It should be clear that all these forms of interaction involve feedback (and hence closed-loop control), though they may also involve predicting performance (i.e. using pseudo-closed-loop control). And each individual controls aspects of the performance, so the control is distributed.

2.5   The Shared Workspace Framework of Cooperative Joint Activity

2.5.1   Introducing the Framework

We now introduce a new systems-based framework for understanding cooperative joint activity and its control. We call this the *shared workspace model* (see Figure 2.4). The figure contains two individuals, each of whom contribute to a *shared workspace* through their own behaviours (thick black arrows), and can perceive those behaviours (downward-facing grey arrows). Each individual can develop and implement plans related to the cooperative joint activity (represented by the two boxes within each individual). Our framework contrasts with the simple sender-receiver model of the relationship between individuals and the system in (two-party) joint action (i.e. Figure 2.2).

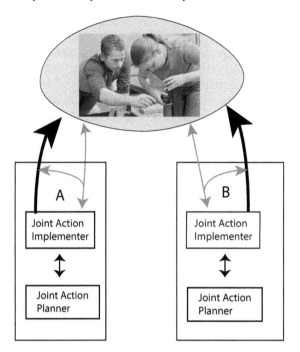

Figure 2.4 The shared workspace model of cooperative joint activity and distributed control.

Instead, we propose a systems analysis of cooperative joint activity in which each individual contributes to this shared workspace.

The shared workspace model makes a key distinction between internal and external aspects of cooperative joint activity. In furniture construction, the shared workspace might contain *A* holding the wood and *B* applying the screwdriver. These behaviours contrast with the internal processes that under-lie *A*'s contribution and *B*'s contribution. In fact, the shared workspace con-tains the individuals' behaviours along with the objects (i.e. the props). The internal processes correspond to the joint action planner and the joint action implementer. The shared workspace provides a changing window on reality. It contains the resources relevant to the current stage of any cooperative joint action. And it develops as the action progresses. It corresponds to what the actors both attend to, over the course of the activity.

In Section 1.2, we introduced the shared workspace in relation to furniture construction. The two individuals set up a shared workspace that contained the components and tools that are relevant for the current stage of the action (e.g. the piece of wood, screw and screwdriver) so that they can both directly use them as needed (without having to search). Thus, the workspace contains the components and tools that both individuals attend to. In addition, the shared workspace contains the individuals' behaviours (holding wood, inserting the screws) that contribute to the joint activity (including communicative behaviours, which we discuss in Chapter 4). And after a behaviour is complete, it contains the results of that behaviour, such as an assembled drawer. There are three essential characteristics of the shared workspace, as we now discuss.

First, the shared workspace is not a mental representation. It is not in one or both individuals' minds, but rather is part of the actual world. It contains objects and events that are relevant for the joint activity. The shared workspace is an external resource. It is a resource because it supports the performance (and fulfilment) of the cooperative joint activity. It is external because its components are in the world rather than in the individuals' minds.

Any aspect of reality can be described in different ways. For example, a particular object can be described as a patch of colour, a lump of metal or a tool. Some descriptions are in terms of physics (e.g. light wavelength) or biochemistry (e.g. compounds), but there are also descriptions at a level appropriate for behaviour and which are meaningful to organisms (Gibson, 1979). Such ecological descriptions afford behaviour: to humans, a chair is a meaningful object, because it affords sitting on; and a screwdriver is a meaningful object, because it affords driving in screws (see Norman, 1988, 2013).

The shared workspace contains constituents at the level that corresponds to their role in the cooperative joint activity. In other words, the objects and events are meaningful with respect to the task at hand, and they constitute the components of cooperative joint activities. These components therefore have *joint affordances*. A chess board and pieces jointly afford a chess game; the instrumentation in a large plane jointly affords flying by the pilot and co-pilot. Such components also correspond to the components of the individuals' cognitive representations.

The shared workspace contains a screw that is individuated (from other available screws) with respect to size and thread (as using a different screw type would be a mistake), and events (typically, behaviours) that are individuated with respect to the task (in this case, holding the wood and inserting the screw). The individuals attend to the type of screw (rather than screws in general or to screw colour), and therefore it is this aspect of reality that is in the shared workspace.

Second, the shared workspace is defined in terms of *parallel attention*, in which both individuals attend to the same element without necessarily being aware of each other's attention. It contains those objects (and events) that both attend to and nothing else. If A attends to the screwdriver and B attends to the same screwdriver, then the screwdriver is in the shared workspace.

Importantly, there is no requirement for either or both individuals to realize that their partner attends to the object.[9,10]

Third, the shared workspace is dynamic. It does not (typically) contain all objects (and events) relevant to the cooperative joint activity at any given point, but rather contains whatever is relevant to the current step. When a chess player uses her queen to capture her opponent's knight, the shared workspace might contain these two pieces. As the game progresses, other pieces (i.e. other meaningful objects) enter and leave the workspace. The individuals' parallel attention shifts over the course of the cooperative joint activity and as it does so, the shared workspace changes as well. These changes are usually incremental during stages in a complex activity (e.g. when the individuals both shift attention from one tool to another) but can sometimes be dramatic (when they turn to a new activity involving different objects).

2.5.2   Acting on the Shared Workspace

Whereas the shared workspace is not a representation, the individuals do represent aspects of the workspace (i.e. objects and events contained in the workspace). These representations enable the individuals to act on the shared workspace (via the black arrows). By doing so, the individuals carry out the cooperative joint activity by manipulating the contents of the shared workspace. The shared workspace is therefore the resource that underpins the activity.

In our example, individual A holds the wood in such a way that B attends to it (as well as A). Therefore, the wood enters the shared workspace. Similarly, B uses the screwdriver to perform the screwing event in the presence of A. The two objects and the event are all in parallel attention. But importantly, these elements actually have a stronger status than simply being in parallel attention. By holding the wood in view of both A and B, individual A puts the wood into parallel attention and also makes it clear to B that A is doing so. Thus, A is confident that B attends to what A is doing. And B does the same for A with respect to the screwdriver and the screwing event.

In a cooperative joint activity, an entity is *manifest* if A is confident that both A and B attend to it and B is confident that A and B attend to it. So when A holds up the wood for B, A acts to make the wood manifest. And by holding up the screwdriver, B acts to make the screwdriver and the screwing event

---

[9] In general, parallel attention is necessary but not sufficient for an element to be in a shared workspace. The shared workspace exists only in the context of a cooperative joint activity. So when two individuals happen to attend to the same event but are not engaged in a cooperative joint activity, there is no shared workspace for the event to be in.

[10] Note that the shared workspace exists in the context of a cooperative joint activity, and such activity requires that both individuals recognize that they are both part of the activity.

manifest. In successful cooperative joint activity, the individuals seek to make elements of the shared workspace manifest whenever appropriate for the activity. We say that those entities are in *joint attention* – they are both manifest and in parallel attention.[11]

Manifestness is not necessary for our weak definition of parallel attention. For example, if A and B do not realize that they attend to the same unremarkable (i.e. non-salient) object in a complex array, then the object is in their parallel attention, but neither is confident that the object is in joint attention. Thus, the unremarkable object is not manifest to either A or B.[12] The reason why we distinguish parallel attention and manifestness is that we will argue that individuals align on entities in parallel attention whether or not they are manifest. Manifestness (and in particular its absence) motivates individuals to act – for example, holding up an object to ensure that it is included in the cooperative joint activity and is jointly attended to.

The shared workspace is a resource that contains objects and events relevant to performing the cooperative joint activity. In the furniture-building example, it might contain the actions of both individuals, including both the current actions and the consequences of earlier ones. It may also contain the objects involved in those actions. More generally, it contains those aspects of reality that are relevant to the activity and that are simultaneously accessible to the individual actors. This of course means that most of reality is outside the shared workspace. Its boundaries are specified at a particular time but are flexible and regularly change as a cooperative joint activity progresses.

The shared workspace is involved not only in acting (i.e. contributing to the workspace) but also in monitoring (i.e. checking and controlling the progress of the activity in the workspace). In other words, individuals can perceive the cooperative joint activity and decide whether and how to contribute to its development. They manipulate the contents of the shared workspace, and they monitor what happens to it. And it constantly develops as the activity progresses.

The individuals put new contributions (i.e. objects or events) into the shared workspace. But those contributions stay in the shared workspace only if they can be monitored by both individuals. This means that they can interpret those

---

[11] In a cooperative joint activity, an entity is manifest if both individuals are confident that both individuals are aware of that entity. We believe that our notion of manifestness corresponds closely to Peacocke's (2005) notion of mutual open-ended availability, which he defined as follows: 'Each perceives that the other perceives that *s* obtains; and if either is occurrently aware that the other is aware that he is aware ... that *s* obtains, then the state of affairs of his being so occurrently aware is available to the other's occurrent awareness' (p. 302).

[12] If our furniture builders both suddenly realize that they should be using the drill rather than the screwdriver, then the drill might be in the shared workspace and in parallel attention, but not be manifest (until one of them refers to it).

contributions with respect to other contributions or their background knowledge (or expertise).

In a cooperative joint activity, the objects and events can be *jointly
manipulated* by the interacting individuals in pursuit of the goal of the activity
and have some meaning with respect to that activity (and this is because those
objects have relevant joint affordances). More precisely, at least one individual
must be able to manipulate any object or event and all individuals must be able
to monitor the object or event, but any manipulations that are part of the
cooperative joint activity are joint manipulations. Our furniture builders make
use of a shared workspace that contains furniture components (such as legs or
drawers), screws and tools, as well as events such as drilling holes. These are
the entities that are represented in the joint action plan and can be jointly
manipulated in a manner that is relevant to the success of the cooperative joint
activity. As we have noted, the workspace does not contain entities corresponding to the colour of the screws or the texture of the wood (or the event of a
radio playing in the background) – and this is because these properties are not
constituents of the plan. (In Figure 2.4, we use the photograph as a proxy for
the meaningful entities.)

The shared workspace contains the actions of both individuals and the
effects of those actions on objects. The workspace does not directly reflect
individual contributions to those actions. When the builders are screwing the
components together (i.e. in Figure 2.4), their actions are individuated in the
workspace. But after they have finished, the resulting bit of furniture does not
reflect their individual contributions – rather, it reflects their (joint) goal – and
so the shared workspace no longer reflects their individual contributions.[13]

2.5.3   Shared and Individual Workspaces

In cooperative joint activities, the shared workspace is defined with respect to a
dyad (or group). It contains those aspects of reality that both individuals attend
to. If *B* is using a screwdriver but *A* does not notice what *B* is doing (or
assumes *B* is using a drill), then the screwdriver is not part of the shared
workspace. *A* is therefore unable to monitor the (complete) component of the
action performed by her partner and hence the progress of their cooperative
joint activity. The intuition is that the shared workspace contains the objects
and events that are directly accessible to both individuals (i.e. that they both

---

[13] We again stress that we distinguish the workspace from the individuals' representations. For
example, they may represent the process of construction and remember each individual's
contribution (separately). But such information is represented within the individuals (as in
Figure 2.4), not in the shared workspace.

can attend to) and relevant to their joint activity. The shared workspace therefore does not contain elements that one individual attends to but the other does not.

However, we now refine our discussion so the workspace as a whole is divided into a shared workspace and two individual workspaces (for a dyad). The shared workspace contains elements that can be manipulated by at least one individual and can be monitored by both individuals. The individual workspaces consist of elements that one but not both individuals can attend to and which are relevant to the cooperative joint activity. In our example, the individual workspaces may contain a screwdriver that individual B can see but individual A cannot, or a preparatory activity (e.g. selecting a screw) that B undertakes and which is not observed by A. In most cooperative joint activities, objects and events in the individual workspace are regularly moved into the shared workspace.[14] In our account, the individual workspaces play a minor role (and in fact it is often unclear whether an object or event is in an individual workspace or outside the domain of the cooperative joint activity).

The shared workspace also plays a role in multi-party activities, for example when three individuals are building furniture. In such cases, the shared workspace contains objects and events that all individuals attend to, but there are workspaces that are shared between some but not all individuals. However, we can often interpret a multi-party joint activity in terms of subordinate dyadic activities, and for each of these sub-activities we can define a shared workspace as involving the two participating individuals (see Chapter 10).[15]

2.5.4   Connecting Individuals to the Shared Workspace

As Figure 2.4 shows, the individuals interact with each other via the shared workspace. The solid (thick) arrows from A and B to the workspace represent the processes involved in producing the actions – in this case, using the screwdriver and holding the wood in place. These therefore represent the outputs of each individual's joint action implementer. They are single-headed, because they represent actual contributions from the individuals to the shared

---

[14] For an entity to qualify for an individual workspace, that individual must be able to introduce it into the shared workspace (cf. Section 11.1, footnote 1).

[15] If someone observes a cooperative joint activity (i.e. without taking part), she may attend to the same entities as one or both of the actors. Such entities are not in a workspace that is shared between the observer and the actors, because there is no such shared workspace. In addition, both actors can attend to an entity that is not part of the cooperative joint activity, in which case it would not be in the shared workspace. (For the furniture builders, background music is unlikely to be in their shared workspace, but the same music would be in the shared workspace of ballroom dancers.)

workspace (i.e. putting behaviours into the workspace). The thin grey arrows, in contrast, represent processes that do not contribute directly to the activity. These additional processes are concerned with monitoring and control of the cooperative joint action (rather than with acting itself). They are double-headed because they can involve feedback to the individual (i.e. downward arrowhead) or prediction from the individual (i.e. upward arrowhead). Importantly, perception of the cooperative joint action is an (important) component of feedback to the individual. The horizontal arrows (i.e. connecting the thick arrow to the joint action implementer) are concerned with 'private' information (i.e. implementation); the vertical arrows are concerned with 'public' information (i.e. the shared workspace).

The horizontal grey arrows (i.e. connecting the solid arrows with the joint action implementer) represent monitoring of the implementer (i.e. the mechanisms involved in implementing an action). In the downward direction, they correspond to proprioceptive feedback. An example would be A's feedback from exerting more torque on the screwdriver (which of course is not available to B). In the upward direction, they correspond to proprioceptive predictions, for example the expected sensation of turning the screwdriver.

The vertical grey arrows (i.e. connecting the shared workspace with the joint action implementer) correspond to perceiving and monitoring the workspace itself. The downward arrowheads represent feedback from the shared workspace, and constitute action perception and monitoring. Most obviously, the feedback can relate to both individuals' contributions at the same time (e.g. holding the board and screwing). Thus it can indicate whether both individuals are acting in a coordinated way. Alternatively it can indicate whether there is a problem, for example if they are not acting at exactly the appropriate time with respect to each other, or are presenting the wrong component or tool for each other's actions. In such cases, the feedback relates directly to the joint action. However, each individual can also receive feedback associated with their own behaviour or their partner's behaviour.

The upward grey arrowheads correspond to predictions of the shared workspace. For example, they might represent that A predicts that A and B will be coordinated (e.g. B will present the wood at the right height and timing for A to screw). However, it is also possible for each individual to predict their own behaviour (e.g. B predicts B will present the wood in 500 ms) or their partner's behaviour (e.g. A predicts B will present the wood in 500 ms).

The arrows connecting the individuals to the shared workspace make it clear how the individuals can access and represent components of the workspace. We have noted that the workspace reflects a cooperative joint activity (e.g. furniture-building), but an individual can predict (via the upward grey arrowhead) or monitor (via the downward grey arrowhead) one individual's contribution to the joint action.

2.5.5   Control and the Shared Workspace

The shared workspace contains behaviours and their physical consequences in relation to the context (i.e. the props). It does not contain plans or their implementation.[16] But the individuals can interpret the workspace (via the vertical arrows) in relation to their own joint action plans and implementation, as well as behaviour. For example, A's joint action plan includes the assumption that that B is planning to construct the drawer. But by perceiving the shared workspace, A determines that B is instead attaching the legs to the base (which would reflect a different joint action plan). Hence, A's joint action planner detects an error (which captures the fact that A and B's plans do not match). Note that on another occasion A might make a prediction error by predicting that B will contribute to the constructing the drawer and then finding out that she does not.

In contrast, if A is holding the board for B to screw and the screwdriver slips, A detects a joint implementation error (which captures the fact that A and B's implementations do not match). Finally, if A assumes that B is inserting the screw appropriately, but notices that B is pointing the screw at the wrong angle, A detects a behavioural error. In all of these cases, A notices a mismatch between the behaviour in the shared workspace and what A assumes on the basis of A's joint action planner and implementer. In this way, the shared workspace plays a key role in distributed control.

The arrows emanating from the shared workspace therefore enable closed-loop control (or pseudo-closed-loop control) over a joint activity. The feedback is necessary for closed-loop control and the prediction facilitates that control by preparing the individual for upcoming contributions to the joint activity. Feedback can affect the process of planning, implementation or behaviour. The monitoring of behaviour takes place via the results of the activities that form part of the shared workspace. So the workspace contains outcomes (e.g. a screw at a particular angle) and each individual monitors those outcomes, so that A may notice a problem (e.g. that the screw is misaligned) that B does not notice. Each individual can also monitor the joint implementation, for example detecting that A is moving the screwdriver to a location higher than B is moving the piece of wood. Finally, each individual can monitor planning, for example detecting that A has chosen the wrong screw to connect the pieces that B has picked up. Note that many acts of monitoring may involve more than one layer. For example, A may notice that

---

[16] An individual can of course explicitly communicate a plan, for example saying *I intend to drill the hole*. Such communication of course constitutes a behaviour that enters the shared workspace.

the screw is wrong at the planning layer because she knows that the screw should have a cross on it (as directed in the instructions) but also because she sees that it will not fit the hole (a problem at the implementational layer). In sum, individuals have great flexibility over their monitoring. They can monitor at the level of planning, implementation or behaviour, and can monitor the joint activity (joint monitoring), their own contribution to the joint activity (self-monitoring), or their partner's contribution to the joint activity (other-monitoring).[17]

2.6 Four Characteristics of Cooperative Joint Action Systems

We now define and discuss four characteristics of cooperative joint action systems that make them successful, and which can be empirically investigated. The four characteristics are *alignment, simulation, prediction and synchrony.* We interpret these characteristics in terms of the shared workspace model, and we illustrate by considering time-critical cooperative joint actions that make the role of the individual cognitive representations clear. Again, we focus on joint construction of flat-pack furniture but discuss other cooperative joint actions when appropriate.

2.6.1 Alignment

As we have noted (see Chapter 1), alignment occurs when two (or more) individuals have similar relevant representations. As it is a property of representations rather than behaviour, it relates to our levels of planning and implementation. It is therefore defined with respect to the individuals-within-the-system rather than the shared workspace or the relationship between the

---

[17] Our use of the shared workspace framework comes by analogy from a method of teaching in which students privately compose their own contributions and then post them to a 'bulletin board' that is publicly accessible (and manipulable). Students can compose on a laptop and then send their contribution to a large screen (the 'bulletin board'). For instance, this approach can be used in teaching scientific writing: each student might have the task of rephrasing a badly worded text on their laptop and pressing return when satisfied. Their contribution then appears alongside the other students' contributions on the screen. Contributions are visible to everyone in the group (cf. traditional 'Blackboard' models in artificial intelligence; Newell, 1962; see Craig, 1995). Each student's contribution can then be assessed by all the students and, of course, the tutor. Moreover, these contributions can be manipulated publicly – the students and tutor can compare different contributions, and the tutor in particular can manipulate (i.e. rework) the contributions. This analogy differs from our proposal in that our workspace changes constantly. The 'bulletin board' also contains an indeterminate amount of information that the students do not attend to. In Chapter 11, we discuss the augmentation of the shared workspace. A 'bulletin board' in the context of teaching provides one such form of augmentation, though we use an example involving a simple whiteboard.

individuals and the workspace.[18] Note that alignment is incompatible with monadic cognitive science, because it is defined with respect to two individuals' representations. Alignment underlies behaviour matching, which is pervasive between interacting individuals, whether engaged in cooperative joint activity or not (e.g. Chartrand & Bargh, 1999; Lakin & Chartrand, 2003; see Dijksterhuis & Bargh, 2001, for a review).

In a successful joint activity, the individuals are well aligned with each other with respect to their joint action planners and joint action implementers. If B has to drill a hole into the board held by A, we propose that both A and B represent the joint plan to drill the hole. In more detail, they both represent the (overall) goal of drilling the hole appropriately. They also represent the plan as a set of plan components which reflect each individual's different role in achieving the goal. In our example, the components might be that A holds the board at location x and time t and that B drills the hole at location x and time t. Importantly, x and t are the same across A and B, which reflects the interdependence of the plan components within each individual, but x and t need not be instantiated to particular values at this point. The goal and the plan components are of course represented in the joint action planner (Figure 2.4).[19] So alignment of joint action plans occurs when A and B represent the same goal and plan components, and cooperative joint activity is much more likely to be successful when this is the case (or at least very nearly so).

In addition, both A and B represent the joint action implementation that A presents the board to B at a specific location and time, and that B holds the drill at the same location and time. In other words, the location and time are necessarily instantiated to particular values in the implementer. Such instantiation can take place in many ways, for example by A saying *Now!* while picking up the board, or by each individual attending to the other's behaviour (e.g. reaching for the board or drill). So the individuals' joint action implementers are aligned when the values are the same (which is a more stringent condition than is necessary for alignment of joint action plans).

Notice also that A realizes that A refers to herself and B to her partner, and B realizes that A refers to his partner and B to himself, both in the planner and the implementer. Thus, A and B's plans are not aligned if both A and B plan to hold the board or both A and B plan to use the drill. Similarly, their implementations are not aligned if both A and B actually hold the board or both A and B actually

---

[18] Our use of alignment therefore contrasts with Gentner and Markman (1997), who are concerned with the relationship between different representational domains within an individual (e.g. between Kepler's representations of planetary motion and light).

[19] In one representational format, both A and B represent the plan components **holds(A, board, x, t)** and **drills(B, board, x, t)**, with the first argument referring to the agent. This 'propositional' format helps emphasize that the representation is abstract and could correspond to different implementations.

use the drill (or try to do so). In other words, alignment of both plans and implementation is defined indexically.

As we have noted, alignment is a property of representations, not behaviour. But alignment is clearly related to behaviour – the behaviour of an aligned dyad is, in general, different from the behaviour of a misaligned dyad. For example, two individuals shaking hands will move their arms similarly (e.g. opening their hands at the same time) only if their representations are well aligned (i.e. they plan and implement the same joint action). In this case, behaviour matching is a consequence of alignment. In other cases, aligned individuals perform complementary actions, as in our furniture construction example. Some aspects of behaviour matching (e.g. acting at the same time) are often indicative of alignment, but the relationship between behaviour matching and alignment is complex (and we shall address it only in relation to language; see Chapters 6 and 7).

The shared workspace records task-relevant behaviour in relation to its environment. The contents of the workspace are perceived and predicted by the individuals. When those individuals are well aligned, they tend to perceive and predict the same contents for the workspace (and at the same time as each other). On occasion, the individuals may perceive or predict differently, for example if their perspectives are different, or if one can see (or hear) better than the other, or indeed if they bring radically different background assumptions to bear on the joint activity (which would of course mean that their joint action planners and implementers would be very different). Such situations will tend to go with misalignment and can often impair successful cooperative joint activity.

We noted (see Section 2.2) that both individuals are aware that they are both taking part in the cooperative joint activity, that they realize when the activity begins and ends, and that they share a commitment to the activity. In other words, they are aligned on their involvement in the task. Second, they are (generally) aware that they are aligning on task performance – they are developing aligned plans and implementations, and therefore engaging in appropriate (matched or complementary) behaviour. We return to these issues of the *meta-representation of alignment* when discussing language (see Chapter 7), when we also consider the relationship between alignment and concepts such as common ground and mutual knowledge (see Clark & Marshall, 1981).

Finally, a general implication of our account is that alignment is related to task success. In other words, the goal (as represented by the joint action planner) is more likely to be realized when the plan components and the joint action implementer are well aligned (and when the individuals perceive and predict the shared workspace in the same way as each other). The less well aligned the individuals are, the less successful the cooperative joint activity is likely to be.

2.6.2   Simulation

An agent simulates an action when he or she undergoes some of the processes involved in performing that action (without actually doing so). The processes may be executed in the same way as the processes involved in the action itself. Alternatively they may be executed differently but produce the same output. Such simulation can be used 'off-line' to imagine (or rehearse) future actions (i.e. in prospective memory; Spreng et al., 2018) or to remember and interpret past actions, for example if they have been partly forgotten. It can also be used 'on-line' to facilitate action and associated motor learning (Wolpert, 1997; see Chapter 3).

Simulation plays a role in action observation, when an individual undergoes some of the processes that the other individual undergoes. Strong evidence for simulation of others' actions comes from studies showing engagement of action-related mechanisms during action observation (see Wilson & Knoblich, 2005), from the extensive literature associated with mirror neurons (Gallese & Goldman, 1998), and from mind reading (Goldman, 2006). It can be used 'on-line' to facilitate action understanding and 'off-line' to imagine another individual's future actions or to interpret their past actions (see Hurley, 2008). Such other-simulation will prove particularly important to our analysis of cooperative joint action. Ultimately, our concern is with joint simulation – that is, simulating a cooperative joint activity in which one individual simulates both individuals' contributions (at the same time).

2.6.3   Prediction (and Postdiction)

As pointed out by Sebanz et al. (2006), many joint activities (such as lifting a heavy object together or dancing a tango) appear to require prediction. It would be impossible to perform such activities by perceiving individual or joint actions and modifying the action on the basis of this perception. For example, reacting to your dance partner's forward step before performing the complementary backwards step would be far too slow. Instead, you must predict how your partner is likely to move and plan your own movement at the same time.

Similarly, consider two people attempting to carry a piano up the stairs. The success of their cooperative joint activity depends on their applying (roughly) the same force as each other at the same time. This is possible only if they predict each other. For example, one piano mover must predict when the other is likely to increase force and increase force himself at the same time. Thus, *A* might realize that *B* is approaching the first step and predict that *B* will increase force in one second in order to accommodate the step. Importantly, *A* also realizes that *B* cannot succeed unless *A* also increases force at this point. In other words, *A* predicts *B*'s upcoming action and modifies his own action accordingly. *B* must also predict that *A* will act appropriately when *B* encounters the step (i.e. *B* must trust *A*). The movement of each person and, importantly, the piano are reflected in the shared workspace. The prediction (and of course the perception) of the movement allows the piano movers to determine the force (which is represented in the joint action implementer). Note that the movers could also use language to support accurate timing. If one of them says *one, two, three* at a constant rate (and they both know the convention to move at *three*), then their cooperative joint activity is likely to succeed.

Such predictions of the content of the shared workspace are represented by the vertical upward grey arrowheads. Like the downward feedback arrowheads, the upward predictive arrowheads typically apply to the cooperative joint activity as a whole, but it is also possible for them to apply to a component of that activity – and that component can be the activity of either individual. In our flat-pack construction example, *A* predicts that *A* and *B* will hold the screw and the wood at the appropriate height, and that the screw has a cross on it. *A* then notices any discrepancy between her predictive monitoring and the contents of the shared workspace – the relative height of the screw and the wood, or the mark on the screw.

Simulation can then be used to facilitate prediction. One possibility is that *A* predicts *B*'s movement on the basis of *A*'s experience seeing *B* or other people like *B* prepare a similar activity in the past. *A* has previously seen *B*'s hand follow a particular trajectory, when performing activities like picking up a screw, and uses the trajectory as a basis for prediction. This does not involve other-simulation. But when people act together, we propose that they emphasize a route that does involve simulation. *A* sees *B*'s hand position and would then determine how she would pick up the screw if it were her hand. Informally, *A* sees the hand and the way it is moving, then thinks of it as her own hand, and uses the mechanisms that she would use to move her own hand to predict *B*'s hand movement. In other words, *A* would simulate *B*'s movements, treating *B*'s hand positions as though they were *A*'s own hand positions. (This idealization ignores the fact that *A* will have to accommodate for differences between *A*'s and *B*'s bodies; see Chapter 3.) We call this *prediction-by-simulation* (following Pickering & Garrod, 2013). And when *A* predicts *A*-and-*B*'s cooperative joint activity, then *A* is using joint simulation to make the predictions.

We have noted that the process of interpreting past events is closely related to the process of predicting upcoming events. The mechanism of prediction-by-simulation can also be used after the event – that is, as postdiction-by-simulation. Under such conditions, the mechanism is used to check that the action occurred as would have been predicted. In other words, it can form the basis of what Halle and Stevens (1959) called analysis-by-synthesis – a framework that was developed for language but which can be applied to other domains in which candidate analyses can be generated.[20] Observing an action leads to a partial analysis enabling the observer to synthesize candidate actions that can then be compared to the observed action. The important point is that in analysis-by-synthesis the action is interpreted on the basis of the observer's prior experience of carrying out that action. So we consider prediction-by-simulation to apply both to instances of prediction and instances of postdiction.[21]

In our account, the use of simulation for prediction is key to understanding joint activity in general (and, as we shall see, dialogue in particular). Simulation provides a mechanism that explains activity that takes place within individuals. Of course, alignment leads to more accurate prediction in joint activity and therefore we can see how alignment, simulation and prediction are closely interrelated. We consider these issues in more detail in Chapter 3.

2.6.4   Synchrony

Finally, many joint activities require *synchrony* between participants' actions. In handshaking, A and B tend to move at the same rate as each other, so that they reach the end point together. The need for synchrony is even more apparent in complex, time-critical activities, such as dancing a tango. In such cases, a failure of synchrony would cause the activity to collapse, even if both participants were performing every individual act flawlessly. Like alignment, synchrony requires a systems analysis and is incompatible with a monadic cognitive science. One possibility would be to treat synchrony as a component of alignment. We do not do so, because we regard alignment as relating to the content of representations, whereas synchrony is concerned with timing, specifically in relation to implementation and its effects on behaviour.[22] (Hence, Chapter 9 concentrates on synchronization.)

Clear examples of synchrony occur in activities such as synchronized diving, clapping in unison or violin playing in an orchestra. Here, the extent of synchronization is reflected in the timing of the solid arrows leading from the individuals to the shared workspace. For example, if B's dive is 100 ms behind A's dive, but all aspects of their plans, execution and behaviour are identical, then B's arrow will be slightly behind A's. In a rhythmical joint

---

[20] Analysis-by-synthesis has applied to vision (see Yuille & Kersten, 2006), but without any obvious commitment to simulation.

[21] Grush (2004) makes a similar point about the mechanisms for simulating action, which he calls emulators. He argues that emulators can be used both predictively and postdictively to help interpret others' actions.

[22] Of course, it is possible to represent time (e.g. I might represent how long it will take us to build the furniture), in which case the representation would be relevant to alignment.

activity, individuals can be in or out of phase; and if they are in phase, their phase angle can be zero (when clapping in unison), 180 degrees (i.e. in counter-phase), or another value in between.

Individuals can synchronize (or desynchronize) as a result of rhythmic entrainment. For example, pairs of participants synchronize the rocking of chairs that initially have different frequencies (Richardson et al., 2007) and start to clap in unison (Néda et al., 2000). Rather than reflecting alignment of representations, such entrainment involves processes by which patterns of oscillations come into phase with each other, in a manner comparable to the entrainment of clocks or the flashing of fireflies (Strogatz, 2002). Like alignment, synchrony is important for prediction – it helps different individuals predict exactly when their partner will act.

2.7   Conclusion

In this chapter, we have argued that accounting for cooperative joint activity requires us to steer between monadic cognitive science (that is concerned only with individuals) and some form of collective cognition (in which the individual ultimately plays no role). To do this, we have treated the dyad as a system in which each individual contributes to a shared workspace and acts on the basis of the contents of that workspace. We have considered the individuals as having representations that allow them to plan and carry out their joint contributions, and have discussed central characteristics of the system and the individuals within that system.

3 Executing, Understanding and Controlling Joint Activity

In Chapter 2 we discussed cooperative joint activities in general to highlight problems associated with understanding dialogue. We emphasized the problem of how pairs of individuals can jointly perform these activities. To reflect the distributed action and control underlying this performance, we introduced a systems framework in which individuals interact via a shared workspace. In Chapter 4 we apply this analysis to dialogue, but in this chapter we consider the principles by which individuals carry out and control their joint actions in terms of the arrows connecting the individuals to the shared workspace.

We first consider individuals' own actions (both isolated actions and components of joint actions) – how they perform, predict and control those actions. We then consider how each individual predicts and interprets their partner's actions. At this point, we are able to put these two components together into a framework for executing, controlling and understanding cooperative joint activity, first in terms of each individual's contribution considered separately and then as a single integrated system in which the control is distributed between the individuals. We end by considering how such distributed control promotes alignment between the individuals' joint action planners and implementers.

Let us first return to Figure 2.4 (repeated as Figure 3.1). Because our interest is in the arrows, we ignore the internal representational structure of the two individuals, apart from the distinction between joint planning and joint implementation. The thick black vertical arrows correspond to the processes leading to an individual contribution to a cooperative joint action (e.g. holding furniture components in place for them to be drilled together) and involve inserting that contribution into the shared workspace.[1] The horizontal grey arrow (within each individual) relates to private processes (before the individual contribution to the joint action has been inserted into the shared workspace), such as the internal representations (i.e. internal states) involved in arm movement. The downward arrowhead refers to perception of those internal states (and

---

[1] We re-emphasize that the workspace is continuously updated by the consequences of action components.

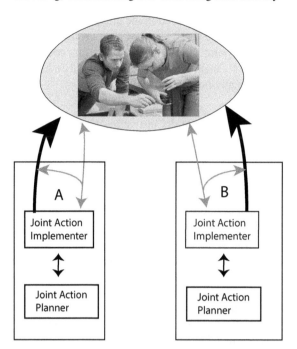

Figure 3.1 The shared workspace framework for joint action.

associated monitoring); the arrowhead pointing to the black arrow refers to predictions of those states. These private processes of course make reference only to the representations of the actor. In contrast, the vertical grey arrows (linking the individuals to the shared workspace) relate to public information and can therefore involve behaviours of either or (importantly) both participants. The downward arrowhead refers to the perception of the behaviours (and is shared with the horizontal arrow); the upward arrowhead refers to the prediction of those behaviours.

But how do the arrows in Figure 3.1 work? In other words, how can people process individual contributions as components of joint actions, and how can they then combine these components? To address this, we explicate our framework in terms of computational theories of motor control (Wolpert et al., 2011) as applied to joint action (Wolpert et al., 2003). We do this by considering individual components of joint action, first from the point of view of the actor and then from the point of view of her partner. We then recombine these components to understand joint action.

Our example is two people shaking hands. Each individual actor has to move their hand to grasp a target. Of course, each individual's target is their partner's hand, which is itself being used in the grasping act. We can therefore analyse each individual's action separately, but we must bear in mind that they form part of a cooperative joint action. We therefore first consider individual A's action, then consider A's interpretation of B's action, then how A integrates A and B's actions, and finally how A and B act jointly.

3.1   Performing, Predicting and Controlling One's Own Actions

Theories of action distinguish fundamentally between the implementation of an act and a prediction of the outcome of that act. This distinction goes back to Von Helmholtz (1867/1962) and underlies many more recent accounts (e.g. Jordan & Rumelhart, 1992). We draw on a specific account from computational neuroscience (Davidson & Wolpert, 2005; Wolpert, 1997), but reframed using psychological terminology concerned with perception and action. For present purposes, the key point is that people construct a prediction of the experience of performing an action and use that prediction to control the performance of the action.[2]

Figure 3.2 is a schematic diagram of our account, which can be seen as corresponding to our account of individual A in Figure 3.1. Using our handshaking example, A generates the action command to move her hand (as part of the handshake). This command emanates from the joint action planner (which plans A's individual contribution to the joint act of handshaking). The command initiates two processes in Figure 3.2: the top process that produces the behaviour (reflected in the shared workspace), and the bottom process that produces the predicted perception (i.e. the predicted action percept). The top process leads from the action command to the shared workspace and corresponds to the thick arrow in Figure 3.1 (and so both are in black). It begins by implementing the action to produce an action representation, which is a representation of the internal states involved in hand movement. These states might include temporal profiles of muscle activity (see Wolpert et al., 2011). This representation in turn provides the input to the motor system that generates the hand movement (i.e. it transduces representations into behaviour), and the hand movement is reflected in the shared workspace.

In addition, the bottom process in Figure 3.2 uses an *efference copy* of the action command to predict the act and the percept of the act, and serves as the basis of action control. The efference copy is inputted into the forward action model to produce a predicted action representation (and corresponds to the

---

[2] Performing the action corresponds to both what we have called execution and behaviour. We treat the action implementer as the process that corresponds to execution and the motor system as the process that brings about the behaviour. These two uses of *action* are natural but admittedly slightly ambiguous.

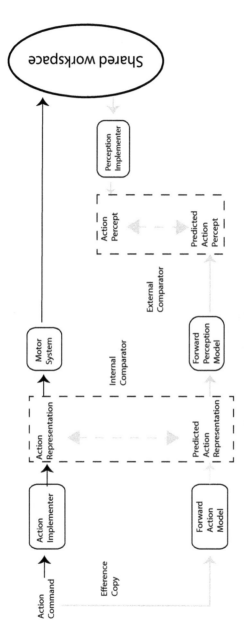

Figure 3.2 A model of action control. Mechanisms occur in closed boxes. Dotted boxes (and dotted arrows) refer to processes that compare representations. The shared workspace is elliptical. The use of black and grey arrows corresponds to their use in Figure 3.1. (Note that the output of the internal and external comparators can be fed back to the action command via an inverse model.)

upward horizontal grey arrowhead in Figure 3.1). This representation might include predictions of some of the temporal profiles of muscle activity. Importantly, it is independent of the muscle activity itself. This predicted action representation provides the input into the forward perception model which outputs the predicted action percept – that is, the predicted perception of the hand movement (such as what it should look or feel like).[3] This process corresponds to the upward vertical grey arrowhead in Figure 3.1.[4] Just as the act depends on the application of the action command to the current state of the implementer (in our example, where the hand is positioned before the command), so the predicted action representation depends on the application of the efference copy of the action command to the current state of the forward action model (corresponding to where the hand is positioned before the command).[5]

Finally, the actor perceives the behaviour (which is reflected in the shared workspace) using the perception implementer (via vision, or even touch or hearing) and produces an action percept (the downward grey arrowhead emanating from the shared workspace). Of course, all of these steps are dynamically updated as the hand moves towards its target – A initiates many action commands and their efference copies, the intermediate processes lead to changes in the representations, and the shared workspace is incrementally updated.

Importantly, the efference copy is (in general) processed more quickly than the action command itself (see Davidson & Wolpert, 2005). For example, the command to move the hand causes the implementer to activate muscles, a process that is comparatively slow. In contrast, the forward models make use of representations of the position of the hand, state of the muscles, and so on (and may involve simplifications and approximations). These representations may be in terms of equations (e.g. using hand coordinates), which the forward models can (typically) solve rapidly (e.g. using a network that represents relevant aspects of mathematics, or even a look-up table). So the predicted action representation is usually ready before the (implemented) action representation, and the predicted action percept is usually ready before the (actual) action percept.

Implementations and predictions can be compared at two points. First, the action representation (e.g. a profile of muscle activity) can be compared with the predicted action representation (e.g. a predicted profile of muscle activity),

---

[3] In Wolpert's (1997) terminology, the forward action model is the forward dynamic model, and the forward perception model is the forward output model (see Pickering & Garrod, 2013).

[4] In fact, the shared workspace reflects behaviour, not the action percept, and so regarding the arrowhead corresponding to the predicted action percept as interfacing with the shared workspace is a diagrammatic simplification, but it should not lead to any confusion.

[5] Note that this predicted percept is compatible with the theory of event coding (Hommel et al., 2001), in which actions are represented in terms of their predicted perceptual consequences.

via the internal comparator. (In Figure 3.1, we regard internal comparison as occurring before external comparison because the horizontal arrow is inside the box.) Any discrepancy between these two representations (as determined by the comparator) can be fed back so that it can modify the next action command accordingly. If the predicted muscle activation profile (i.e. the profile that the actor judges is needed to direct the hand to the target) is inconsistent with actual muscle activation profile (e.g. because of fatigue), then the comparator registers a discrepancy that can be fed back to modify the action command. This process involves an inverse model, which is the (paired) inverse copy of a forward model (i.e. mapping from percept to action command), discussed below. It could, for example, prevent the actor implementing an action command that would lead to the hand falling short of the partner's hand. Note that in fact the actor might perform more than one internal comparison (e.g. with respect to different muscles).

Second, the action percept can be compared with the predicted action percept, via the external comparator. In our example, the actor predicts the experience of the hand on a certain trajectory towards the target. The actor performs the hand movement and the predicted action percept is compared to the actual action percept, using the external comparator. Any discrepancy (as determined by the comparator) can also be fed back and used to modify the next action command. If the hand is experienced as being to the left of its predicted position (e.g. through vision or proprioception), the next action command can move it more to the right (though in practice such correction may well be too late).

As we have noted, the process of making predictions and comparing them with outcomes takes place repeatedly. Our example of hand movement focused on a single act of moving to a target (the partner's hand). But in reality, the actor compares the prediction with the (implemented) movements dynamically. For example, the actor might first open the hand and direct fingers towards the target, and then compare the experience of these movements with the predicted experience. If a finger were mis-positioned, the output of the comparator could in turn lead to a correction of the action command, and so on.

3.1.1   Other Functions of Forward Modelling of Action

Importantly, forward (and inverse) modelling has other functions besides predicting the outcomes of an action and helping repair errors. First, forward models can cancel the sensory effects of self-motion (reafference cancellation) when these sensory effects match the predicted movement. This cancellation enables people to differentiate between perceptual effects of their own actions and those reflecting changes in the world (and can therefore help explain why self-applied tickling is not effective; Blakemore et al., 1999). But also it can be used to help estimate either the current state or a past state, given that perception is not entirely accurate. The best estimate of the current position of the hand combines the estimate that comes from the percept (i.e. the estimate of the current hand position) with the predicted percept (i.e. before the hand movement). For example, a person can estimate the position of her hand in a dark room by remembering the action command that underlay her hand movement to its current location (along with proprioceptive feedback, of course). Similarly, the best estimate of a past (intermediate) position (i.e. a postdiction) combines the evidence that comes from the current (final) position with the predicted percept (i.e. before the hand movement). In other words, both current estimate and postdiction can make use of forward models generated at a prior point (and recall that we treat prediction as including postdiction; see Section 2.6.3).

To illustrate further, we use the analogy of an old-fashioned sailor navigating across the ocean (see Grush, 2004; Pickering & Garrod, 2013). He starts at a known position which he marks on his chart (which is his model of the ocean) and sets a compass course and speed. He lays out the corresponding course on the chart and traces out where he should be at 12.00 (his predicted act), and determines what his sextant should read at this time and place (his predicted percept).[6] He then sets off at 09.00 through the water until 12.00 (his act). At 12.00, he uses his sextant to estimate his position in relation to the sun (his percept) and compares the predicted and observed sextant readings (using the comparator). He can then use this comparison in various ways. The first use is error correction: if he is not confident of his course keeping, he pays more attention to the actual reading, and uses it to change his course accordingly. If he is not confident of his sextant reading (e.g. it is misty), he pays more attention to the predicted reading, maintains his current course and estimates his current position on the basis of the prediction rather than the sextant reading. This procedure is equivalent to estimating current hand position following movement in a dark room. Finally, if the mist subsequently clears and he becomes confident about his final location (at 15.00) but wishes to determine his intermediate location (at 12.00, because a crew member fell overboard at that time), he combines his previously predicted course (i.e. made at 09.00) with the final accurate sextant reading (at 15.00) to postdict his intermediate location. This procedure is equivalent to estimating an intermediate hand position following movement in a dark room.

---

[6] He can use this prediction (before he sets off), for example to inform the coastguards of where he plans to be and when. The prediction is available before the event and can be used for other purposes.

Forward modelling also plays an important role in motor learning (Jordan & Rumelhart, 1992; Kawato et al., 1987; see Wolpert, 1997). Learning how to grasp a target requires learning a model that maps the target location onto an action command to move one's hand to that location, which is of course the inverse model. The inverse model could in principle be developed directly through trial-and-error learning. However, in learning to execute rapid movements (e.g. learning to move the eyes quickly and precisely to a target) such real-world feedback will be too slow to allow for on-line modification of the inverse model. Therefore motor control theorists argue that learning initially involves tuning the forward model on the basis of discrepancies between the sensory outcomes of the action and the forward model prediction of those outcomes (Haith & Krakauer, 2013). It is only at this point that the forward model is used to generate an appropriate inverse model for executing that action. For example, our actor might move her hand slightly to the left of the target, tune her forward model on the basis of this discrepancy (which leads to on-line corrective movement), and incorporate the change into the inverse model (which leads to better targeting in future). In fact, the inverse model is also used in postdiction – in our example, by 'tracing back' from the final state to the action command that leads to that final state via the intermediate state and thereby providing a postdiction of that intermediate state.

The relative use of internal versus external comparison depends on skill level (which is a consequence of learning). For unskilled performance, there is no accurate forward model, so the actor can control the action only by determining how closely the action percept matches a fixed goal (e.g. grasping a target). But as an actor repeatedly performs the task successfully, she develops a forward model that predicts the action percept from the specific action command, and the accuracy of this forward model gradually increases. This increased accuracy allows the actor to compare the action percept with the predicted action percept (i.e. external comparison) and feed back the results of this comparison to modify the action command, thus developing an accurate inverse model. The inverse model is therefore the mechanism by which the output of the internal or external comparator is fed back to the action command.

But repeatedly applying the action command does not only lead to regular action percepts that can be predicted. It also leads to regular action representations (internal states) that can be predicted as well. Initially, the relationship between the action command and the predicted action representations is not stable, but over time it stabilizes. The actor therefore learns to compare the action representations with the predicted action representations (i.e. using internal comparison) and feeds back the results of this comparison to modify the action command (again, developing an accurate inverse model). Such internal comparison is fast, because the action representations are developed earlier than the action percepts. As the actor becomes more skilled, the control and monitoring of behaviour tends to increasingly emphasize internal comparison, though external comparison remains important. (Below, we shall argue that external comparison is more important in joint action.)

Actors can dynamically change their interpretation of an unfolding action using forward-inverse model pairs. In their Modular Selection and Identification for Control (MOSAIC) account, Haruno et al. (2001) proposed that actors run sets of model pairs in parallel, with each forward model making different predictions about how the action might unfold in different contexts. By matching actual movements against these different predictions, the system can shift responsibility for controlling the action towards the model pair whose forward model prediction best fits that movement. For example, an actor starts to pick up a small (and apparently light) object using a weak grip but subsequently finds the grip insufficient to lift the object. According to MOSAIC, she would then shift the responsibility for controlling the action to a new forward-inverse model pairing, which produces a firmer grip.

The same principles apply to more complex structured activities such as the process of drinking a cup of tea. Here the forward model provides information ahead of time about the sequence and overlap between the different stages in the process (moving the hand to the cup, picking it up, moving it to the mouth, opening the mouth etc.) and represents the predicted action percept at each stage (i.e. the sensory feedback). To account for such complex sequences of actions, Haruno et al. (2003) developed the Hierarchical MOSAIC (HMOSAIC) model. HMOSAIC extends MOSAIC by having hierarchically organized forward-inverse model pairings that link 'high-level' intentions (goals) to 'low-level' motor operations (implementations). Again, this process is dynamic, so that these pairings can be computed and recomputed on-line.

In sum, forward modelling in action allows the actor to predict her upcoming action, in a way that allows her to modify the unfolding action if it fails to match the prediction. In addition, it can be used to facilitate estimation of the current state, to cancel reafference and to support short- and long-term learning. The outputs of the internal and external comparators feed into the mechanism that generates the action command (not illustrated in Figure 3.2), and can thus modify the action command. Therefore, the process of generating the action command and its efference copy and then comparing their consequences constitutes a control loop through which the individual can monitor and correct her actions as they unfold. The system uses what we referred to in Chapter 2 as pseudo-closed-loop controllers (Grush, 2004) because they control the action implementation using forward models.

To conclude, the top (black) line in Figure 3.2 (i.e. the action implementational pathway) corresponds to the solid upward black arrow in Figure 3.1, and leads into the shared workspace. The grey line emanating from the workspace (i.e. the perception implementation pathway) corresponds to the downward vertical grey arrowhead. The bottom line (i.e. the forward model pathway) corresponds to both upward grey arrowheads, with the internal comparator corresponding to the contact between the horizontal grey arrowhead and the solid upward black arrow (i.e. the private action implementer) and the external comparator corresponding to the vertical grey line (with the comparison occurring between the upward predictive arrowhead and downward perceptual arrowhead). The inverse models (which map the outputs of the comparators to the action command) are a component of the downward arrowheads (again, with a distinction between the external and internal comparator loops).[7]

3.2   Predicting and Interpreting Others' Actions Using Simulation

The handshaker also needs to process her partner's hand movements. We have already argued that the perception of the other actor's contributions to many joint actions involves prediction (Chapter 2), and this applies to handshaking. We suggested two ways in which such prediction can happen, one based on the handshaker's prior experience of perceiving handshaking movements by her partner or by other similar people (the association route) and the other based on simulation of that movement (the simulation route) (see Hesslow, 2002, for a discussion of this distinction). We now concentrate on the simulation route, because it requires the handshaker to predict her partner using the same processes that she uses to predict her own action. We do this because joint actors need to integrate self- and other-representations (see Section 3.3).

In theory, the perceiver could simulate by using her own action implementer (and inhibiting its output). However, this would usually be too slow for prediction – much of the time, she would determine her partner's action after he had performed that action. Instead, she can use her forward action model to derive a prediction of her partner's act (and the forward perception model to derive a prediction of her percept of that act). To do this, she derives her partner's action command (intention) from her perception of the previous and current states of his arm (or from background information such as knowledge of his state of mind and the broader context) and uses it to generate an efference copy of the intended act.

Figure 3.3 characterizes the process of predicting another's actions by simulation. *A* observes *B*'s hand moving towards her at time *t* (e.g. in a partly closed position) and incorporates appropriate background knowledge

---

[7] Apart from the inverse model, we have not considered the downward horizontal grey arrowhead. This would be used if the actor used proprioception to perceive an internal state (e.g. muscle activation), in the absence of any prediction.

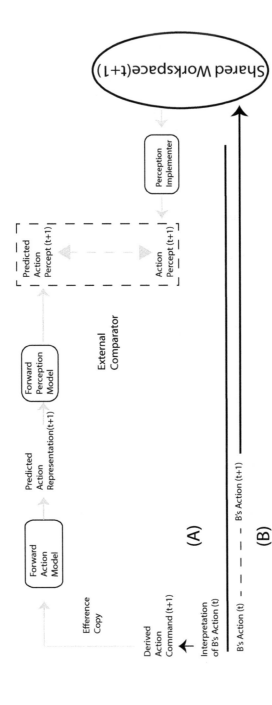

Figure 3.3 A model of the system for action prediction-by-simulation. Mechanisms occur in closed boxes. Dotted boxes (and dotted arrows) refer to processes that compare representations. The shared workspace is elliptical. The use of black and grey arrows corresponds to their use in Figure 3.1.

(e.g. about cultural norms) to interpret it as the precursor to a handshake (in an open position). A uses this interpretation (along with appropriate background knowledge) to derive the handshaking action command – specifically, the derived action command at $t + 1$ that A would use if she were B. A does not of course perform B's act, but instead generates an efference copy of this derived action command to predict some representations underlying the open hand at $t + 1$ (such as the upcoming pattern of muscle activation) and the percept of the open hand at $t + 1$. In general, these predictions are computed before the hand moves (i.e. before $t + 1$). B moves his hand, and the position (and orientation) of the hand at $t + 1$ is reflected in the shared workspace. A then perceives the actual hand position (using the perception implementer) and compares this percept with the predicted percept (using the external comparator). Notice that there is no internal comparator for predicting another's action, even when it contributes to a joint action. This is because A has no access to B's action representation.[8]

The important difference between Figures 3.2 and 3.3 is that Figure 3.3 includes the process of interpreting B's action and deriving the upcoming action command (as the command itself is used in the same way as in Figure 3.2). In our example, how can A derive B's intention to move his hand in a particular way? This process is computationally highly complicated – and may of course turn out to be wrong. A can predict that B will proffer an open hand for shaking by perceiving B's initial hand movement and covertly imitating that movement. In other words, at time t, A covertly imitates some of the processes that B used to prepare his hand. Of course, A does not do exactly the same as B, because their bodies are different, but instead transforms muscle activation to an extent that compensates for their differences. Alternatively, A can derive B's intention from aspects of the context apart from B's behaviour. For example, B could be standing in a line, in a formal situation in which handshaking is expected. A also assumes that B understands both his role and A's role in this situation and therefore assumes that B has the intention of handshaking. In this case, A does not covertly imitate B, but still derives B's intention. In our framework, action commands are the outcome of the joint action planner (Figure 3.1), and derived action commands have a similar origin (see Section 3.4). So A can derive B's intention as part of a joint action to which both A and B are committed. A and B could have arranged to come into a room and immediately shake hands, for example to publicly declare a political agreement. In this case, A represents the joint action plan that A and B will shake hands, and as part of that plan represents B's

----

[8] When we consider dialogue (Chapters 5 and 9), we make use of (ordered) steps rather than (precise) times. Some joint activities may be best characterized in terms of steps and others in terms of times (and in this chapter we make use of times).

contribution to proffer his hand. When the appropriate time comes, A activates that plan component by deriving B's action command.

Wolpert et al. (2003) developed a similar account using the HMOSAIC system to make predictions about how different intentional acts unfold over time. In their implementation, the perceiver runs parallel, linked forward-inverse model pairings from movements to intentions. By matching actual movements against these predictions, HMOSAIC determines the likelihood of different possible intentions (and dynamically modifies the space of possible intentions). This in turn modifies the perceiver's predictions of the actor's likely behaviour. For example, the first level might determine that a movement of the shoulder is likely to lead to a movement of the arm (and would draw on information about the actor's body shape); the second level might determine whether such an arm movement is the prelude to a proffered handshake or a punch (and would draw on information about the actor's state of mind). At the second level, the perceiver runs forward models based on those alternative intentions to determine what the actor's hand is likely to do next. If, for example, A predicts B is more likely to initiate a handshake but then B's fist starts clenching, A modifies her interpretation of B's intention and now predicts that B will likely throw a punch. At this point, A has determined B's intention and confidently predicts the upcoming position of B's hand, just as A would do if A were predicting her own hand movements.

In terms of our framework, the output of the external comparator feeds into the mechanism that interprets B's action and generates the derived action command (not illustrated in Figure 3.3). It therefore can be used to modify this command. Therefore, the process of generating the efference copy of the derived action command and comparing it with the action percept constitutes a control loop through which the individual can track her partner's actions as they unfold. But it is a limited control mechanism: it cannot correct her partner's actions through this 'perceptual' mechanism (in contrast to controlling her own actions). Again, this system uses pseudo-closed-loop controllers (Grush, 2004) because they control the process of action simulation using forward models.

This section is about both prediction and interpretation but has so far been framed in terms of prediction. We argue that the process of predicting another's action via simulation leads to interpretation of that action. So when A predicts B will move his hand in position for a handshake by simulating that movement, then A interprets B's ongoing action as a handshake. More strictly, it is the act of simulation rather than prediction that underlies interpretation (see Goldman, 2006). So if A (successfully) simulates what B has already done, then this constitutes interpretation (and in fact, interpretation involves both simulating what has happened and what will happen). Simulation under-lies interpretation because it involves computing (and testing) the intention behind an act – and people understand an act if they understand why it happens.[9]

With respect to Figure 3.1, the black arrow from the interpretation of *B*'s action to the derived action command corresponds to *A*'s upward arrowhead from the joint action planner to the joint action implementer. The forward model pathway from the derived action command to the predicted action percept corresponds to *A*'s vertical upward grey arrowhead. The grey line emanating from the shared workspace (i.e. the perception implementation pathway) corresponds to *A*'s downward vertical grey arrowhead. The external comparator corresponds to *A*'s vertical grey line (with the comparison occurring between the upward predictive arrowhead and downward perceptual arrowhead). The inverse model (which maps the outputs of the external comparator to the derived action command) is a component of *A*'s vertical downward arrowhead. Finally, the bottom line in Figure 3.3 represents *B*'s action implementational pathway (i.e. the solid upward black arrow from *B* to the shared workspace).

3.3   Individual Prediction and Interpretation of Joint Actions

We have considered in some detail how each individual can independently predict their own unfolding action and that of their partner. In our handshaking example, *A* can predict both her own hand movement and *B*'s hand movement. But this is not enough for joint activity: instead, *A* must predict *A* and *B*'s joint activity (the upcoming handshake). Our framework lends itself naturally to these situations by combining prediction in action and prediction in action perception. Figure 3.4 is a composite of Figures 3.2 and 3.3 which shows how A can predict A's upcoming action together with B's upcoming action.

In our example, both *A* and *B* have partly closed hands at time *t* and their hands are far apart. At time *t* + 1, they will have open hands which are closer together. *A* predicts her own hand movement at the top of Figure 3.4 and *B*'s hand movement below (i.e. immediately above the dividing line between *A* and *B*). The shared workspace contains both hand movements, but the top perception implementer acts on *A*'s hand movement and the bottom perception implementer acts on *B*'s hand movement. Notice that the two external comparators involve identical mechanisms – the process *A* uses to predict, perceive and compare *A*'s actual hand movements is the same as the process *A* uses to predict, perceive and compare *B*'s actual hand movements. But there is only one internal comparator – *A* can use the internal comparator only on herself, as she has access to her own internal states (e.g. muscle activation) but not to *B*'s internal states.

---

[9] In relation to Pickering and Garrod (2013), the intention underlying what will happen is the derived action command at *t* + 1, and the intention underlying what has happened is the derived action command at *t*. (Figure 3.3 does not represent the derived action command at *t*.)

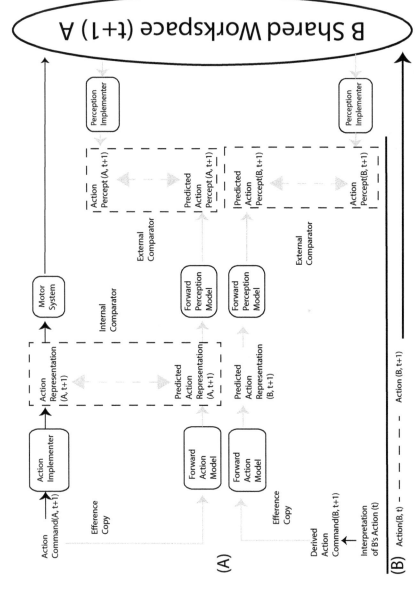

Figure 3.4 A model of one individual predicting own and other's action. Mechanisms occur in closed boxes. Dotted boxes (and dotted arrows) refer to processes that compare representations. The shared workspace is elliptical, with *B*'s contribution at the bottom and *A*'s contribution at the top. The use of black and grey arrows corresponds to their use in Figure 3.1. Everything above the solid line refers to *A*'s representations and processes (e.g. Action Percept (*B*, *t* + 1) refers to *A*'s percept of *B*'s action at *t* + 1).

In individual activity, the actor concentrates on both internal and external comparisons. She can compare sensations associated with action preparation and the sensations associated with the action outcomes with her predictions (see Figure 3.2). In joint activity, the actor can still make both comparisons (Figure 3.4). But the actor has to concentrate on the outcome of the joint activity, because the joint activity involves combined contributions from both the actor and her partner, and she cannot assess sensations associated with her partner's action preparation (Figure 3.3). Therefore the only way to assess the joint activity is via external comparison. In joint activity, there is still a role for internal comparison, but it is less important because it relates only to one part of the action. For example, actors are concerned with the success of handshaking (as a joint activity) and they focus their attention on this process rather than on their individual hand movement. In sum, internal comparison 'withers away' in joint action.[10]

In this analysis, A is separately predicting A's contribution to the joint action and B's contribution to the joint action. But A is not yet making a single prediction of the joint action. At this point, our model appears complicated, and it appears to suggest that A has to perform two unrelated acts of comparison. But we now show how it can be simplified, with A's grey pathways (forward modelling, perception, and comparison) becoming interwoven in the context of cooperative joint action. When this happens, A uses prediction-by-simulation for the joint action.

For this to happen, A will have learnt a plan associated with the action to help her monitor the progress of both her own and her partner's contributions to the joint activity. Underlying the model in Figure 3.4 is the fact that A represents a plan for the cooperative joint action. In our example, the plan is that both A and B should proffer their hands for each other by moving them together and opening them at the same time (as it is a symmetric joint action). Other (asymmetric) joint actions involve complementary moves: when building flat-pack furniture, A represents the joint plan that A will hold the furniture at a particular position, and B will hold the drill at a related position (e.g. just in front of a mark in the furniture). In both cases, A represents a sub-plan for A and a sub-plan for B, and meshes these sub-plans into a single joint action plan. And the joint action plan leads to two interdependent action commands (A's action command and A's derived action command for B) – commands that are interdependent precisely because they both support aspects of the joint action plan.[11]

---

[10] This suggests that actors are likely to pay more attention to internal comparison when performing solo activities than when performing joint activities.

[11] In a cooperative joint activity, both A and B play appropriate roles in the action (i.e. typically do the right things at the right times). In chess, players have the common knowledge that they have to take turns and therefore White has a joint plan that Black moves after White and that White

Because these action commands are interdependent, they can be merged. In addition, both *A* and *B* place their interdependent contributions into the shared workspace, and therefore *A*'s two perception implementers can be merged as well. Before merging (Figure 3.4), *A* compares (1) her action percept for herself with her predicted action percept for herself (using the top external comparator) and (2) her action percept for *B* with her predicted action percept for *B* (using the bottom external comparator). After merging, *A* compares her joint action percept for *A* and *B* with her predicted joint action percept for *A* and *B* – and we take this up in detail below.[12]

3.4   Joint Performance, Prediction and Control of Joint Action

So far, we have considered one individual's prediction and interpretation of joint action, and our analysis is compatible with monadic cognitive science. But this ceases to be the case when we include the second individual. Both *A* and *B* are predicting both *A* and *B*, and those predictions can be used to perform and control the joint action. We therefore now present a systems analysis of joint action – an analysis that is not compatible with monadic cognitive science. At this point, we have a complete, distributed, control mechanism. We do this by representing the merged comparator mechanisms in relation to *A*, and represent the same for *B* (Figure 3.5).

We can now develop a model of distributed control with associated feedback loops. In Section 3.3, we treated the shared workspace as involving individual components of joint actions (e.g. *A*'s hand position and *B*'s hand position). But we now treat the shared workspace as involving joint actions (e.g. *A* and *B*'s handshake). Therefore, each individual represents a joint action percept for the joint action (i.e. via the perception implementer, shown as the left-facing grey arrows). If *A* and *B* have the same perception of the joint action (perhaps because they see it from the same perspective), then their joint action percepts will be the same.

Either individual's joint action percept needs to be compared with a predicted joint action percept (via the external comparator). *A* first performs joint simulation: she uses the joint action planner to construct an action command for herself (i.e. reflecting her commitment and leading to her contribution) and

---

moves after Black (except initially). Therefore a component of White's forward model of White is a prediction of when White will move, and a component of White's forward model of Black is a prediction of when Black will move. These components are represented as separate pathways in Figure 3.4 but of course they actually constitute two components of a cooperative joint action.

[12] Such merger specifically relates to cooperative joint activity (and is linked to the feeling of joint agency). If *A* acts while perceiving *B* acting independently, then *A* may perform separate acts of self- and other-comparison.

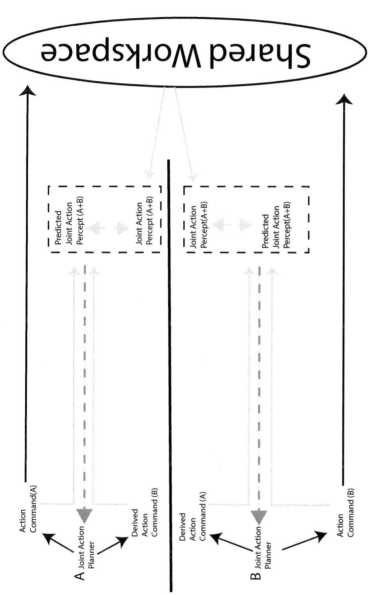

Figure 3.5 A model of the joint action control system. *A* is above the central line, and *B* is below it. *A*'s and *B*'s action commands lead to action components (solid black lines) that feed into the joint action recorded in the shared workspace. *A*'s and *B*'s perceptions of the joint action (grey left-facing arrows) feed into their external comparators (in dotted boxes). The efference copies of their action commands (i.e. self-predictions) and the efference copies of the derived action commands (i.e. other-predictions) are both represented with grey right-facing arrows. They combine to provide the predictions that also feed into the external comparators. The comparisons between perceptions and predictions (i.e. the prediction errors) feed back to *A*'s and *B*'s Joint Action Planners (dotted dark grey left-facing arrow).

61

her derived action command for *B* (i.e. reflecting his commitment). *A* combines the efference copy of her action command (strictly, the associated forward model) with the efference copy of her derived action command for *B* to predict the joint action percept. For example, *A* combines her prediction of the percept of her own hand movement and her prediction of the percept of *B*'s hand movement to produce a prediction of the percept of the handshake. At the same time, *A* uses her action command to move her hand and update the shared workspace. *B* of course does all of the same things as *A* and therefore predicts the joint action percept and moves his hand.

Now consider the acts of comparison using the external comparators. *A* determines the discrepancy between the predicted joint action (e.g. a success- ful handshake) with the actual joint action (e.g. *A*'s hand is slightly above *B*'s hand). The discrepancy is fed back to *A*'s Joint Action Planner. This can lead to two corrections. Most obviously, it can enable *A* to update her action (moving her hand down) and an associated updating of the efference copy, which allows *A* to predict the effect of this update.[13] In addition, it can lead to *A* updating her derived action command for *B* and the associated efference copy, which allows *A* to predict the effect of an update in *B*'s contribution (e.g. that *B* will move his hand up). As before, *B* of course does all of the same things as *A*.

We now have 'closed the loop' and so the two actors can perform joint actions with repeated updates. This system enables distributed control. *A* uses the joint contribution to drive her own contribution, and *B* does too. So they are both exercising some control over the joint action – they each control their own contribution, but their contribution is continuously affected by the rela- tionship between the effects of their own contribution and their partner's contribution.

Let us now interpret furniture construction in terms of this account. In this task, *A* and *B* have different roles, using a drill and holding furniture compon- ents, respectively. They each know their own and their partner's roles (and their roles are common knowledge; Lewis, 1969). Therefore *A*'s action command is to start the drill and *A*'s derived action command for *B* is to hold the components appropriately; similarly, *B*'s action command is to hold the components and *B*'s derived action command for *A* is to start the drill. These commands are a consequence of the current state of the joint action planner. The shared work- space reflects the current state of the joint action, for example *A* moving the drill towards the components that are held by *B*, and the actors represent the percept of this joint action. In addition, they combine the consequences of the efference copies of the action command and derived action command to construct the

---

[13] Performing this corrective movement serves the function of keeping the cooperative joint activity on track, which is a responsibility for each individual (Bratman, 1992).

predicted joint action percepts and assess any discrepancies from the percepts. For example, if *A* aims the drill above the target mark on the component held by *B*, one or both of them can alter their action command.

This account focuses on the external comparator, because it can be equated across self- and other-generated components of the joint action. In contrast, we have noted (see Figure 3.4) that individuals can compare the predicted representation of their own action with the actual representation of their own action, but they cannot compare the predicted representation of their partner's action with the actual representation of their partner's action, because they do not have access to this representation. Therefore they can perform an additional internal comparison and use the feedback from this comparison to update their action command and the efference copy of this command, but this comparison has no effect on the derived action command and is not directly related to the joint action (and is therefore omitted from Figure 3.5).

In practice, such internal comparison involves monitoring of one's own unfolding movement, typically early in the process. An example would be if *A* went to pick up the drill and underestimated its weight. *A* might then revise the action command underlying her arm movement and grip to compensate (see Haruno et al., 2001), before actually raising her arm. This process takes place without *A*'s arm raising and therefore is not accessible to *B*. This comparison corresponds to the relationship between the vertical black arrow and the horizontal grey arrow in Figure 3.1.

In sum, Figure 3.5 represents a system involving distributed control of joint cooperative activity. Both individuals use joint simulation and forward action perception models to predict the unfolding joint activity in relation to their joint actions (right-facing grey arrows). They monitor the unfolding activity in relation to their joint actions (left-facing dotted dark grey arrows) and then use this to control the way the joint activity unfolds by modifying each of their contributions to it as a whole.

3.5   Alignment in Joint Activity

Finally, we turn to how this control system relates to alignment between the actors' joint action planners and related joint action implementers. In Section 2.6.1, we said that alignment occurs when two (or more) individuals have similar relevant cognitive representations. Alignment is defined with respect to planning and implementation rather than behaviour, and so relates to all of Figure 3.5 except the shared workspace. We assume that the control system in this figure serves to enhance alignment (as we are considering cooperative joint action).

We therefore consider alignment both with respect to the joint action plan and with respect to the actual and derived action commands associated with that plan. *A* and *B* are aligned if they have the same joint action plan – for example, they both plan that *A* will drill and *B* will hold the wood. With respect to the action commands, *A* and *B* are aligned if (1) *A*'s action command (i.e. of *A*) and *B*'s derived action command (i.e. of *A*) are the same and (2) *B*'s action command (i.e. of *B*) and *A*'s derived action command (i.e. of *B*) are the same. In this case, *A* and *B* are aligned if (1) *A*'s planned movement (positioning the drill in front of the mark) and *B*'s prediction of *A*'s planned movement are the same (i.e. with respect to trajectory and timing) and (2) *B*'s planned movement (positioning the wood at a particular height) and *A*'s prediction of *B*'s planned movement are the same. (Note that *A* and *B* do not need to do the same thing as each other to be aligned.)

In this ideal state, (1) *A*'s actual and predicted joint action percepts match and (2) *B*'s actual and predicted joint action percepts match. Thus, no discrepancy is fed back to their joint action planners. This means that any change in the actual or derived action commands comes about only as a result of a regular update in the joint action planners (e.g. that the next step is to drill the hole).[14]

Alignment of the action commands is typically a consequence of the actors having aligned joint action plans. In other words, they have agreed to work together on a particular task and are both aware of both their roles within that task. In the furniture construction task, they are both aware that it is *A*'s role to manage the drill and *B*'s role to present the furniture component appropriately. This joint plan then feeds into each action command and derived action command (so that each change in an action component is a combination of the joint plan and the outcome of the feedback from the external comparators).

Now let us turn to misalignment, which will lead to a situation in which each actor's action command does not match the other actor's derived action

---

[14] We do not assume that *A*'s percept matches *B*'s percept. In much joint action, *A* and *B* have different perspectives on the joint action – *A* may be behind the drill and in front of the board, whereas *B* may be on the other side of the board (and so be facing the point of the drill). The shared workspace is the same for *A* and *B* (as it contains the meaningful entities that are implicated in the joint action) but they have different views of what it contains. In this example, *A* and *B* have complete but different perspectives on the joint action (they can both perceive the drilling) but sometimes one participant does not have a complete perspective (for example not seeing the drill). Because *A* and *B* have different joint action percepts, they are also likely to be have different predicted joint action percepts (even when they are aligned). Thus, alignment of action commands (i.e. *A*'s action command and *A*'s derived action command matching *B*'s action command and *B*'s derived action command) does not require matched predicted joint action percepts.

These complexities relating to perspective are important for joint actions that are primarily perceived visually. They are much less important for joint actions that are primarily perceived auditorily. *A* may hear more than *B* (if *B* is hearing-impaired) but *A* and *B* are unlikely to hear different things. Perspectival differences tend not to be fundamentally important to spoken dialogue (see Chapter 5).

command. For example, A and B might not have agreed on the height at which the drilling should occur, so that A assumes height X and B assumes height Y. As a consequence, A issues an action command that moves the drill to X and issues a derived action command that predicts that B will present the furniture at X, whereas B issues an action command that presents the furniture at Y and issues a derived action command that predicts that A will move the drill to Y. They then start to perform the joint action and each constructs a joint action percept. For both actors, this percept mismatches the predicted joint action percept and a large prediction error ensues.

We can now see how misalignment can be corrected. Each actor can use this prediction error to change the action command, for example changing the target height for the drilling. This change is not simply a consequence of the prediction error but is instead due to a combination of the prediction error and the joint action plan, which is concerned that the drill and the furniture are at the same height and not that they are specifically at X or Y. Importantly, a good plan will contain some strategy for resolving such misalignments, perhaps that A always accommodates to B (i.e. A's action command is updated but B's is not).[15] So we now have an account of distributed control, in which the joint actors (i.e. in a cooperative activity with a shared plan) control the joint action between them.

Finally, joint actors may be more or less aware that they are aligned or misaligned. We regard such awareness of the degree of alignment as *meta-representation of alignment* (which is defined with respect to each individual, in contrast to alignment itself). Such awareness may follow from the output of the external comparator, with an actor being more likely to assume alignment if the prediction error has been low and misalignment if it has been high. In other words, joint actors are likely to believe they are aligned if they successfully predict the (unfolding) joint action, and misaligned if they do not.[16]

Additionally, we speculate that meta-representation of alignment relates to the feeling of joint agency – in other words, that A (at least partly) produces B's act and vice versa (see Bolt & Loehr, 2017). But joint agency is an illusion – individuals do not actually produce each other's contributions.

3.6   Conclusion

In Chapter 2, we developed a systems framework for joint activity built around a shared workspace. In this chapter we showed how individuals can use the

---

[15] If the actors' plans do not contain such a strategy, then a coordination problem will ensue (Lewis, 1969).
[16] We note that other frameworks assume some awareness of alignment. A good example is shared reality, as discussed by Echterhoff et al. (2009).

arrows connecting them to the shared workspace to execute and control joint activities in collaboration with each other. The discussion led to a model of the joint action system that enables both individuals to contribute to the cooperative joint activity, monitor its progress and modify their contributions to reflect that monitoring process. We have now completed our consideration of joint activities in general and can now apply our framework to dialogue.

4 Dialogue as a Joint Activity

The topic of this book is the understanding of the nature of dialogue (primarily in dyads). To do this, we need to understand how dialogue is processed within each individual interlocutor. That is, we need to understand language processing in individual minds, but under the circumstances in which those individuals are interacting. Of course, cognitive scientists have spent much time studying language processing in individual speakers and listeners – this is the basis for almost all textbook treatments of the psychology of language in the last half century (e.g. Fodor et al., 1974; Traxler, 2011). But most of these treatments focus on one individual's activity in isolation, without appreciating their role in relation to another individual (the target or source of the activity).

This approach is unable to provide an overarching understanding of language use. Language use is an act of communication, and communication logically requires (at least) two participants. So even when one individual is producing or comprehending language in isolation, that individual's representations make reference to another individual (the presumed audience or designer). Thus any adequate theory of language processing must make reference to two participants. In other words, language processing is incompatible with monadic cognitive science.

However, our focus is not merely on pairs (or groups) of individuals (i.e. the system). Instead, we are also concerned with individual cognitive processes that make reference to other individuals (i.e. the individual-within-the-system). These concerns are the same whether we focus on language processing in dialogue (our primary interest) or monologue (which we return to in Section 10.3).

Dialogue is a form of joint activity (Clark, 1996) and bears important similarities to the cooperative joint activities considered in Chapter 2. But in fact the cooperative joint activities that we discussed (Table 2.1) are actually quite specialized. On specific occasions, people play tennis, move a heavy table or construct furniture together. Some activities, such as jointly piloting a plane or performing an operation, require extensive training or special authorization and are not possible for most people. Other activities such as handshaking are highly circumscribed – they are associated only with a particular purpose or stage in a social encounter. Moreover, in many cases there are closely related individual activities such as constructing furniture on one's own or solo piloting – and in fact the cooperative joint activities are sometimes offshoots of the individual activities that are performed primarily when the activity is too complex (for physical or cognitive reasons) for a single person. One might therefore argue that such forms of cooperative joint activity are derived from solo activity.

In contrast, dialogue is not derived from monologue. It is clearly more basic than isolated speaking and listening. As we noted in Pickering and Garrod (2004), 'every language user, including young children and illiterate adults, can hold a conversation, whereas reading, writing, preparing speeches and even listening to speeches are far from universal skills' (p. 169). People spend a great deal of time holding conversations, the ability develops before the ability to engage in monologue, and animal communication systems make it clear that language must have evolved for interactive use rather than for giving soliloquies. And infants learn language via dialogue (and its precursors) when interacting with caregivers. It is therefore very important to study dialogue in its own right. To do so, we now consider the parallels between cooperative joint activity in general and dialogue in particular (and this is of course an important reason why we have considered cooperative joint activity in detail).

Dialogue is an excellent example of a cooperative joint activity (see Chapter 2). Recall that such activities need not be cooperative 'all the way down' and in this sense they differ from shared cooperative activity (Bratman, 1992).[1] In dialogue, both interlocutors have the goal of understanding each other via communication. Some dialogues may be fully cooperative, for example when interlocutors are solving a crossword puzzle together (and believe they are more likely to succeed by 'pooling their resources'). Dialogue may also involve argument, when interlocutors have different goals (each trying to convince the other of their position) – and such an argument is not fully cooperative (any more than is chess). But even in such dialogues, the interlocutors cooperate on communication.

---

[1] Bratman's focus is on activities that need not be cooperative but can be. This appears to mean that there is an equivalent solo activity (e.g. painting a house on one's own) rather than one that is defined cooperatively (and his example is cooperative problem solving). Clearly dialogue is an example of an activity that has to be a joint activity, in that the concern is with a process of communication that requires two participants. (In monologue, there are still two participants, whether there is a silent audience or the utterances are being recorded or written down 'for posterity'.)

Note that our account excludes some uses of language, for example when one person is shouting at another who is trying not to listen, or perhaps when two people are shouting at each other about different things and are not responding to each other. These uses of language do not involve dialogue. In dialogue, both parties want each other to understand what they are talking about. This is the case in argument as well as agreement, and even in lying or deception (in which the thing to be understood is false; Tomasello, 2010).[2] In all dialogue, the interlocutors are committed to communicative success.

4.1   What Kind of Cooperative Joint Activity Is Dialogue?

In Chapter 2, we discussed a range of cooperative joint activities and their properties. How does dialogue relate to other activities? Its most distinctive characteristic is that it is communicative. Although many cooperative joint activities incorporate dialogue (see Table 2.1), most other activities have a primary goal that is separate from communication.

Like all cooperative joint activity, dialogue requires that the interlocutors commit to a joint goal. In many non-linguistic activities (e.g. shaking hands, moving a heavy table, playing tennis), this overall goal is established before the activity begins. It defines the activity and is our starting point. In contrast, the goal of dialogue is almost always determined by the interlocutors as part of the dialogue itself. Sometimes, interlocutors agree this goal early on, for example if they agree to work out a route to a destination, actually work out the route, and then stop talking and follow the route. But more typically, interlocutors develop the goal opportunistically – they might determine sub-goals (such as intermediate locations) or new goals (such as what they will do after reaching their destination). The process of determining and developing goals of course involves planning (see below).

We also considered general dimensions over which cooperative joint activities vary. An example such as Table 4.1 (repeated here) shows how dialogue can be cooperative, internally managed, largely sequential, locally asymmetric but globally symmetric, time-critical, and with fairly tight coupling (see Table 2.2 and Section 2.1).

We regard this example as representative of dialogue in general and treat dialogues that do not have these characteristics as special cases. In this respect we echo Sacks et al. (1974) and use informal conversation as a model for all

---

[2] A speaker can be deliberately confusing (obfuscating), perhaps to assert intellectual superiority, to evade an awkward question, or to sound mystical. In triadic dialogue, a speaker may aim to inform one addressee but be unintelligible to another (see Clark & Schaeffer, 1987). But even in these cases, the interlocutors want each other to understand most of what is said (otherwise they are not communicating at all).

Table 4.1 *An example conversation*

1 -----**B:** .... Tell me where you are?
2 -----**A:** Ehm : Oh God (<u>laughs</u>)
3 -----**B:** (<u>laughs</u>)
4 -----**A:** Right : two along from the bottom one up:
5 -----**B:** Two along from the bottom, which side?
6 -----**A:** The left : going from left to right in the second box.
7 -----**B:** You're in the second box.
8 -----**A:** One up :(<u>1 sec.</u>) I take it we've got identical mazes?
9 -----**B:** Yeah well : right, starting from the left, you're one along:
10 -----**A:** Uh-huh:
11 -----**B:** and one up?
12 -----**A:** Yeah, and I'm trying to get to ...

Source: from Garrod and Anderson (1987) and repeated from Table 1.1.

forms of interactive language. In Chapters 10 and 11, we discuss forms of dialogue that deviate from 'pure' informal conversation.

As discussed, this example is cooperative because both interlocutors want their partner to interpret their descriptions correctly (and therefore reach their goals). It is internally managed because there is no external control, and of course this is the case for any informal conversation (in contrast to situations such as an appointment panel in which the chair controls who speaks when). It is largely sequential because interlocutors take turns to speak and there is little overlap. (Note that the transcript does not actually indicate when the interlocutors overlap.) Extensive overlap is very rare, presumably because simultaneous comprehension and production typically exceeds processing capacities. When two interlocutors begin to speak at the same time, one or other tends to yield the floor within a few syllables (Schegloff, 2000). However, one interlocutor can provide contributions (so-called backchannel contributions; Yngve, 1970) while the other is speaking (i.e. holding the floor). Such feedback can take the form of affirmations (*OK, yeah*), continuers (*mmm, go on*), or queries (*eh? What?*), and can be non-linguistic (nods, frowns, claps). The contributions can have considerable effects on the speaker's behaviour (e.g. Bavelas et al., 2000) but do not cause the speaker to yield the floor (see Chapter 8).

Our example is locally asymmetric because *A* and *B* do not do the same thing at the same time – something that is necessary in sequential interactions. Local symmetry occurs in choric contributions (see discussion of collectives in Section 10.2.4), for example when more than one addressee answers a question in the same way at the same time. (Choric chants and prayers are scripted and are not part of dialogue; Cummins, 2003.) However, the example is not merely asymmetric because one interlocutor 'holds the floor', but also because the interlocutors play different roles at any point, for example when *A* asks a question (e.g. 5) and *B* answers (6).

In contrast, the example is globally symmetric because both participants make the same types of contribution to the dialogue – any contributions made by *A* can be made by *B* and vice versa. This is the case for informal conversation in general. Of course global symmetry depends on the level of analysis. In a teacher-student dialogue, the interlocutors make different contributions because of their different social roles or degree of specialist knowledge, and in this sense teacher-student dialogue is globally asymmetric. But it is globally symmetric in the sense that they both have the ability to make contributions of various types (questions, responses, brief interjections etc.).

The example is time-critical because the interlocutors need to make contributions at particular times, for example taking the floor rapidly after their partner finishes, or producing a query just after an ambiguous utterance. Failing to respond rapidly would make conversations unacceptably slow, and would also violate social norms, such as the norm of responding to a direct question within about five hundred milliseconds in many cultures (see Bögels et al., 2017, for an experimental investigation). In fact, inter-turn intervals are extremely close to zero milliseconds in most exchanges (e.g. Stivers et al., 2009). Finally, the example involves fairly tight coupling because the contributions are quite short, though of course longer utterances sometimes occur (see Levinson, 2016).

4.2   A Systems Analysis of Dialogue

As discussed in Chapter 2, the two key characteristics of a system are that the components must be understood in relation to each other (i.e. they are not merely an aggregate) and that the system has some degree of stability (i.e. is obligate). Like other forms of joint activity, dialogue is recurrently stable – its structure remains the same when individual interlocutors are replaced. We focus on the dyad, and assume that similar principles apply to larger groups (see Chapter 10). Moreover, we assume that all conversing dyads share essential properties, and this is why we can construct a cognitive theory of dialogue.

Both interlocutors are aware that they are engaged in the dialogue and that they are both part of the system. In other words, they accept that they are both interlocutors and assume that their partner does too.[3] They realize that both their acts and their partner's acts are communicative (and believe that their

---

[3] One way of characterizing this is to say that the speaker communicates both a message and the fact that he is communicating that message (see Grice, 1957), and that the addressee understands both of these aspects of the act of communication. But this characterization is rooted in a monological approach to communication (and specifically speech acts).

partner realizes this too). This means that they are committed to trying to communicate with each other and are jointly responsible for the dialogue being successful.

Like all other joint activities, dialogue has a lifetime, with the interlocutors coming together and eventually splitting apart, and they have to indicate that their commitment begins and ends; the practices that underlie openings and closings have been documented by conversation analysts (e.g. Sacks et al., 1974; Schegloff, 1968). Furthermore, the same or different interlocutors can subsequently engage in a fresh dialogue (i.e. because the system is recurrently stable).

The dialogue system necessarily involves loops between the interlocutors, in which each interlocutor's contribution is subject to feedback by the other interlocutor. Such loops are (temporally) fairly tight. They cannot be any longer than the length of individual contributions (as in Table 4.1), but in fact some loops are much tighter than this, as addressees can give feedback at any point during a speaker's turn. Properly working loops appear essential for fluent, successful dialogue, as is illustrated by the disruptive effects of interfering with timing and feedback (e.g. Krauss & Glucksberg, 1969).[4]

We have already considered and rejected a simple model of a closed-loop system for joint activity in general (see Figure 2.1). Not surprisingly, the equivalent model (in which individuals are replaced by interlocutors) is also inadequate for dialogue. In this 'sender-receiver' model, Interlocutor A's utterance affects Interlocutor B, whose utterance in turn affects Interlocutor A, and so on. This model might be compatible with interaction in which each interlocutor contributes serially and in which there are no props. An example is communication via half-duplex walkie-talkies (where each interlocutor can either send or receive at any instant; see Section 10.3.1). Such a form of communication involves a closed-loop system in which the arrows represent language that is produced by the interlocutor at the blunt end and comprehended by the interlocutor at the sharp end.

But the 'sender-receiver' model does not capture dialogue well, because it assumes discrete contributions – in other words, serial monologue. We noted that dialogue is not fully sequential and that both interlocutors can make simultaneous contributions when their turns overlap or when they are giving feedback. In addition, this model cannot deal with props – that is, objects that are integral to the dialogue (e.g. the furniture components being discussed during assembly). Such objects could be represented only as separate inputs to each individual, and there is no way of indicating that they might be the same

---

[4] Even small delays in transmission (around 200 ms) can be very disruptive, as occurred in traditional long-distance telephony.

for both individuals. The model also cannot represent additional people who are not contributing at this point (e.g. side-participants; Goffman, 1976).

Another problem with this model is that it is limited to dialogues involving information transfer. For example, if A asks B 'where did we go for dinner when we were last here?', and B responds 'Kalpna', then B transfers information to A (as a result of A pointing out her missing information). But if A asks B 'where shall we go for dinner?', then this is most likely a request to start a negotiation, and there is no straightforward sense in which either A or B is transferring information to the other. In Section 4.5 we consider a more appropriate model of the dialogue system.

4.3   The Interlocutors-within-the-Dialogue

Just as we eschew monadic cognitive science, so we eschew monadic psycholinguistics. Instead, our goal is to compare and relate the individual cognitive representations and processes across interlocutors (including representations of the interlocutors themselves). In doing so, we aim to develop an account of the dialogue system, as well as accounts of the individual interlocutors.

Traditional psycholinguistics is largely monadic, in that it is concerned with one isolated speaker or one isolated listener, and the theories of how that speaker or listener processes language does not take much account of a communicative partner – a partner who is essential to the act of communication even when he or she is absent. For example, theories of word production (e.g. Levelt et al., 1999) are informed by picture-naming experiments (e.g. Schriefers et al., 1990), but such theories make no essential reference to an addressee, and participants in the experiments are simply asked to name pictures as quickly as possible. Similarly, theories of sentence interpretation focus on the representations of the structure of the sentence and are informed by experiments in which participants simply read what is put on a screen in front of them (e.g. Frazier & Rayner, 1982).

Some psycholinguistics does, of course, make reference to other participants, usually addressees. Speakers' utterances are affected by their beliefs about whom they are addressing: parents, educators, and broadcasters use what is termed *audience design* to decide what to say and how to say it (Clark & Murphy, 1982).[5] In psycholinguistic terms, speakers represent aspects of their addressees' linguistic and non-linguistic knowledge, and researchers have proposed theories of how and when such representations are used (e.g. Horton & Keysar, 1996; Isaacs & Clark, 1987). Such theories are concerned

---

[5] Sacks et al. (1974) refer to this as recipient design.

with one individual's representations of more than one individual – something that is compatible with monadic psycholinguistics. But we aim to go beyond this and to make reference to more than one individual's representations at the same time. We do so by considering the individuals as part of a system.

This systems-based approach allows us to consider the relationships between individual cognitive representations. For example, two interlocutors may develop the same representations as each other (i.e. become aligned), or they may develop different representations that are related in specific ways (e.g. when producing a question and an appropriate answer). We can also investigate the effects of the relationship between the interlocutors: for example, the representations associated with an instruction-follower may come to be aligned with the representations associated with an instruction-giver (more than the other way round). Such investigations are possible only when we consider the representations of more than one interlocutor, as part of a dialogue system.

We therefore now interpret dialogue using a systems analysis. Just as for joint activity in general, we distinguish between an analysis of the structure of the dialogue system as a whole, and an analysis of the interlocutors as part of that system. This second aspect of the analysis is concerned with linguistic and non-linguistic representations within each interlocutor, and the way in which those representations are interpreted with respect to the rest of the dialogue system (both its structure and the representations of the other interlocutors). Therefore our analysis is cognitive, but it is not monadic.

4.4   Distributed Control for Dialogue

4.4.1   Control of Isolated Speech

To understand control in dialogue, we first briefly discuss control in monologue. Consider a broadcaster announcing the emergency procedures for evacuating a sports ground over a loudspeaker. He establishes the overall goal of communicating how this evacuation should take place, and set of sub-goals, such as indicating where each emergency exit is and discouraging running. He has to make a plan to achieve the overall goal and its sub-goals. This plan specifies the processes involved in producing an appropriate sequence of utterances. These processes in turn lead to the production of utterances themselves, as sequences of speech sounds. This scheme corresponds to Levelt's (1989) account of language production, which is divided into conceptualization (i.e. message generation), formulation and articulation.

The broadcaster's plan could be inflexible, for example specifying the location of the exits before the instruction about running. But if he forgot to mention one of exits before telling people not to run, he would fail to achieve his goal. To avoid this, he needs to attend to the process of indicating the exit locations. Specifically, he has to monitor his utterances, identify problems and repair them. He therefore needs a *control* mechanism that is separate from the mechanisms that are used to *implement* the utterance.

This control mechanism makes use of feedback, either about the utterance itself or about the process (the plan and its implementation) that leads to the utterance. Specifically, the feedback provides evidence about whether everything is working as expected (i.e. the goal is being achieved). If everything is not working as expected, either the plan or its implementation can be modified and the utterance can be changed. In other words, there is a split between implementing and monitoring the utterance (just as there is for other actions).

The broadcaster may encounter a problem at any of the three levels (i.e. layers) of planning, implementation or articulation. He monitors for planning errors, for example planning to say *Row M* rather than the correct *Row N*. He may notice this error while planning (he suddenly remembered that the exit had changed last week), while implementing (he activated the lexical entry *M* and then realized that it was wrong), or while articulating (he started to say *M* and realized that it was wrong). He also monitors for implementation errors, for example noticing that his plan to say *Row* does not match the activated lexical entry *Level* or the sound /l/. Finally, he monitors for articulation errors, for example that he has uttered /w/ rather the intended sound /r/. This analysis demonstrates that speakers can go wrong at any of the three levels. But in addition, it makes clear that an error can be detected at that level or a different level – for example, the broadcaster can tell that his plan is wrong internally (i.e. during planning or implementation) or externally (i.e. in relation to his speech). Thus, the plan, implementation and articulation are all linked together, though a specific act of monitoring is directed at one of these levels, and in this respect the task of the broadcaster is similar to the task of the solo furniture builder. The broadcaster can then reformulate (i.e. self-repair) – he can change any aspect of the speech process. Monitoring and self-repair in isolated speech therefore involves closed-loop control (or pseudo-closed loop control), with the loop being fairly tight (typically operating at fractions of a second).

4.4.2   Distributed Control for Dialogue

The broadcaster exercised solo control over his utterances. But in dialogue, both interlocutors have to exercise control, over both their own and their partner's contributions. As we have already noted, dialogue is collaborative at the level of the overall goal – the interlocutors both intend to communicate about something with each other (even if arguing). They may initially share some more specific goals (i.e. sub-goals). For example, two holidaymakers may share the goals of visiting three tourist destinations, but need to discuss the itinerary. Alternatively, one may have more specific goals (e.g. to visit the Colosseum, St Peter's Cathedral and the Trevi Fountain) than the other (who simply wants to see Rome). Furthermore, some goals may be more apparent to one interlocutor than the other (e.g. in a didactic context). Of course they plan different utterances from each other, as during question-answering. Thus, they also implement differently (i.e. formulate their own utterances but not their partner's) and behave differently (i.e. say different things). This process is analogous to the planning, implementation and behaviours associated with other cooperative joint activities, such as our furniture-building example in Chapter 2.

In many such activities, the overall goal is clearly established before it takes place. For example, the furniture builders have the joint intention of building the furniture before they begin to do so. But as we have noted, dialogue is much more fluid. Our tourists initially have the goal of establishing an itinerary around Rome, but might move on to discuss the artwork in the Sistine Chapel.

Therefore the goals of a dialogue change dynamically and in this sense are more complex than isolated utterances. They can develop during the course of the conversation, for example when one interlocutor becomes aware that she has to pose a sequence of questions to her partner (see Clark, 1996, chapter 7, on joint projects). Interlocutors cannot of course construct rigid plans for achieving those goals before engaging in the dialogue, because they have to be prepared to modify their plans opportunistically, depending on their part- ner's contributions.[6] This means that control is especially necessary for dia- logue, with each interlocutor using closed-loop control, so that they can use the feedback from their own and their partner's performance to direct subsequent activity. In fact, they must be able to monitor their own and their partner's utterances and determine whether they are appropriate, not merely on their own (e.g. is an answer meaningful?), but with respect to each other (e.g. is it relevant?). If an interlocutor realizes that there is problem with his own contribution, his partner's contribution or the combination of their contribu- tions, then he must modify his plan or implementation, or indicate that his partner must modify her plan or implementation (or both). Control is exercised by both interlocutors – perhaps at the same time, or at different times during the dialogue. As in other forms of joint activity, the control is *distributed* across the interlocutors.[7] This distributed control provides a basis for dialogue

---

[6] Of course, people plan and implement ceremonial or theatrical interactions in a largely ballistic manner (though even then they are able to dynamically respond to off-script contributions). But such non-spontaneous interactions fall outside our definition of dialogue.

[7] Again, there are unusual circumstances in which control is largely or entirely limited to one interlocutor, for example in some forms of military communication or interrogation. In such cases, the officer or interrogator is able to control what is said and at what time.

as a cooperative joint activity, in particular allowing mutual responsiveness and a commitment to mutual support.

In Chapter 2, we discussed distributed control in relation to the coordination of autonomous robots performing different parts of a single task. Recall that our analysis (following Simmons et al., 2002) was that each robot had three layers or levels (corresponding to planning, implementation and behaviour) that were linked to each other. The presence of these links therefore allowed the emergence of distributed control. Interlocutors, like joint actors in general, also need to link their planning, implementation and behaviours. When discussing joint actors, we referred to the planner as the joint action planner and the implementer as the joint action implementer. In interlocutors, we now refer to the layers as the dialogue planner and the dialogue implementer. The behaviours are specifically communicative behaviours, most notably utterances. Obviously, interlocutors cannot directly interact at the dialogue planning or implementation layers (in the absence of direct brain-to-brain connections such as telepathy), because they involve representations that can be observed only as a consequence of behaviours.

In dialogue, links can emerge as a consequence of interactions at different layers. An example of interaction at the behavioural layer would be when a speaker utters something inaudible, an addressee provides feedback (e.g. *eh?*), and then the speaker repeats more clearly. Interaction at the layer of the dialogue implementer occurs when the addressee elaborates on the speaker's contribution, and the speaker indicates agreement. Interaction at the layer of the dialogue planner occurs when one interlocutor attempts to negotiate a change of topic, and the other counters this suggestion. It should be clear that all these forms of interaction involve feedback (and hence closed-loop control), though they may also involve predicting performance (i.e. using pseudo-closed-loop control). But most importantly, each interlocutor is controlling aspects of the performance, so the control is distributed.

4.5   The Shared Workspace Framework for Dialogue

Instead of adopting the simple dyadic model illustrated in Figure 2.1, we propose a version of the shared workspace model introduced in Chapter 2 (Figure 2.4). The shared workspace model allows us to address the nature of distributed control within a dialogue system. Figure 4.1 illustrates the shared workspace framework for dialogue, which has the same structure as the shared workspace framework for cooperative joint activity. The rectangles refer to the interlocutors *A* and *B* and their individual dialogue planners and dialogue implementers (which correspond to the joint action planners and implementers in Figure 2.4). The arrow between the planner and implementer is of course the vertical link between these layers, and it is double-headed because information

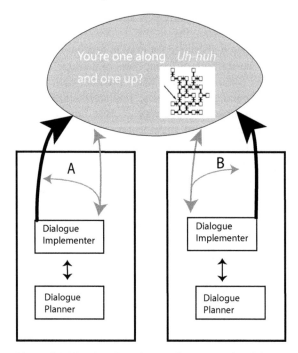

Figure 4.1 The shared workspace framework for dialogue.

can flow in both directions – planning can be used to implement (when preparing to produce utterances), and implementation can affect planning (in relation to comprehension).

The interlocutors use the dialogue planner to determine the joint conversational goals. If our tourists agree to determine an itinerary, then they both establish this goal as part of their dialogue planner (including a representation of their commitment). But as we have noted, interlocutors develop sub-goals and additional goals throughout conversations, and when this happens, their plans change accordingly.

The oval contains a record of the shared workspace during the interaction. In Figure 4.1, the oval contains the contributions by both interlocutors (with the contribution by interlocutor A italicized), together with the relevant aspect of the context being discussed (in this case the overall maze configuration).[8]

---

[8] In Garrod and Anderson (1987), the interlocutors saw the same maze configuration, though there were differences of detail (e.g. they saw only their own position token). The shared workspace contains manifest information, including the configuration (which is shared) but not the position tokens (which are not shared).

The contributions come from the dialogue in Table 4.1, lines 9–11. The shared workspace changes dynamically, and at any given point reflects the current contribution – which is the contribution that the interlocutors jointly attend to.

In this figure, we depict the linguistic contributions (e.g. *you're one along*), including backchannel contributions (*uh-huh*; *A*'s contributions underlined), but the shared workspace can also include non-linguistic contributions (e.g. laughs, facial expressions, hand gestures) or voice quality. Moreover, it can include the relevant props (such as the maze configuration). It is therefore equivalent to the shared workspace discussed in Chapter 2, in that it contains the contributions of more than one individual as well as task-relevant aspects of context.

In dialogue, the shared workspace captures the publicly accessible communicative behaviours, together with relevant aspects of the context. For example, it might reflect both turns in a question-answer pair. In this case, the interlocutors first attend to the question and then the answer, so the question enters the shared workspace before the answer. A similar situation occurs when one interlocutor requests an object and the other holds it up (i.e. as a demonstration). Sometimes, the interlocutors can jointly attend to two contributions that take place at the same step in the dialogue (e.g. a statement with concurrent feedback); if so, the shared workspace can reflect both contributions together.

Both interlocutors can then act with respect to the shared workspace, considering the contributions of both interlocutors together (and not merely their own or their partner's individual contribution). In addition, aspects of the external context can form part of the shared workspace and are therefore integral to the system. We now describe the detailed framework and then use it to explain production, comprehension and distributed control in dialogue.

The thick black arrows from *A* and *B* to the shared workspace correspond to the processes involved in producing the contributions. In other words, they correspond to the implementation of language production (and other aspects of communication). The thin grey arrows, in contrast, correspond to additional processes that do not contribute directly to production. The downward arrowheads correspond to processes by which each individual comprehends what has been uttered and which are used in monitoring the progress of the dialogue. The upward grey arrowheads correspond to processes by which each individual predicts the progress of the dialogue (see Chapter 5). The horizontal grey arrows correspond to the processes by which the interlocutors perceive and predict their own contributions.

Importantly, the vertical grey arrows (unlike the black arrows or the horizontal grey arrows) make reference to the dialogue as a whole (i.e. the current content of the shared workspace), not to the contributions made by one or other interlocutor considered as an individual. For example, either interlocutor could comprehend the joint contribution *along uh-huh* and thus infer that the dialogue at this point is progressing satisfactorily or that *A* understands *B*'s use of *along*. Either individual could also comprehend (or indeed predict) an interlocutor's contribution (e.g. *uh-huh*) rather than a joint contribution – the important point is that comprehension and prediction are not limited to contributions by a single interlocutor.

The vertical grey arrows are comparable to processes of comprehension and prediction in traditional psycholinguistic theories, but they differ because they operate on joint contributions by different individuals rather than on a contribution by a single individual. But in a true monologue (i.e. in total absence of listener feedback, as in a radio broadcast), the contribution is made by a single individual (the speaker) and the other individual (the listener) is silent; in Figure 4.1, one of the black arrows would be removed (as well as the associated horizontal grey arrow). For example, if interlocutor *A* produced a speech, this speech would appear in the shared workspace, there would be no solid arrow from interlocutor *B* to the workspace, and the grey arrows would constitute *A*'s comprehension and prediction of her own speech and *B*'s comprehension and prediction of *A*'s speech (see Section 10.3).

4.5.1   Implementing Dialogue in the Shared Workspace Framework

As in other forms of cooperative joint activity, interlocutors interact with each other via the shared workspace. The workspace records behaviour, and in dialogue such behaviour involves language (as well as gesture and relevant props). Just as the shared workspace for cooperative joint actions contains those entities that the agents can manipulate, so the shared workspace for dialogue contains those entities that the interlocutors use to communicate.

The relevant entities are signs – physical entities with meaning. When *A* utters *I take it we've got identical mazes* (8) when talking to *B*, the sign for *mazes* enters the shared workspace. This is because the interlocutors jointly attend to the sign and they are engaged in dialogue as a form of cooperative joint activity. The sign has a joint affordance – that is, it can be interpreted as part of the current dialogue. Typically, such a sign is manifest (as the speaker ensures that it is heard as a meaningful entity). In Section 7.3, we present a more detailed discussion of signs and their relationship to the workspace.

The sign *mazes* enters the shared workspace because it is meaningful (hence, the sound /m/ does not enter the workspace instead). The sign includes the fact that *A* uttered it, hence the sign is *mazes$_A$*.[9] It is necessary that both

---

[9] When there is no ambiguity, we leave out the speaker subscript.

interlocutors interpret *mazes* as a meaningful expression, but it is not necessary that they give it the same interpretation. For example, *A* could use a homonym (*bank*) intending one interpretation (money bank) and *B* could give it a different interpretation (river bank), but there is a unique sign in the workspace (*bank$_A$*). (*A* and *B* have different representations corresponding to *bank*, but this difference is not reflected in the workspace.) If *B* subsequently uttered *mazes* when talking to *A*, then the shared workspace would now contain *mazes$_B$* as well as *mazes$_A$* (because they are distinct meaningful objects by virtue of being uttered by different people).

In (8), *A* utters *I* as referring to herself (as well as *we* as referring to *A* and *B*), and therefore *I$_A$* enters the shared workspace. If *B* subsequently uttered *I*, then *I$_B$* would also enter the workspace. The status of *I* with respect to the workspace is the same as the status of *mazes*. (However, the distinction between *I* as uttered by *A* versus *B* is important for both individuals' representations, with the effect of indexicality on interpretation being 'read off' the shared workspace directly; see Chapter 7.) Similarly, the workspace contains meaningful gestures as well as words. Such gestures can also be indexical (e.g. pointing) and the workspace reflects the gesturer, just as it reflects the speaker.

In Figure 4.1, the shared workspace therefore contains a record of who contributed what – for example, that *B* contributed *You're one along* and *A* contributed *Uh-huh*. Processes that put information into the workspace are represented by the thick black upward pointing arrows in Figure 4.1. They correspond to making spoken and other communicative contributions to the dialogue. Pointing to this arrow is a horizontal grey two-way arrow that reflects the processes by which the speaker can monitor the (private) imple-mentation of her productions before the result enters the shared workspace. The upward arrowhead corresponds to an internal monitoring process involved in making intermediate sensory predictions about implementation, which can be tested as it proceeds, as we will argue (Chapter 5). In other words, the upward arrowhead predicts the result and the downward arrow-head feeds back any discrepancy between prediction and implementation. Processes by which each individual interprets the shared workspace are reflected in the remaining vertical two-way grey arrow. These processes relate to comprehension, prediction and external monitoring of the work-space's content. It is a two-way arrow because we propose that the moni-toring process (like that used for private speech monitoring) involves predicting the upcoming content of the shared workspace and then checking those predictions as the content arrives.

Now return to the exchange in Table 4.1. The process of conceptualizing the contributions (e.g. Levelt, 1989) corresponds to the dialogue planner and the arrowhead leading to the dialogue implementer. For example, *B* determines that she wishes to check *A*'s position, and makes particular assumptions about the situation model in doing so (e.g. assuming a 'path' scheme; Garrod & Anderson, 1987). Similarly, *A* wishes to convey understanding or acceptance.

The thick arrows emanating from the dialogue implementer represent the processes underlying *B*'s production of *you're one along* and of *and one up?* and *A*'s production of *uh-huh*. For example, *B* accesses lexical items such as *you*, *are*, *one*, and *along*, as well as syntactic rules (or constraints) that allow these items to be combined and ordered, a phonological rule allowing contraction of *are*, and so on. Thus, the thick black arrows correspond to the stages of formulation and articulation (Levelt, 1989). Of course, the processes involved in producing *uh-huh* may be less complex than those involved in producing a longer utterance, but both involve formulation and articulation and are therefore captured by the same thick arrows emanating from an interlocutor. Note that the arrow is one-directional because it stands for processes involved in the act of production that starts in the individual and ends in the shared workspace (we ignore internal feedback at this stage). The processes represented by the arrow are private – they place utterances in the public workspace but are not themselves accessible to anyone except the producer.

The thin two-way grey arrow emanating from the thick arrow represents any processes that monitor these mechanisms of production. The downward arrowhead represents internal comprehension-based processes involved in self-monitoring (and is therefore an 'internal loop'). For example, *B* might construct a phonological (or phonetic) representation of the word *one* and treat it as the starting point of comprehension (i.e. then constructing syntactic and semantic representations). She can then determine whether there is a mismatch between a representation used in production and a representation resulting from comprehension (e.g. Levelt, 1989; Levelt et al., 1999); in this case, there does not seem to be. The upward arrowhead represents internal production-based processes involved in self-monitoring. For example, the speaker may decide that she wishes to produce a phonological representation corresponding to the meaning SINGLE. She predicts (using the thin grey arrow) that she will construct the phonological form /wɒn/, quite separately from formulating the phonological form /wɒn/ (using the thick black arrow). As we shall see below, the predicted representation need not always match the formulated representation. For now, the important point is that the prediction is of a representation that is private to the speaker. Thus, this two-way grey arrow represents speaker-internal processes involved in (internal) self-monitoring (see Chapter 5).

In contrast, we have noted that the other two-way grey arrow represents processes involved in comprehending (downward arrowhead) or predicting (upward arrowhead) the content of the shared workspace. In other words, it relates to public events associated with communication. Primarily, these activities are utterances, though they also include bodily movements and gestures and relevant aspects of the context such as objects or events that the utterances may refer to.

For now, we focus on the utterances themselves, as in our maze game example. Each interlocutor has access to the same contents of the shared workspace, which we represent as *you're one along uh-huh and one up?*, though of course it also includes timing, loudness, voice characteristics and so on. Thus, *B* can comprehend one or both of his own utterances (*you're one along* and/or *and one up?*). This process of listening to oneself involves what Levelt (1989) calls the 'external loop' – it involves actual sound and is therefore public – and is hence external self-monitoring. Similarly, *A* can self-monitor her own utterance *uh-huh*. Either *A* or *B* could therefore have revised (or corrected) what they have uttered (though they did not do so on this occasion). The process of external self-monitoring is represented by the downward grey arrowheads.

In addition, *B* can comprehend *A*'s utterance (*uh-huh*), during what we call *other-monitoring* (see Pickering & Garrod, 2014). Again, this is represented by the downward grey arrowheads. (Unlike self-monitoring, other-monitoring of course has to be external, and so other-monitoring is not represented in the horizontal grey arrows.) Similarly, *A* other-monitors *B*'s utterances – a process that involves comprehension, but can also trigger responses to those utterances such as suggested repairs (see Schegloff et al., 1977). In our example, *A*'s utterance *uh-huh* is a consequence of other-monitoring. Presumably, *A* believes (wrongly, as it turns out) she understands *B*'s utterance (as an indicator of horizontal position) and provides a confirmation of this understanding.[10]

The shared workspace framework allows us to introduce an important new concept of *joint monitoring* – that is, monitoring a joint contribution. In our example, *B* might monitor *you're one along uh-huh* and use it to conclude that *A* and *B* have reached some degree of alignment – that is, shared understanding. On another occasion, it might be that one interlocutor joint monitored a contribution followed by a query and concluded that they were not aligned with each other and that some form of expansion or repair was necessary. Joint monitoring is captured by the fact that the downward grey arrowhead emanates from the shared workspace. It is particularly appropriate for our framework, which allows either interlocutor to focus on any aspect of the workspace (see Chapters 5 and 8).

---

[10] Speakers can also monitor their addressees for understanding (see Postma, 2000). This is a different sense of other monitoring and can lead to other-initiated repairs (Schegloff et al., 1977), which we consider in relation to negative commentaries in Chapter 8.

Note also that the shared workspace framework allows either interlocutor to monitor the combination of either or both interlocutors' utterances with the context (including non-linguistic joint actions such as constructing furniture). For example, if *A* realizes that *B* refers to an object incorrectly (e.g. *look at that lovely azalea!* when she realizes he is pointing to a hydrangea), then she comprehends the combination of *B*'s utterance and her interpretation of the object and monitors the inconsistency. In our maze game example, one interlocutor might detect a discrepancy between the joint contribution (in effect, *A*'s acceptance of *B*'s *You're one along*) and the maze configuration. In such a situation, our framework allows monitoring to reflect a combination of both interlocutors and the context. Note that interlocutors can produce utterances that are distributed between them, for example when one interlocutor assists the other by retrieving a problematic word or when *A* points at a rare plant and *B* says *That's called a Jellyfish Tree*.

In addition, each interlocutor can predict the contents of the shared workspace. So for example, *B* might predict what he will utter and how *A* will respond. Informally, *B* might think 'if I describe her position in such-and-such a way, then *A* will probably affirm'. Such a joint prediction is easy to accommodate in our framework, because the prediction is of future states of the shared workspace that includes contributions by both partners. Such joint prediction is captured by the upward grey arrowhead. Notice that joint monitoring is incompatible with monadic psycholinguistics.

Above, we noted that the control of dialogue is distributed across interlocutors, and that they can exercise such control at the layers of planning, implementation and behaviour. Within the shared workspace framework, such distributed control is brought about by the flow of information through the arrows.

Distributed control therefore allows either interlocutor to attempt to repair errors (or for them both to decide not to repair) at any of the three layers. For example, a potential house purchaser asks *Can you open the windows?* (as he is hot), the estate agent answers *Yes, they open easily*, and the purchaser says *No, I meant, would you mind doing so?* Here, the purchaser recognizes a pragmatic error, which we interpret as an error of planning. If the purchaser says *I like that house best*, the agent responds, *Yes, it's more spacious than No. 4*, and the purchaser says, *No, I meant No. 4*, then the purchaser recognizes a referential error, which we interpret as an error of implementation. And finally, if the purchaser and the agent speak at the same time and the purchaser yields to the agent, then the purchaser recognizes an error of behaviour. Importantly, all of these errors are joint errors, with first two being errors of alignment and the third being an error of synchrony. It is not correct to regard either the agent or purchaser as individually responsible. This concept of a joint error cannot be explained in monadic psycholinguistics.

4.6   Four Characteristics of the Dialogue System

In Chapter 2, we considered four characteristics of successful joint action systems: *alignment, simulation, prediction* and *synchrony*. We now consider them in relation to dialogue and the shared workspace framework, focusing both on the individual interlocutors and on the dialogue system.

4.6.1   Alignment

The dialogue planner and implementer make use of various representations concerned with the content of what is being discussed and the form of the utterances that the interlocutors produce. When interlocutors are well aligned, their representations are similar to each other. They represent the same dialogue plans (and if they develop the plan during the conversation, they do so in the same way as each other). In the dialogue implementer, they represent linguistic information in the same way as each other. For example, they would tend to use the same words to refer to the same entities and understand their partner's use of those words in the same way as their partner. Alignment is therefore a property of the relationship between the interlocutors' representations. It is not a property of the shared workspace: the workspace contains behaviours, and alignment is not a property of behaviours – though of course alignment can be reflected in behaviours such as speech (aligned interlocutors tend to speak in similar ways).

When interlocutors are aligned, the flow of information to and from the shared workspace will be similar. For example, aligned interlocutors are likely to make use of prediction in similar ways to each other. Additionally, they are likely to have access to similar information in the workspace. They are both likely to hear everything that is said, and both have access to the same props (e.g. one will not have privileged access to relevant information). Thus the downward arrowheads from the shared workspace to the dialogue implementer will convey similar information. Similarly, they will tend to make the same predictions about the joint contents of the workspace. Informally, the two sides of Figure 4.1 will function in the same way.

As with other cooperative joint activity, both interlocutors are aware that they are participating in dialogue and that their partner is too. They realize when the dialogue begins and ends and are both committed to the dialogue. So they are aligned on their involvement in the dialogue. Moreover they are generally aware when their understanding of the dialogue is similar to their partner's and when they are using appropriately similar forms (e.g. the same words to refer to the same things). In such cases, they both come to meta-represent their alignment. Finally, we assume that in general alignment is closely related to conversational success. Alignment is the central to our account of the dialogue processing system (following Pickering & Garrod, 2004) and so we devote Chapters 6 and 7 to it.

4.6.2   Simulation

Simulation occurs when an agent undergoes some of the processes involved in performing an action (without actually doing so) in order to model that action. The process of forward modelling therefore is a form of simulation. So an agent simulates language by conducting some processes involved in planning (i.e. conceptualizing) or implementing (i.e. formulating) language but does not articulate. As when simulating other forms of action, an agent can self-simulate during language production or can other-simulate language production during language comprehension. Self- and other-simulation can also be used 'off-line' to imagine (or rehearse) future utterances, for example when preparing to give a speech or anticipating another's speech, and to remember and interpret past utterances (see Gambi & Pickering, 2016). Self- and other-simulation are combined in joint simulation – to represent dialogue, an interlocutor must simulate both interlocutors' contributions.

In terms of the shared workspace framework, self-simulation uses the planner and implementer to predict (via the upward horizontal grey arrowhead) the content of the solid black arrow and to predict (via the upward vertical grey arrowhead) the speaker's contribution to content of the workspace. So if *A* prepares to speak, she may predict associated representations, such as the meaning, grammar or phonology associated with a word or longer utterance. Alternatively, she may predict the actual sound (i.e. of her own voice) as recorded in the workspace. To do this, *A* self-simulates some of the processes involved in speaking. Similarly, if *B* listens to *A*, then *B* uses other-simulation (via the upward vertical grey arrowhead) to predict *A*'s contribution to the contents of the workspace. Other-simulation is closely related to alignment: if *A* simulates *B*'s language, then *A* develops similar representations to *B*.

4.6.3   Prediction (and Postdiction)

As we have discussed, many cooperative joint activities require prediction (see Sebanz et al., 2006). In our example from Chapter 2, two people carrying a piano up the stairs have to predict each other's actions, for example because they can only exert the necessary force if they both lift at the same time. Their actions – that is, both of their contributions and the movement of the piano itself – enter the shared workspace via the solid black arrows and they predict, perceive and monitor this outcome via the vertical grey arrow. In Chapter 3, we proposed that agents make use of prediction-by-simulation in order to control cooperative joint actions.

Importantly, prediction is also crucial for dialogue. At any given point, the current addressee has to predict when the speaker is going to end in order to initiate a turn without extensive delay or overlap. So when *B* is saying *You're one along*, *A* presumably predicts that *B* is about to end (or at least, that *B* is about to reach a transition-relevant point) and uses this prediction to prepare an appropriate response. And when *A* is responding *uh-huh:*, *B* can likewise predict *A*'s ending and prepare a response. The unfolding utterances enter the shared workspace via the solid black arrows (see Figure 4.1). The predictions of the content of the workspace (in this case, the utterances) are represented by the vertical upward grey arrowheads. These arrowheads can apply to an individual contribution (e.g. when *A* predicts the ending of *You're one along:*) or a joint contribution (e.g. when *B* predicts the ending of *You're one along: uh-huh:*) – and it is also possible to predict one's own content or end point.

We argue that prediction of language (and in particular dialogue) is primarily conducted using prediction-by-simulation. To predict that *B* will finish speaking after *along*, *A* simulates the production of *You're one*. Specifically, *A* goes through some of the processes that *B* is using to produce *You're one* and determines what *B* would be likely to say next and how long it will take. Of course, *B* also uses prediction-by-simulation when *A* is speaking.

Interlocutors can also use postdiction-by-simulation to aid comprehension, to check that the utterance occurs as the comprehender would have predicted (given the following as well as preceding information). For example, *A* might have failed to hear *one* but postdicted it after hearing *You're ... along:* (presumably in the context of the maze, which is also in the shared workspace). Evidence that comprehenders can use subsequent information to resolve ambiguities and disfluencies comes from studies of phoneme restoration effects (e.g. Samuel, 1981) and word recognition in connected speech (Bard et al., 1988).

We have already noted that prediction-by-simulation (including postdiction) is compatible with analysis-by-synthesis (Halle & Stevens, 1959). In a more recent discussion, Poeppel and Monahan (2011) reconsidered its relevance to speech processing (and processing language more generally). For example, they note that analysis-by-synthesis may account for audio-visual interactions in speech perception, such as van Wassenhove et al.'s (2005) finding that more predictable articulatory configurations yield more rapid auditory speech perception. In other words, the more predictable the earlier lip movements, the easier it is to identify later speech sounds. In conclusion, prediction appears to be central to dialogue and interlocutors appear to simulate each other when deriving such predictions. We elaborate on this framework in Chapter 5.

4.6.4   *Synchrony*

Like other joint activities, dialogue depends on timing. As argued above, interlocutors need to predict precisely when someone is going to say something and when they will finish speaking. Conversational turns rarely overlap and on average the gap between them is around 200 ms (Stivers et al., 2009). A major part of the explanation for why conversation is so fluent (given that it takes much longer to plan utterances) is that interlocutors often predict when their partner is going to finish speaking and initiate their response accordingly (see Levinson, 2016).

We argue that the synchronization of interlocutors' speech rates is very important for dialogue timing. If A's speech rate is the same as B's, then either can use prediction-by-simulation (running at their own speech rate) to estimate when to complete an utterance whose content is predictable. Either interlocutor can also ensure that their response will synchronize with their partner's utterance – that is, following on at roughly the same rate or interrupting the utterance at an appropriate point. In fact, some evidence from corpora shows that conversational partners adapt their baseline speech rate to converge with that of their partner (e.g. Cohen Priva et al., 2017). In other words, naturally slow speakers speed up and naturally fast speakers slow down when conversing with each other. We consider the details of such synchronization in Chapter 9.

4.7   Conclusions

In this chapter, we have applied the shared workspace framework to communication. We developed the framework in the context of cooperative joint activity in general, and showed how it can be used to explain dialogue. To do this, we extended the systems analysis from individuals cooperating to interlocutors communicating. Importantly, the shared workspace for dialogue involves signs as well as other entities. In the final section, we interpret alignment, simulation, prediction and synchrony in relation to dialogue.

5 Producing, Controlling and Understanding Dialogue

In Chapter 4, we introduced a framework for dialogue that was derived from our framework for joint activity. Actors perform collaborative joint activities by interacting via a shared workspace, and interlocutors engage in dialogue in the same way. We now consider how interlocutors can engage in dialogue and control its progress in terms of the arrows connecting them to the workspace. In Chapter 3, we considered action, action perception, and joint action, and in the same way we now consider production, comprehension, and dialogue.

We therefore first consider each speaker's language production (both in isolation and as part of dialogue) – how they perform, predict and control what they say. We then consider how each comprehender predicts and interprets their partner's speech. We then put these two components together into a framework for producing, controlling and understanding dialogue, first in terms of each interlocutor's contribution considered separately and then as a single integrated system in which the control is distributed between them. It should be clear that this structure is parallel to the way that we interpreted joint activity in Chapter 3.

We first re-present the shared workspace framework, as applied to dialogue (Figure 5.1). Because our interest is in the arrows, we leave the internal representational structure of the two interlocutors until Chapter 6, except that we distinguish between dialogue planning and dialogue implementation. The thick vertical arrows correspond to the processes leading to an individual utterance (e.g. *You're one along*) and involve inserting that utterance into the workspace. They implement the stages of language production – constructing its semantics, syntax and phonology. The horizontal grey arrow (within each individual) relates to these private stages of implementation (before the utterance has entered the shared workspace). The downward arrowhead refers to perception of these stages (and associated monitoring); the upward arrowhead refers to predictions of these stages. In contrast, the vertical grey arrows (linking the interlocutors to the shared workspace) relate to public behaviours reflected in the workspace, and can therefore involve behaviours of either or (importantly) both participants. These public behaviours are of course speech and its communicative context (as illustrated in the shared workspace of

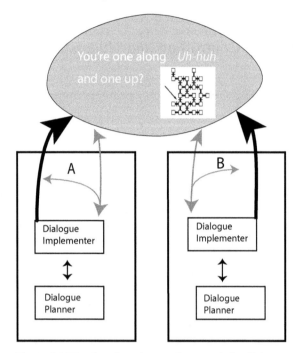

Figure 5.1 The shared workspace framework for dialogue.
Reproduced from Figure 4.2.

Figure 5.1). The downward arrowhead refers to the perception of these behaviours; the upward arrowhead refers to the prediction of these behaviours.

An important difference between the shared workspace framework for nonlinguistic joint action and for dialogue is that it is unclear what levels of structure are involved in most forms of (non-linguistic) joint action.[1] In contrast, dialogue (and language use more generally) has a well-established internal structure with multiple levels of representation.[2] The three important

---

[1] Note that *layers* refers to planning, implementation and behaviour, whereas *levels* refers to components within these layers.

[2] Even if detailed research can uncover levels of representation for specific joint actions, they may not be the same as the levels involved in other forms of joint action. Of course, some joint actions have an obvious structure just as individual actions do. For example, preparing a meal involves different steps (e.g. slicing vegetables, boiling water, adding the vegetables to the water) and these steps can be distributed across two chefs. So there may be well-specified levels of representation involved in such a task. But these levels will of course be quite different in other forms of non-linguistic joint activity and generalizations across joint activities may be difficult. For example, Hutchins (1995) provides a structured interpretation of co-pilots landing a plane, which can applied to other joint activities. But the specific representations that he assumed are different in other joint activities. In contrast, all forms of dialogue involve the same linguistic

levels are concerned with meaning, grammar and sound, and we refer to them as *semantics*, *syntax* and *phonology*, respectively (we assume spoken language). In this chapter, we do not focus on the details of these levels of representation, but rather focus on the structure of the dialogue system as a whole. We discuss their details in relation to alignment in Chapter 6, and now consider how the arrows in Figure 5.1 work by developing more detailed models in Figures 5.2–5.5.

5.1 Performing, Predicting and Controlling One's Own Utterance in Dialogue

To analyse how interlocutors control their utterances in dialogue, we apply the model for action control to language production (see Figure 5.2). We therefore begin with a distinction between implementing (i.e. producing) an utterance and predicting the outcome of that act of production (via an efference copy). The action command is specified as the production command, the action implementer is specified as the production implementer, and the perception implementer is specified as the comprehension implementer. Similarly, the forward action model is specified as the forward production model, and the forward perception model is specified as the forward comprehension model. The motor system is replaced by the articulator, and internal and external comparators are replaced by internal and external monitors (using standard psycholinguistic terminology; Levelt, 1989). As noted, we simply assume that the linguistic representations are semantics, syntax and phonology.

In Figure 5.2, the production command is the output of the dialogue planner (see Figure 5.1). It is the dialogical equivalent to the message (Levelt, 1989), and serves as the input to the production implementer. The production implementer is part of the dialogue implementer (Figure 5.1) – specifically, the component concerned with putting utterances into the shared workspace. In more detail, the production implementer converts the production command into a series of linguistic representations (semantics, syntax and phonology). It corresponds to the *formulator* in traditional psycholinguistic theories of language production (e.g. Bock & Levelt, 1994). These representations are computed (roughly) in sequence and take time (roughly 600 ms for a word; Indefrey & Levelt, 2004).[3]

---

representations, irrespective of the form or content of the dialogue. In Section 11.1, we discuss the integration of linguistic and non-linguistic cooperative joint activity and argue that language tends to structure non-linguistic activity.

[3] Indefrey and Levelt (2004) estimate that semantics (including message preparation) takes about 175 ms and syntax (so-called lemma access) takes about 75 ms. They estimate that phonology (including syllabification) takes around 205 ms and that phonetic encoding and articulation take an additional 145 ms, but notice that our use of *phonology* includes phonetic encoding. These timings are based on isolated single-word production and may be somewhat different in richer

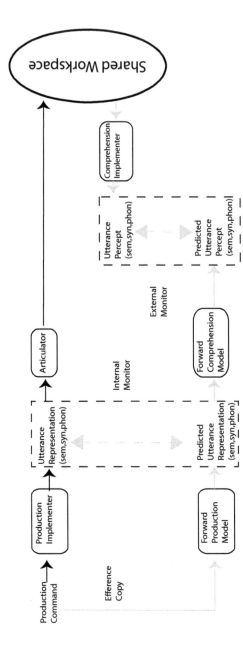

Figure 5.2 A model for controlling language production. Mechanisms occur in closed boxes. Dotted boxes (and dotted arrows) refer to processes that compare representations (i.e. monitors). *Sem*, *syn* and *phon* refer to the semantics, syntax and phonology of the utterance. The shared workspace is elliptical. The use of black and grey arrows corresponds to their use in Figure 5.1. (Note that the output of the internal and external monitors can be fed back to the production command via an inverse model.)

As noted, we simply assume that speakers construct a semantic representation, followed by a syntactic representation, and then a phonological representation. Theories of sentence formulation typically assume further sound-based representations and may also assume other syntactic or semantic representations (e.g. concerned with grammatical functions such as subject and object; Bock & Levelt, 1994). Moreover, some theories propose that representations overlap in time (i.e. involve cascading), and some allow information to flow backwards as well as forwards between representations (i.e. involve feedback); see Dell (1986).[4] Eventually, the production representations feed into the articulator, which produces the utterance that enters the shared workspace.

The speaker then comprehends what she has uttered via the comprehension implementer and constructs an utterance percept containing phonological, syntactic and semantic representations. We consider language comprehension in detail in Section 5.2 (here, our focus is solely on the role of self-comprehension in production). Comprehension is illustrated by the grey left-pointing arrowhead from the shared workspace (with self-comprehension involving the components of the workspace that were produced by the speaker, in this case *you're one along*). All theories of language comprehension assume a staggering of phonological, syntactic and semantic processing, though they differ in the extent to which the representations overlap in time or how much feedback occurs (e.g. Frazier, 1987; MacDonald et al., 1994).

Alongside the processes of implementation, an efference copy of the production command feeds into the forward production model, which outputs predicted production representations – predictions of the semantics, syntax and phonology of the utterance. The predicted production representations are input into the forward comprehension model, which outputs the predicted comprehension representations – predictions of the percept of the semantics, syntax and phonology of the utterance. The efference copy is in general processed more quickly than the production command itself.

Importantly, we assume that many production representations and comprehension percepts involve the same information. For example, B's utterance *you're* has a syntax (noun phrase plus verb) that is the same whether B is producing it or comprehending it (i.e. his own utterance). This assumes that the speaker does not mishear herself (which would be a mistake at the level of the comprehension implementer).[5] But the production representation for syntax (i.e. the representation corresponding to the experience of producing syntax) is

---

contexts. Other studies provide slightly different estimates (Sahin et al., 2009; Indefrey, 2011; cf. Strijkers & Costa, 2016).

[4] Pickering and Garrod (2013, Figure 1) represented feedback as a small arrow embedded in a larger arrow.

[5] Such a situation can in fact be experimentally induced (see Lind et al., 2014).

different from the comprehension percept for syntax (i.e. the representation corresponding to the experience of perceiving syntax) – they draw on the same information (noun phrase plus verb) but construct two different representations (one action-based, the other perception-based). Informally, the information in the production representation and the comprehension percept are equivalent but the 'perspective' on that information is different. In this normal situation, the forward comprehension model simply involves changing the 'perspective' (but involves an identity mapping of information). Just as production representations and comprehension percepts are normally equivalent, so predicted production representations and predicted comprehension percepts are also normally equivalent – and when this is the case, the forward comprehension model does no work (i.e. it instantiates the identity mapping).

In contrast, many researchers assume different sound-based production representations and comprehension percepts (e.g. Hickok et al., 2011; Mitterer & Ernestus, 2008; Tourville & Guenther, 2011). Therefore, the production representation and the comprehension percept for aspects of sound may be different with respect to information and not merely the 'perspective' on the information. If so, the predicted production representation and the predicted comprehension percept would also not be equivalent, and so the forward comprehension model would do more than change 'perspective' (i.e. not instantiate the identity mapping of information).

Implementations and predictions can be compared at two points. First, the utterance representation (its semantics, syntax and phonology) can be compared with the predicted utterance representation (its predicted semantics, syntax and phonology), via the internal monitor. Any discrepancy between these two representations (as determined by the monitor) can be fed back so that it can modify the next production command accordingly. If the predicted phonology (e.g. /j/ when producing /j . . ./, corresponding to *you're*) is inconsistent with actual phonological representation (e.g. the speaker prepares /w/) then the monitor registers a discrepancy that is fed back and can be used to modify the production command (so that the speaker can now correctly prepare /j/). This modification could prevent the speaker uttering /w/ but might lead to a hesitation or disfluency. In addition, the speaker might use comprehension to interpret utterance representations (i.e. without involving forward modelling). This is the 'inner loop' as assumed by Levelt (1989), in which the speaker interprets a sound-based representation in the absence of articulation.[6]

---

[6] Some researchers assume that monitoring can involve other internal mechanisms such as conflict-monitoring (Nozari et al., 2011), in which the mechanisms involved in production are alert to difficulties caused by competition between potential alternatives. Whatever way this proposal would be represented in Figure 6.1, it would relate to the mechanisms of production and would not relate to the shared workspace, as they are concerned with representations rather than

Second, the utterance percept can be compared with the predicted utterance percept, via the external monitor. For example, the speaker may produce the sound /w/ when intending to utter /j . . ./. She has predicted that she would hear herself utter /j/ and in fact perceived herself utter /w/. She therefore compares the predicted percept and actual percept using the external monitor and feeds back the discrepancy so that it can be used to modify the next production command. The speaker would then produce /w/, followed perhaps by a disfluency or self-repair, and then /j/ (e.g. /w/ . . . *I mean you're*). In sum, both internal and external monitoring take place continuously. (Note that we are assuming that the production representations and comprehension percepts of these phonemes are equivalent.)

An obvious criticism of this account is that if the speaker is computing a forward model, why not just use that model in production itself? The response is that the predictions are not the same as the implemented production representations, but are easier-to-compute 'impoverished' representations. They leave out (or simplify) many components of the implemented representations, just as a forward model of predicted hand movements might encode coordinates but not distance between index finger and thumb, or a forward model for navigation might include information about the ship's position and perhaps fuel level but not its response to the heavy swell.

For example, if the speaker is attempting to utter *you're*, then the important properties of the sounds are that they are /j/, /a/, and /w/, rather than their phonetic features (e.g. the height of each formant or the length of each phoneme within certain limits) – as such changes would not lead to the perception of a different word. Our proposal is that the speaker would predict the phonemes. For example, she might be aware that being in the state to generate a particular production command (in this case, to produce *you're*) ought to lead to the construction of /j/, /a/, and /w/. In the process of internal monitoring, she would compare the predicted phonemic representations with the phonemic representations that she constructs during production. In external monitoring, she would perceive the phonetic features but would use them to construct the phonemes and then compare these with the predicted phonemes – but there would be no prediction of the phonetic features.

As with action more generally, the role of forward modelling is not limited to predicting and helping repair speech errors. It can be used to estimate what is being uttered in a noisy environment and to reduce the sensitivity to one's own speech (e.g. Flinker et al., 2015). It can also be used in speech acquisition (see Tourville & Gunther, 2011).[7]

---

behaviours (or context). A similar conclusion holds for the older node-structure theory (Mackay, 1987).

[7] Two neuro-computational accounts of isolated word and phoneme production use forward modeling and control (of phonology). Tourville and Guenther's (2011) DIVA (Direction of Velocities of Articulators) model (and its extension, the Gradient Order DIVA model), uses

The outputs of the internal and external monitors feed into the mechanism that generates the production command (not illustrated in Figure 5.2), and can thus modify the production command. These outputs constitute inverse models and function in the same way as in action in general (see Chapter 3). Therefore, the process of generating the production command and its efference copy and then comparing their consequences constitutes a control loop through which the individual can monitor and correct her actions as they unfold. Language production therefore uses pseudo-closed-loop controllers (Grush, 2004).

Now compare Figure 5.2 with Figure 5.1. The production implementer and the articulator correspond to the thick black arrow in Figure 5.1, with the speech (e.g. *you're one along*) appearing in the shared workspace. The grey line emanating from the workspace (i.e. the comprehension implementation pathway) corresponds to the downward vertical grey arrowhead. The bottom line (i.e. the forward model pathway) corresponds to both upward grey arrowheads, with the internal monitor corresponding to the horizontal grey line (i.e. going into the 'private' production implementer) and the external monitor corresponding to the vertical grey line (i.e. going into the 'public' shared workspace). The inverse models (which map the outputs of the monitors to the production command) are a component of the downward arrowheads (again, with a distinction between the external and internal monitor loops). The downward horizontal grey arrowhead would also be used to comprehend the utterance representations (without prediction), as in the inner loop (Levelt, 1989).

5.2   Predicting and Interpreting Others' Utterances Using Simulation

As in action perception more generally, comprehenders can predict other's utterances in two ways (see Pickering & Garrod, 2013). They can predict on the basis of their experience comprehending others – in other words, prediction-by-association. For example, if they have previously heard the speaker, or speakers in general, talking about a topic in a certain way, then they can predict

---

somatosensory and auditory forward modeling for speech production and acquisition. Their account assumes target maps for the predicted somatosensory phonology (in our terms predicted utterance (phon)) and predicted auditory phonology (predicted utterance percept (phon)) of the upcoming utterance. The target maps are compared with the actual somatosensory state (in our terms utterance (phon)) and actual auditory state (utterance percept (phon)) as the speech unfolds and the discrepancy is fed back into the speech implementer. Similarly, Hickok et al.'s (2011; Hickok, 2014) State Feedback Control model of word production involves both predicted somatosensory phoneme targets (predicted utterance (phon)) and predicted auditory syllable targets (predicted utterance percept (phon)) for comparison with the utterance articulation and acoustics as it unfolds. Both accounts assume distinct phonological representations for articulation and acoustic comprehension. (In Hickok's model, articulatory predictions are based on somatosensory phoneme targets whereas acoustic predictions are based on auditory syllable targets.)

how the speaker is likely to continue. If speakers have tended to say word or sound X after word or sound Y, and they hear Y, they can predict X. We assume that prediction-by-association plays a fairly minor role in dialogue and is not our current concern.

More important, comprehenders predict on the basis of their experience producing utterances. According to such prediction-by-simulation, a comprehender predicts speakers by using the same processes that he uses to produce his own utterances. The comprehender can simulate by just using his own utterance implementer (and inhibiting its output). But we have just argued that the producer also computes an efference copy of the production command to predict what she is going to say. And if the comprehender simulates the producer using production mechanisms, then he can make use of this efference copy to predict his partner's utterances. We therefore propose that he uses his forward production model to derive a prediction of his partner's utterance (i.e. an action-based representation) and the forward comprehension model to derive a prediction of his percept of that utterance (i.e. a perceptual representation). To do this, he derives the speaker's production command from his comprehension of her previous and current utterance (or from background information such as knowledge of her state of mind and the broader context) and uses this to generate an efference copy of the intended utterance.

Importantly, our analysis now requires us to consider when the construction of percepts and predicted percepts takes place. Language involves discrete steps (such as words) and so we analyse utterance prediction in terms of such steps rather than times. In this respect, our analysis contrasts with our analysis of joint action in Chapter 3 (though see footnote 8 in that chapter). As will become clear, steps constitute units of analysis for the dialogue planner, and it is the planner that drives the production command that underlies prediction and monitoring.

Figure 5.3 characterizes the process of predicting another's utterance using on-line simulation. *B* is uttering *Harry wants to go into the garden to fly his kite*, in a context in which *A* knows that Harry is a keen kite-flier (i.e. an intentional component of the context) and in which this kite is on a table (i.e. a physical component of the context). At step *s*, *A* interprets *Harry ... his* in relation to this contextual knowledge and uses their combination to derive the production command for *s* + 1 that *A* would use if she were *B* – specifically, the command to utter *kite*. *A* does not of course utter *kite*, but instead generates an efference copy of this derived production command to predict some of *B*'s representations at *s* + 1 – both the predicted utterance representation (i.e. the action-based representation of what *B* would say) and the predicted utterance percept (i.e. the perceptual representation of what *A* would hear).[8] *A* could predict the meaning (flyable, unitary, toy), the syntax (singular noun), or the

---

[8] Note we assume that that the forward production model feeds into the forward comprehension model. It may be possible to by-pass the forward production model (cf. Jaeger & Ferreira, 2013).

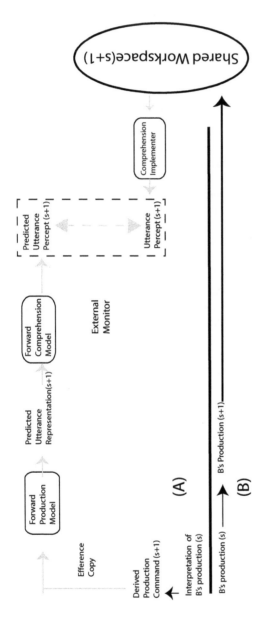

Figure 5.3 A model of the system for utterance prediction via on-line simulation. Mechanisms occur in closed boxes. Dotted boxes (and dotted arrows) refer to processes that compare representations. The shared workspace is elliptical. The use of black and grey arrows corresponds to their use in Figure 5.1. Note that we leave out the internal structure of the representations (i.e. *sem*, *syn* and *phon*) for simplicity. The subscripts *s* and *s* + 1 refer to the current and subsequent step, respectively.

phonology (/**kaɪt**/). However, *A* need not predict all of these representations, or might predict components of the representations (e.g. noun but not singular, or just the first phoneme /**k**/). These predictions can be computed well before *B* completes the utterance. *B* then utters *kite* (assuming *A* is correct, of course) and *kite* enters the shared workspace. *A* then comprehends *kite* and computes the utterance percept (specifically, its semantics, syntax and phonology) which she can then compare with the predicted utterance percept (using the external monitor).

As with action (Section 3.2), the computationally complex problem is deriving the upcoming production command on the basis of the utterance and its context (as the command itself is used in the same way as in Section 5.1). In our example, how can *A* determine *B*'s intention to utter *kite*? *A* covertly imitates *B*'s utterance so far (i.e. up to *fly his*) and draws on her knowledge that Harry likes kite-flying and that there is a kite at hand. On this basis, *A* determines the production command that she herself would use at *s* + 1 and treats this as the derived production command for *B*. She then predicts *B*'s utterance representation and associated utterance percept. The external monitor then compares this predicted utterance percept with the actual utterance percept. Its output (i.e. the discrepancy between the predicted and actual utterance percept) is used to interpret *B*'s utterance.

As when considering action (see Section 3.2), *A* interprets *B*'s utterance by simulating *B*'s utterance, both in relation to what *B* will say (our primary interest) and in relation to what *B* has said. If *A* is able to simulate *B* successfully, then *A* has understood what *B* has said. So when *A* simulates *B*'s utterance (up to *his*) to predict that *B* will say *kite*, and *B* actually says *kite*, then there is evidence that *A* understood *B*'s complete utterance (*Harry wants to go into the garden to fly his kite*) correctly.

Thus, the simulation of others' utterances constitutes interpretation. As we noted in Section 3.2, simulation is necessary for interpretation but prediction is not necessary. Note that a comprehender can interpret an utterance by simulating it after it has occurred (i.e. using postdiction).[9]

We now need to relate Figure 5.3 to Figure 5.1. The black arrow from the evaluation of *B*'s production to the derived production command in Figure 5.3 corresponds to *A*'s upward arrowhead from the dialogue planner to the dialogue implementer in Figure 5.1. The forward model pathway from the derived production command to the predicted utterance percept corresponds to *A*'s vertical upward grey arrowhead. The grey line emanating from the shared workspace (i.e. the comprehension implementation pathway) corresponds to *A*'s downward vertical grey arrowhead. The external monitor corresponds to

---

[9] This means that our account contrasts with proposals in which prediction is necessary for understanding (Altmann & Mirkovics, 2009; Elman, 1990) or where it always occurs (Jaeger & Kuperberg, 2016).

A's vertical grey line (with the monitoring occurring between the upward predictive arrowhead and downward comprehension arrowhead). The inverse model (which maps the outputs of the external monitor to the derived production command) is a component of A's vertical downward arrowhead. Finally, the bottom line in Figure 5.3 represents B's production implementational pathway (i.e. the solid upward black arrow from B to the shared workspace).

5.3   Individual Prediction and Interpretation of Dialogue

We have considered how an individual can independently predict their own unfolding utterances and those of their partner. This account is adequate for an account of isolated language production and comprehension, but is insufficient for dialogue. Instead, A must predict A's and B's contributions to the dialogue as a whole. Our framework allows us to do this by combining prediction in production and prediction in comprehension, and is illustrated by the composite Figure 5.4. We do not need to explain each component in detail because they correspond straightforwardly to the components of individual prediction of joint action (Figure 3.4). For example, the derived production command corresponds to the derived action command, the predicted utterance percept corresponds to the predicted action percept, and so on.

Consider our example, but now let us assume that A utters *you're one along* and B responds *uh-huh*, so that we can interpret these contributions in terms of Figure 5.4. At step s, we assume A has uttered *you're one* and therefore A predicts the rest of A's utterance at the top of Figure 5.4 and B's utterance below (i.e. immediately above the dividing line between A and B). A therefore predicts A's upcoming word *along* and we assume that A also predicts that B will respond with an affirmation or rejection (because A has produced a 'try-marker' that A believes B will accept; Sacks & Schegloff, 1979). The shared workspace contains both utterances, but the top comprehension implementer acts on A's utterance and the bottom comprehension implementer acts on B's utterance. The two external monitors involve identical mechanisms – A's process of predicting, perceiving and monitoring A's and B's utterances is the same. But as with joint action, A can internally monitor herself but cannot internally monitor B – she has access to the utterance representations that she constructs when producing *you're one along* but not to the utterance representations that her partner constructs when producing *uh-huh*. As we shall see, the grey pathways concerned with forward modelling, comprehension and external monitoring become interwoven in the context of successful dialogue. But the grey pathway concerned with internal monitoring 'withers away', just like the internal comparator in Chapter 3.

Underlying our account is the fact that A represents the dialogue plan – roughly that A will suggest what B's position is, and that B will respond (i.e. two sub-plans that are meshed into a dialogue plan). The dialogue plan

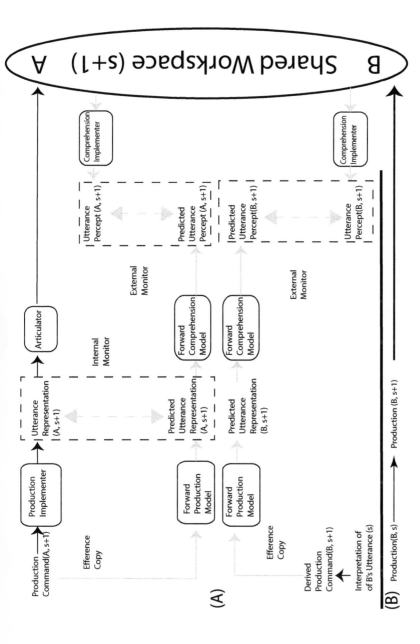

Figure 5.4 A model of one interlocutor predicting dialogue. Mechanisms occur in closed boxes. Dotted boxes (and dotted arrows) refer to processes that compare representations. The shared workspace is elliptical. The use of black and grey arrows corresponds to their use in Figure 5.1. Everything above the solid line refers to A's representations and processes (e.g. Utterance Percept (B, s + 1) refers to A's percept of B's utterance at s + 1).

therefore leads to two interdependent production commands (*A*'s production command and *A*'s derived production command for *B*). As the shared workspace contains related contributions (*A* and *B*'s contributions to an adjacency pair), the comprehension implementers are related, as are the utterance percepts. In this successful interchange, both *A* and *B* play their appropriate roles (i.e. they say the right things at the right times). The dialogue plan is not reflected in Figure 5.4, but it will emerge below.

5.4   Joint Performance, Prediction and Control of Dialogue

So far, we have considered one interlocutor's prediction and interpretation of dialogue, in an analysis that is compatible with monadic cognitive science. Just as we did for joint action, we now need to include the second interlocutor. At this point, *A* and *B* are predicting both *A*'s and *B*'s contributions, and those predictions can be used to produce and control the dialogue. We are therefore now in a position to present a systems analysis of dialogue in the context of a complete, distributed, control mechanism.

We have presented *A*'s representation of *A* and *B* in Figure 5.4, and *B*'s representation of *A* and *B* is identical to *A*'s. Figure 5.5 combines both perspectives on the dialogue, and includes both interlocutors' dialogue planners. Each planner represents both interlocutors' roles in the dialogue and is responsible for control. Just as when considering joint action, we now merge the predictions and develop an account of control that is distributed across the interlocutors, and focus on the external monitor because it relates to the shared workspace. The shared workspace reflects the dialogue as a whole (and can include props such as the maze configuration). Therefore, each interlocutor represents a joint utterance percept for the dialogue (i.e. via the comprehension implementer, grey leftward-pointing arrows). If *A* and *B* understand the dialogue in the same way, then their joint utterance percepts will be the same. This is not always the case – *B* might not hear everything *A* says, *A* and *B* might have access to different props (as in Garrod & Anderson, 1987), or the interlocutors may not have the same access to the dialogue plan. We leave discussion of such issues until we have considered alignment (i.e. Chapters 6 and 7).

As we have noted, speakers can monitor what they say internally and externally (cf. Levelt, 1989) but listeners can monitor what other people say externally but not internally. Interlocutors need to concentrate on the combination of what they and their partners say, and therefore primarily monitor externally. As Figure 5.4 is concerned only with monitoring of the combined dialogue percept, it represents external monitoring but not internal monitoring.[10]

---

[10] Interlocutors can of course internally monitor their own utterance and use the feedback to update their production command and the efference copy of this command. For example, they can use internal monitoring to prevent speech errors, just as in isolated language production. But

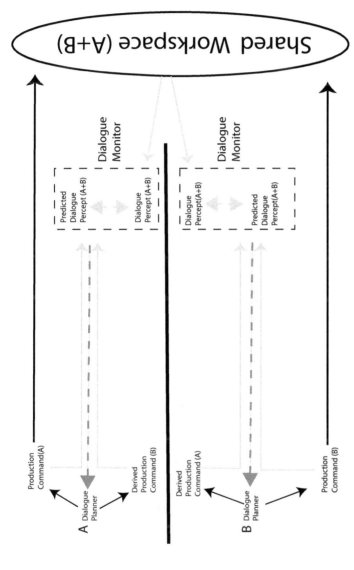

Figure 5.5 A model of the dialogue control system. A is above the central line, and B is below it. A's and B's production commands lead to utterance components (solid black lines) that feed into the dialogue recorded in the shared workspace. A's and B's comprehension of the dialogue (light grey left-facing arrows) feeds into the dialogue monitors. The efference copies of their production commands (i.e. self-predictions) and the efference copies of the derived production commands (i.e. other-predictions) are both represented with light grey right-facing arrows. They combine to provide the predictions that also feed into the dialogue monitors. The comparisons between dialogue percepts and predicted dialogue percepts feed back (via the dark grey dotted arrows) to A's and B's dialogue planners (potentially leading to changes in the utterance components and to changes in self-predictions as well as changes in other-predictions).

The dialogue percept can be compared with a predicted dialogue percept (via the joint external monitor). So far, we have assumed that each individual predicts utterances independently (e.g. *you're one along* and *uh-huh*, with *B*'s contribution underlined). But we now integrate these components into a joint prediction of the dialogue (*you're one along uh-huh*). To construct this joint prediction, *A* combines the efference copy of her production command (strictly, the associated forward model) with the efference copy of the derived production command to predict the dialogue percept. At the same time, *A* uses her production command to speak (*you're one along*) and update the shared workspace. *B* also predicts the dialogue percept (*you're one along uh-huh*; i.e. the same percept as *A*) and uses his production command to speak (*uh-huh*) and update the shared workspace. This process of prediction, comparison and subsequent contribution to the interaction results from what we call *dialogue monitoring*.

Now consider the acts of comparison using such dialogue monitors. In our example, if *A* predicts that *B* will utter an affirmation (which *A* presumably regards as the most likely or default response to a try-marker), then there is no discrepancy and hence no error-based feedback at the level of semantics. (*A* might expect *yes* rather than *uh-huh*, and if so there would be a phonological discrepancy.) But in other cases, the speaker might predict a response that the addressee does not make. In Example 1.1 (4–5), *A* uttered *two along from the bottom one up:* and *B* responded *Two along from the bottom, which side?* Assuming that *A* expected an affirmation, the discrepancy between the expected response and *B*'s actual response caused (semantic) feedback to *A*'s dialogue planner. This led to a new production command, and hence to updating both of *A*'s utterance (black arrow) and associated forward model (grey rightward-pointing arrow). In fact, *A* produced a clarification (*The left : going from left to right in the second box*, 6). In addition, *A*'s dialogue planner led to a new derived production command for *B* and hence a new forward model of *B*'s utterance – that is, *A*'s prediction of what *A* would likely hear *B* say next. We assume that *B* also predicted the progress of the dialogue in a similar fashion.

We have shown how interlocutors can manage dialogue, just as two actors can manage other forms of cooperative joint action. This system enables distributed control, with *A* using the dialogue to drive her own contribution, and *B* doing the same thing. So they are both exercising some control over the cooperative joint action – they each control their own contribution, but their contribution is continuously affected by the relationship between their own

---

this internal monitoring has no effect on the derived production command, and we propose that it plays a smaller role in dialogue than monologue. (It would be interesting to compare self-repair in dialogue vs monologue.)

contribution and their partner's contribution. Note that the system involves dialogue monitoring as a consequence of both interlocutors committing to the dialogue as a cooperative joint activity, and in particular where success of the dialogue (as an act of communication) is a result of a joint intention (in which *A* and *B* succeed if the dialogue is successful).

5.5   Conclusion

We have now presented an analysis of dialogue that follows from a more general analysis of cooperative joint activity. The framework depends on two central diagrams that we have developed over Chapters 4 and 5. Figure 5.1 captures the private representations of the interlocutors and the public shared workspace. In contrast, Figure 5.5 captures the control structure of dialogue.

Figure 5.1 provides the basis for the theory of alignment that we develop in Chapters 6 and 7. The interlocutors do not interact directly but rather post contributions to the shared workspace and interpret each other's contributions. As a result of such activity, their representations become aligned. Figure 5.5 captures the way in which information flows from one interlocutor to the other and back again, in a way that allows each to draw on their predictions of utterances and information about actual utterances. As we shall see, it provides the basis for the theory of division of labour and timing that we develop in Chapters 8 and 9. In sum, we have now completed the groundwork for a theory of dialogue processing – a theory that is cognitive but not monadic, and which treats language as a part of social interaction.

Part II

Alignment during Dialogue

6 Interactive Alignment and Linguistic Representations

People constantly become aligned with each other. When they engage in a joint activity, such as going to a safari park together, they set out for the same venue, they sit next to each other on the tour bus, and they of course observe the same animals. Their intentions become aligned as a result of deciding to go to the park together, and their understanding of animal behaviour becomes aligned on the basis of having the same experiences. They therefore align in part as a result of the language that they use (*look at the lions playing*) and in part because they see the same things (the behaviour of the lions).

Alignment need not be the result of interaction. Strangers in different rows on the bus become aligned because they see and hear the same animals and the same commentary from the tour guide, even if they do not see or hear each other. But our interest is in *interactive alignment* – when the alignment is due (at least in part) to the participants themselves. Such alignment results from the way in which the interlocutors behave towards each other. It occurs in many forms of joint action, but is particularly apparent when the participants communicate with each other, using language. In other words, interactive alignment occurs between interlocutors in dialogue.

Participants in any cooperative joint activity are aligned with each other to the extent they activate the same task-relevant representations, and so participants in dialogue are aligned to the extent that they activate the same dialogue-relevant representations. In our example, these representations relate to the trip to the safari park (both the plan for the activity and the specific experiences of seeing the animals). This means that the study of alignment is incompatible with monadic cognitive science, because it is defined with respect to the relationship between two individuals' representations. Instead, it is compatible with the system-based approach that analyses both the system (as a whole) and the individual-within-the-system. More specifically, we can interpret alignment with respect to the shared workspace framework.

As we have noted, alignment relates to representations rather than behaviours. We have argued that cooperative joint activity depends on representations concerned with joint action planning and joint action implementation,

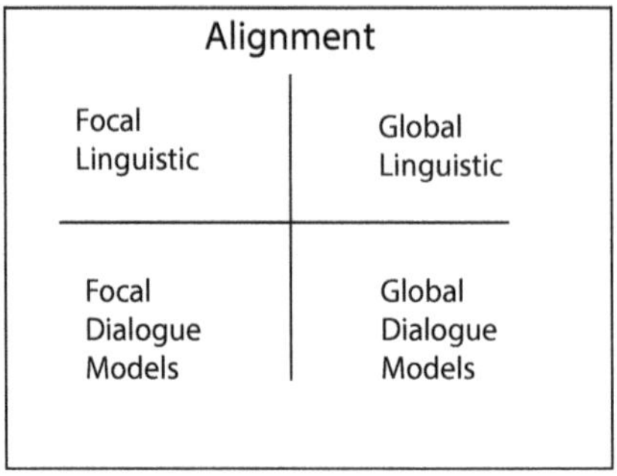

Alignment	
Focal Linguistic	Global Linguistic
Focal Dialogue Models	Global Dialogue Models

Figure 6.1 Two dimensions of alignment.

and alignment occurs when these representations are similar across the actors. Similarly, dialogue depends on representations concerned with dialogue planning and dialogue implementation, and alignment occurs when these representations are similar across the interlocutors. We refer to the representations underlying dialogue planning as *dialogue models* (which we divide into two components in Section 6.1.1) and the representations associated with dialogue implementation as *linguistic representations*. We use the term *model* (in accord with its use in *mental model* and *situation model*) to indicate that the planning representations model reality (Craik, 1943/1967; Johnson-Laird, 1983).[1] We treat *linguistic* in a broad sense to include co-speech gestures as well as language.

In this chapter and the next, we distinguish two dimensions of alignment (Figure 6.1). The first relates to the distinction between the implementer and the planner, with linguistic alignment taking place at the level of the implementer and dialogue model alignment taking place at the level of the planner. The second relates to the timescale over which alignment occurs, and we distinguish between focal alignment (which relates to individual steps in the process of alignment) and global alignment (which takes place over the course of the dialogue as a whole). This chapter describes the nature of the representations that can become aligned in dialogue, and then considers focal and global linguistic alignment. Such alignment is concerned with representations of meaning, grammar and sound, as well as with co-speech gesture (which we do not discuss in detail). It is central to our account (following Pickering & Garrod, 2004) that alignment of such linguistic representations leads to alignment of dialogue models. We leave the discussion of model alignment (and conversational success) to Chapter 7.

---

[1] Note that this sense of model is different from its use in *forward model* and *inverse model*.

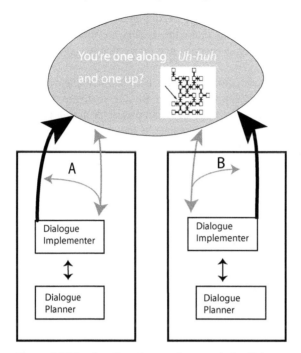

Figure 6.2 The shared workspace framework for dialogue.
Reproduced from Figure 4.2.

6.1   Individual Cognitive Representations in Dialogue

Figure 6.2 illustrates two interlocutors engaged in dialogue. In this chapter, we
are concerned with the relationships between the structures within the interlocutors (i.e. the dialogue planners and the dialogue implementers). In other
words, we do not discuss the shared workspace or the ways in which individual and joint behaviours contribute to shared workspace (via the arrows).

Both interlocutors access information associated with planning (represented
by the lower rectangles) and information associated with implementing the
dialogue (represented by the upper rectangles). So if interlocutor *A* wishes to
communicate that John has gone away, she may represent the fact of John's
leaving and the decision to communicate this information in her dialogue
models (i.e. the representation associated with dialogue planning), and formulate the utterance *John left* by accessing linguistic representations using the
dialogue implementer. (The utterance then enters the shared workspace.) By
comprehending this utterance, interlocutor *B* is likely to access the same
linguistic representations as *A* using his dialogue implementer, and to construct

the same dialogue models as *A* using his dialogue planner. This means that *B*'s linguistic representations and dialogue models are similar to *A*'s linguistic representations and dialogue models, and hence that *A* and *B* are aligned (see Section 6.3).

Note that each interlocutor in Figure 6.2 has a single rectangle for the dialogue planner and a single rectangle for the dialogue implementer. Of course interlocutors are engaged in different processes during production from comprehension, but they use the same set of representations, both at the level of implementation and planning.[2] We therefore assume *representational parity* (following Liberman & Whalen, 2000), an assumption that is equivalent to common coding within integrated theories of action and perception (Prinz, 1997).[3] Traditional psycholinguistic theories are concerned with either production or comprehension (see Traxler, 2011) and rarely commit to parity. However, some recent accounts that integrate production and comprehension show more commitment to parity (e.g. Dell & Chang, 2014; MacDonald, 2013; Pickering & Garrod, 2013; see Gambi & Pickering, 2017) and they do so even when their primary concern is with monologue.

In the context of dialogue, it is obviously beneficial for interlocutors to have at least extensive overlap between the representations involved in production and comprehension (Garrod & Pickering, 2004) – informally, it makes it easier to reuse representations developed during comprehension when producing and vice versa. We now explicate these mental representations within the individuals and then turn to the relationship between representations across speakers.

6.1.1   Representations Used by the Dialogue Planner

The *dialogue planner* draws on two dialogue models. The *situation model* corresponds to the 'informational' content of the model itself and represents what the interlocutors are discussing. The *game model* represents the current dialogue game – the interactive device (e.g. question plus answer) used to achieve the current goal of the dialogue (e.g. seeking information from your partner). We illustrate this in Figure 6.3.

The situation model. The situation model for dialogue is similar to the traditional individualistic notion of a situation model or mental model – a bounded (i.e. limited) representation that captures key elements of a situation. As noted in Section 2.3, the notion of a mental model originates in Craik

---

[2] During comprehension, people are concerned with interpreting a plan rather than executing it. However, we use the term planning to refer to both execution and interpretation.

[3] In our framework, the rectangle corresponding to the dialogue implementer serves as output from the arrow coming from the dialogue planner and as input to the arrow going to the shared workspace, but it also serves as output from the arrow coming from the shared workspace and as input to the arrow going to the dialogue planner.

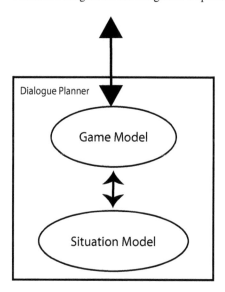

Figure 6.3 The dialogue planner, containing the situation model and the game model. Collectively, the situation model and the game model constitute the dialogue models.

(1943/1967) and was developed by Johnson-Laird (1983). They proposed that people apprehend and reason about their world using representations which model reality by sharing relational structure with the state of affairs being modelled. Hence such models can be used as internal surrogates for the real world, and the modeller can use them to fill out the details and determine how the world would change under different circumstances. Importantly, these models are impoverished and contain only some information about reality. For example, a model of a person might include gender and some distinctive characteristics, or it might just include location (e.g. a dot that moves around a street map on a mobile phone). The modeller might not know anything else about the person being modelled, or might model only those aspects of the person that are relevant for current purposes (e.g. gender or location). Such models have been used, among other things, to explain how people understand mechanical systems or use analogical mappings between domains (see Gentner & Stevens, 1983).[4]

---

[4] For example, Gentner and Stevens (1983) includes chapters on how mental models can explain qualitative reasoning (Forbus, 1983), problems in physics (Larkin, 1983), naïve theories of motion (McCloskey, 1983) and Micronesian navigation (Hutchins, 1983).

We adopt the term *situation model*, as standard in the psychology of language. It has primarily been used to refer to the representations that readers construct during text comprehension (e.g. Sanford & Garrod, 1981; Van Dijk et al., 1983; and also Johnson-Laird, 1983). For example, in understanding a novel, the reader maintains representations of main characters and their attributes, as well as information about the causes, consequences and settings of important events. Based on an extensive literature review, Zwaan and Radvansky (1998) proposed that comprehenders represent time, space, causality, intentionality and the main characters. Thus, when a new character is introduced, the reader adds a token to the model; when this character meets another character, the reader adds a new token and a link between them that reflects the interaction (including when and where it happened). Importantly, the situation model is distinct from linguistic semantics (which forms part of the dialogue implementation); it can be derived from a non-linguistic basis (e.g. a silent film) and incorporates encyclopaedic knowledge as well as semantics.

Dialogue of course differs from most texts in that it is simultaneously constructed and interpreted by two (or more) interlocutors. Partly for this reason, it tends to be quite different in form from at least formal texts.[5] Moreover, each interlocutor develops an understanding of something that they have contributed to. But the informational components of a situation model for dialogue are fundamentally similar to those for texts – interlocutors make reference to time, causality, and 'characters' (i.e. particular individuals) just as writers do, and so interlocutors need to represent them just as readers do.

The situation model resides in long-term working memory, which means that its contents can be accessed rapidly but also that it is limited in capacity (Ericsson & Kintsch, 1995; see Section 7.1.3). It is therefore distinct from long-term knowledge 'as a whole' (which is of course primarily outside the dialogue planner). The situation model often 'uses up' most available working memory. For example, people reading a complex novel with many characters and events may be unable to remember enough to understand the plot sufficiently (and may therefore re-read). And in dialogue, interlocutors may fail to understand their partner's contributions (though in practice they may query each other and obtain clarifications). But the most important effect of working memory limitations on dialogue is to prevent interlocutors holding two

---

[5] This means that dialogues are polyphonic (i.e. multi-voiced) in a concrete sense – they involve the voices of more than one individual. The term polyphonic is often used in a different way, namely that speakers and writers appropriate expressions and their interpretations that have been previously established by someone else (Bakhtin, 1981; Linell, 1998; cf. Goffman, 1981). Note also that many texts are constructed by multiple authors (e.g. instruction manuals, the US Constitution, this book), but readers can interpret them monophonically (though they might of course identify the hand of Jefferson or Garrod).

situation models corresponding to their own and their partner's beliefs about a situation – something that would be particularly difficult if those views were very different or contradictory. Of course, people know that they disagree about a particular issue or fact, and teachers realize that much of their knowledge may not be shared with their students, but in such circumstances they can represent a single situation model and tag part of it as shared (see Section 7.3). In contrast, interlocutors do not (typically) construct and use more than one situation model – and a major reason for this is that holding multiple incompatible models would often exceed working memory limitations.

Of course the dialogue (like a text) need not be about events in people's lives. For example, the components of the situation model in the maze game dialogue from Example 1.1 (as in Figure 6.2) are elements of the maze itself and the (purported) locations of the players (Garrod & Anderson, 1987). The model breaks down the situation (i.e. the maze configuration) into significant spatial entities – points, lines, or areas or volumes of space – associated with the various objects in the scene, and then represents significant spatial relations between them. Importantly, the model represents spatial relations that reflect how the objects in the scene can interact and how the players can interact with the objects in the scene. In other words, the model represents what the players can do (e.g. how they can move about the maze) as well as the maze's geometry.

In fact, Garrod and Anderson (1987) noted that maze game players adopted quite different schemes (i.e. frameworks) for describing their current positions in the maze. For example, they might describe their position thus:

1.   See the bottom left, go along one and up one, that's where I am.

Or alternatively thus:

2.   I'm on the second level, second from the left.

In (1), the speaker appears to represent the maze as a network of paths connecting the positions along which one can travel. In (2), the speaker appears to represent the maze as set of levels (or lines) ordered from the bottom to the top and made up of positions ordered from the left or right. Garrod and Anderson assumed that the two speakers adopted different types of situation models, with the speaker in (1) adopting a 'path' model and the speaker in (2) adopting a 'line' model. A speaker uses a model scheme to provide an interpretation of her position in the maze, and the addressee interprets the speaker's position with respect to this model scheme. In this way, choice of situation model type reflects the speaker's perspective with respect to the mapping between the spatial entities and tokens in the model and with respect to the relations between those tokens. For example, a related study in monologue found that people adopted different perspectives to describe the

Table 6.1 *Examples of dialogue games from Levin and Moore*

---

1. *Helping:* Person 1 wants to solve a problem, and interacts with Person 2 in an attempt to arrive at a solution.

2. *Action-seeking:* Person 1 wants some action performed and interacts with Person 2 to get him to perform it.

3. *Information-seeking:* Person 1 wants to know some specific information, and interacts with Person 2 in order to learn it.

4. *Information-probing:* Person 1 wants to know whether Person 2 knows some particular information, and interacts with him to find out.

5. *Instructing:* Person 1 wants Person 2 to know some information, and interacts with him to impart the information.

6. *Griping:* Person 1 is unhappy about some state of affairs, and interacts with Person 2 to convey that unhappiness.

Source: Levin and Moore (1977, pp. 399–400).

layout of an amusement park or convention centre (e.g. as a route through it, a survey from on top, or a mixture of both) (Taylor & Tversky, 1996).

The game model. In contrast to the situation model, the game model has no clear parallel in theories of text comprehension. It is used to manage the progress of the dialogue (and therefore we treat it as interfacing with the dialogue implementer in Figure 6.3). For this purpose, each interlocutor has a representation relating to what the interlocutors are trying to achieve at that point in the dialogue. For example, *A* might be seeking information from *B*, and *B* might be providing that information. Both interlocutors represent this *dialogue game* – a term which we take from Levin and Moore (1977),[6] but which is derived from Wittgenstein's (1953/1958) notion of a language game. Importantly, the game incorporates both interlocutors' contributions (here, seeking and providing information). The game is of course represented in each interlocutor's mind. But the representation is dialogical – it relates to both interlocutors. Dialogue games are therefore distinct from speech acts, which are not dialogical but are defined with respect to a speaker (in this case, interlocutor *A*). For example, the information-seeking game in Table 6.1 is the (rough) dialogical equivalent of the monological interrogative speech act (together with its monological response).[7]

Levin and Moore (1977) mentioned six examples of dialogue games, but these are illustrative rather than exhaustive. Dialogue games are (presumably) found in all cultures and occur early in communicative development (e.g. Shatz, 1978). We therefore we assume that all interlocutors use such games.

---

[6] The same concept is called a 'conversational game' by Kowtko et al. (1993).

[7] This monological (unilateral) interpretation of speech acts is consistent with Grice (1975) and Searle (1979). It is less clear whether Austin (1962) assumed this monological interpretation or whether he defined speech acts with respect to two interlocutors (see Clark, 1996, pp. 137–138).

Of course, interlocutors may use more specific versions of such games – for example, different ways in which one interlocutor can help another or two interlocutors can gripe. Such games are types of joint projects (Clark, 1996) and are related to Linell's (1998, Chapter 12) concept of a communicative activity type (which is based on Levinson, 1979).[8] We discuss dialogue games in a more fine-grained manner in Chapter 11.

When using the information-seeking game (3), both interlocutors represent that A (i.e. Person 1) is seeking information from B (i.e. Person 2) and that B is expected to supply relevant information in response. In fact, a dialogue game sets up conditions that need to be fulfilled for the game to be complete. The interlocutors need to draw on representations that allow them to determine their move in the current game. In this case, A has to plan how to seek the specific information from B, and therefore has to draw on information-seeking representations. Subsequently, B has to draw on representations concerned with responding to an information-seeking request. These representations are concerned with planning but serve as the input to the dialogue implementer, which is used to construct utterances such as questions and answers.

Another game can then be concatenated to the first game. For example, the information-seeking game might be followed by another information-seeking game in which the interlocutors switch roles, or it might be followed by an action-seeking game (e.g. if A asked B how long the soup had been cooking, B responded, and A persuaded B to take it off the stove). Alternatively, another game can be embedded into the first game, with B seeking more detailed information (or clarification).[9] The interlocutors need to be able to keep track of complex game structures, and they appear to be fairly good at doing so (see Levinson, 2013).

Using the dialogue models. When preparing an utterance, the dialogue planner draws on both dialogue models to generate what Pickering and Garrod (2013) call the *production command* – the instruction to use the dialogue implementer to produce the utterance. In other words, the production

---

[8] In a different framework, Tomasello (2008, p. 87) identifies three basic (evolved) communicative motives (his italics):

   i. Requesting: I want you do something *to help me* (requesting help or information);
  ii. Informing: I want you to know something because *I think it will help or interest you* (offering help including information);
  iii. Sharing: I want you to feel something so that *we can share attitudes/feelings together* (sharing emotions or attitudes).

[9] In practice, many dialogue games can be manifested as adjacency pairs (Schegloff & Sacks, 1973; see Clark & Schaefer, 1989; Levinson, 2013). The dialogue game constitutes part of the representation within the lower rectangle of both interlocutors and the associated adjacency pair is constructed by their dialogue implementers and posted to the shared workspace (see Figure 6.2).

command is the upward arrowhead leading from the dialogue planner to the dialogue implementer. This command corresponds roughly to what Levelt (1989) calls the *message* (informally, the content and function of the proposed utterance) and is therefore the output of the *conceptualizer* (which corresponds to our planner). However, our account contrasts with many (but not all) applications of Levelt's account (e.g. most literature discussed in Bock & Levelt, 1994; Levelt 1999), because they are concerned with preparing a command for a monological act and we are concerned with the preparation of a command for a dialogical act (and therefore the command involves a collective intention; see Section 2.1). Similarly, when comprehending an utterance, the dialogue models are the result of the application of the dialogue implementer (in this case performing comprehension) as represented by the downward arrowhead in Figure 6.2 leading to the dialogue planner.

The dialogue models also serve as the interface between the dialogue implementer (which manipulates linguistic representations) and background (general) knowledge (which we do not represent in our figures). Such background knowledge includes both factual (episodic and semantic) information that primarily feeds into the situation model (e.g. about a known person who is being introduced into a conversation) and procedures and conventions that underlie dialogue games (e.g. relating to politeness). For example, when *A* instructs *B* about a particular procedure (e.g. that a screw is needed to join two furniture components), she uses her background knowledge and intention to describe the event to construct the dialogue models. These then form the basis of a production command that is used to construct linguistic representations involved in uttering the instruction *you now need to screw the components together*. In turn, *B* listens to this utterance, and constructs a situation model by combining the linguistic representations associated with the sentence and his background knowledge (or assumptions) about furniture construction, and a game model that determines that *A* is producing an instruction and that he should respond to that instruction, either linguistically (e.g. *which screw?*) or non-linguistically (e.g. holding up two different screws with a quizzical expression). Note that the combination of language and non-linguistic demonstrations is compatible with the non-linguistic nature of situation models (see Section 11.1).

The situation model corresponds to the interlocutor's understanding of the situation under discussion. This understanding occurs because the interlocutor can access the appropriate content of long-term memory (or information directly from the context). Metaphorically, long-term memory is an enormous store that requires the organizational support of the situation model to 'point' the retriever to the relevant component of this store. It is like a library that is too extensive and not sufficiently organized for a reader to navigate without 'pointers' to particular aisles. For example, if the situation model contains a token corresponding to a known person (e.g. John), then the 'pointer' directs the retriever towards information associated with John (as for example when a novel refers to a character who has been previously discussed).[10]

6.1.2   Representations Used by the Dialogue Implementer

Linguistic representations. The dialogue implementers (in Figure 6.2) are responsible for linguistic processing, and are therefore the dialogical equivalent of the formulator in theories of language production (e.g. Bock & Levelt, 1994) and of the processing mechanisms involved in language comprehension (e.g. word recognition, parsing). In other words, they transform the representations in the dialogue models into behaviours (such as sounds) or vice versa. These representations are concerned with language, and primarily correspond to the levels assumed by theoretical linguistics. Specifically, they involve both comprehension and production mechanisms together, for example allowing the construction of utterances across interlocutors (as when *B* completes *A*'s utterance, or *B* establishes co-reference with an entity introduced by *A*).[11] The implementers also manage the process of turn-taking – a process that has no equivalent in monologue (see Chapter 8).

We assume three linguistic levels, concerned with meaning, grammar and sound. We refer to them as semantics, syntax and phonology. We also assume representations underlying arguably non-linguistic aspects of communication, including gesture (McNeill, 1992), depictions (Clark, 2016), and perhaps paralinguistic aspects of language such as tone of voice. We (somewhat loosely) refer to all of these as *linguistic representations*, in contrast to representations associated with the dialogue model (which are pre- or post-linguistic).

These representational assumptions are consistent with psycholinguistic theory about language production and comprehension. Most theories assume representations corresponding to semantics, syntax, phonology (or orthography), and the lexicon. For example, theories of comprehension assume separate representations of syntax and semantics, even though they disagree about the extent to which syntactic processing is completed before semantic processing (e.g. Frazier, 1987; MacDonald et al., 1994). Theories of production are similar: there is controversy about the degree of feedback from phonology to semantics (e.g. Dell, 1986; Levelt, 1989), but much less about

---

[10] There is perhaps a sense in which direct access is necessary for (full) understanding. Such understanding occurs when a person 'grasps' a complex idea (such as a mathematical principle) without having to work through steps 'on-line'.

[11] In examples such as *A: Who does John love most? B: Himself*, the exchange is 'grammatical' across interlocutors, and is treated as such by their dialogue implementers (see Morgan, 1973; Pickering & Garrod, 2004, pp. 185–186).

the levels of linguistic representation. In fact, our proposals have much in common with Levelt et al. (1999), who assume that lexical entries involve conceptual, lemma and word-form strata, which correspond fairly closely to semantics, syntax and phonology.

The parallel architecture. We assume the parallel linguistic architecture proposed by Jackendoff (2002; see also Jackendoff, 2007; Culicover & Jackendoff, 2005), in which semantics, syntax and phonology each constitute a single, linked level (or tier). The semantic representation includes the meanings of both individual words and more complex expressions. It incorporates aspects of formal semantics such as quantifier scope, as well as lexical semantics (the components of the meanings of words). The syntactic representation is relatively 'flat': it involves constituent-structure trees that avoid highly complex hierarchical structure or many empty categories (such as in Chomsky, 1981). The phonological representation captures aspects of sound structure such as individual phonemes and the intonation of utterances. We ignore the representation of phonetic information and do not assume underlying (deep) levels of syntax (as in traditional transformational grammar; Chomsky, 1965) or of grammatical functions such as subjects and objects (as Culicover & Jackendoff, 2005, tentatively assume). Our linguistic assumptions are supported by evidence from experimental studies of the tendency to prime linguistic structure (some between interlocutors), as discussed in Branigan and Pickering (2017).

These linguistic representations are used by the dialogue implementer to construct an utterance (i.e. to place it in the shared workspace) and to interpret utterances (i.e. with respect to the shared workspace) during comprehension. Figure 6.4 captures the way in which semantics, syntax and phonology are linked in the representation both of individual words (or morphemes) and longer expressions (such as phrases). For example, the word *John* has the semantics $JOHN_1$, the syntax NP_1, and the phonology $/\text{dʒɒn}/_1$, and the word *walks* has the semantics $WALKS_2$, the syntax VP_2, and the phonology $/\text{wɔːlkz}/_2$ (using the notation of Jackendoff, 2002). The subscripts indicate that the co-indexed representations correspond to the same word (e.g. $/\text{wɔːlkz}/$ means WALKS). We write linguistic representations as [semantics, syntax, phonology], hence *John* is $[JOHN_1, NP_1, /\text{dʒɒn}/_1]$. In Figure 6.4, the co-indexation is indicated by the central node, and captures the fact that all three levels are co-indexed (in this respect, our diagram differs from Jackendoff, 2002, who relates each pair of levels to each other via 'interface' components).[12]

---

[12] Jackendoff (2002) argued that some expressions have only two (linked) tiers. For example, *ouch!* has semantics and phonology but no syntax; *it* (in *it's fine*) has syntax and phonology but no semantics.

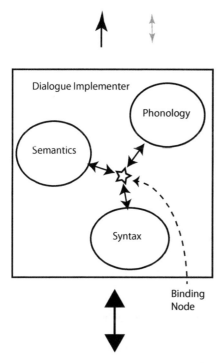

Figure 6.4 Linguistic representations used by the implementer.

The representations for *John* and *walks* are lexical entries. Lexical entries are stored and are therefore forms of long-term knowledge – knowledge that is different from but complementary to the long-term general knowledge that feeds into the dialogue model. The central node binds the semantic, syntactic and phonological representations together and we therefore refer to it as a binding node. For individual words, these representations are stored (i.e. as part of the lexicon).

However, Figure 6.4 also captures representations that are not stored (lexicalized) but are built up during production or comprehension. The utterance *John walks* has the semantics $(WALKS_2(JOHN_1))_3$, the syntax $[[NP_1][VP_2]]_3$, and the phonology $//\textbf{dʒɒn}/_1/\textbf{wɔːlkz}/_2/_3$, in which the subscript 3 relates the levels involved in the complex utterance. In such cases, the central node does not refer entirely to lexical information (i.e. subscripts 1 and 2 are lexical, but subscript 3 is not).

Importantly, Jackendoff (2002) proposed that people represent many multiword expressions in long-term memory, such as idioms (e.g. *kick the bucket*) and frequent but literal 'stock phrases' (e.g. *don't worry*). Such expressions tend to be more frequent than would be expected on the basis of the frequency of their components; Aijmer, 2014). Jackendoff assumes an 'extended lexicon' that may involve redundancy for literal expressions (because people also represent the individual words).[13] In the previous paragraph, we assumed that *John walks* was not stored in the lexicon, but in fact some people might store this complex expression. When a complex expression is stored, the central binding node in Figure 6.4 is a lexical node that refers to an item in the extended lexicon. Following Pickering and Garrod (2004, 2005), we treat such complex lexical entries as routines (see Section 7.1.4).

The flexible lexicon. The traditional view of the lexicon assumes it is fairly static – adults have a 'dictionary' in their minds that stores all the expressions that they know, and they only occasionally learn new expressions or forget old ones. Jackendoff's (2002) extended lexicon is somewhat more flexible, as people learn complex expressions (e.g. in marriage rituals) made up of familiar words but can later forget the complex expressions when they are not used any more. But our view of the dialogic lexicon is more flexible still. We note that interlocutors often introduce expressions with novel meanings for a specific purpose and so propose that the lexicon can rapidly expand (and contract) in a particular interaction. Thus, maze game players extended their lexicon to include *right indicator* to mean a maze configuration in Garrod and Anderson (1987), and they might then also establish related expressions such as *left indicator*. In terms of Figure 6.4, this expansion involves novel bindings between linguistic representations, and is captured by the binding node. The binding node can of course capture both novel simple expressions (e.g. nonce words) and complex expressions. We refer to the process of developing novel expressions as *routinization* (Pickering & Garrod, 2004).

Activating linguistic representations. Finally, a linguistic representation has a specific level of activation. The higher the level of activation, the easier it is to use – for example, it is more likely to be used during production or to lead to easier comprehension. A consequence of representational parity is that there is a single level of activation associated with both production and comprehension. In general, more frequent words, sounds or grammatical constructions have higher activation than less frequent ones – and such activation underlies frequency effects (e.g. Rosenweig & Postman, 1957). Importantly, the frequency effect occurs for complex expressions, and is not due to the frequency of the constituent words (Arnon & Snider, 2010).

In addition, activation is flexible and can vary extensively during dialogue (or in fact monologue). Importantly, the use of a representation (during either

---

[13] In fact, people may access the components as well as the phrase as a whole during processing. For example, experimental evidence suggests that people access the internal structure of idioms (Konopka & Bock, 2009). The important point is that there can be representational structure internal to lexical nodes.

production or comprehension) temporally raises its level of activation, and such activation can persist. Persistence of activation underlies many priming effects, such as repetition priming of words during comprehension (Neisser, 1954) or syntax during production (a form of structural priming; Bock, 1986). However, level of activation can be raised not only by repetition priming but also by semantic priming (Meyer & Schvaneveldt, 1971).

To clarify the way in which activation affects language use, consider the noun *cook*. This has the representation [PERSON-WHO-COOKS$_1$, N$_1$, /kuːk/$_1$]. Activation of the semantics PERSON-WHO-COOKS facilitates the production or comprehension of language with this meaning – perhaps the word *cook*, or its (near) synonym *chef*. Similarly, activation of the phonology /**kuːk**/ facilitates the production or comprehension of language with this sound – which could be the noun *cook* or the verb *cook*. To facilitate the production or comprehension of the noun *cook*, the whole lexical entry needs to be activated. Such activation specifically includes the co-indexed relationship among the three components (i.e. the subscript 1), as indicated by the binding node in Figure 6.4. The role of activation is of course the same for complex expressions as for individual words. Level of activation will prove central to the theory of alignment (see Section 6.3).

Reference and the planner-implementer link. Reference occurs when an expression is used to correspond to an entity. The entity can exist in the world, but it also can be represented in a person's mind. In our account, the expression is represented in terms of the linguistic components of the dialogue implementer, and its referent is represented in the situation model component of the dialogue planner. For example, if *A* uses *the sofa* to refer to a particular piece of furniture, then she represents [DEFINITE-SOFA$_1$, NP$_1$, /θəsəʊfə/$_1$] using her implementer and a token in her situation model corresponding to that piece of furniture (which may include details such as its colour or location). But importantly, she also represents the link between these two representations. We capture this by assuming the link occurs between the binding node (Figure 6.4) and this token. Thus when *A* subsequently uses the phrase *the sofa* as part of a particular exchange, it activates the semantics, syntax and phonology of *sofa* via the binding node, the token in the situation model, and the link between the node and this token. Note that there are also links between the implementer and the game model, for example if a particular utterance type (e.g. a *Wh*-question) is used to express a particular dialogue move (e.g. information-seeking) as part of the exchange.

6.2   Alignment of Cognitive Representations

The discussion in Section 6.1 is compatible with monadic cognitive science (or psycholinguistics), because it relates to individuals considered independently. Although we have referred to two individuals (*A* and *B*), we have not considered the relationship between them. Alignment occurs when two individuals activate the same cognitive representations as each other, at a similar time and to a similar extent, in their planners and implementers (and interactive alignment occurs when such alignment occurs as the result of dialogue). In other words, alignment (or, more strictly, degree of alignment) is defined with respect to the relationship between two (or more) individuals' representations. Therefore any account that incorporates alignment is incompatible with monadic cognitive science.

Alignment refers to cognitive representations, not behaviours. When interlocutors activate similar representations at any level (at a similar time and to a similar extent), they become aligned at that level. So interlocutors can be aligned with respect to their dialogue planners (i.e. the lower rectangles in Figure 6.2) or their dialogue implementers (i.e. the upper rectangles). In fact, they can be aligned with respect to the situation model or the game model, or with respect to semantic, syntactic, or phonological representations. They can also be aligned with respect to links between representations, either the binding node (within the implementer) or the planner-implementer link.

We restrict alignment to the representations involved in planning and implementation. Interlocutors can of course share more or less background knowledge, most of which is not directly relevant to a particular dialogue. But of course shared background knowledge tends to support alignment. For example, experts know terms with specialist meanings (e.g. *powder* for skiers) and so they share such background knowledge. When they are discussing something unrelated to their expertise, this shared knowledge does not influence alignment. But if they start to discuss a relevant aspect of their expertise (e.g. today's skiing conditions), they can readily align on these terms and their interpretation.

Figure 6.5 is an extension of Figure 6.2 to reflect (interactive) alignment. In this figure, the dotted arrows correspond to what Pickering and Garrod (2004) call *channels of alignment*. These channels reflect the fact that interlocutors align both with respect to their linguistic choices (e.g. using the same words) and with respect to how they understand and address the aspect of the world under discussion (using their dialogue models). The channels do not correspond to processes. They therefore do not capture production or comprehension (or indeed monitoring or prediction) and therefore contrast with the arrows within each individual and the arrows connecting each individual to the shared workspace.

To make this absolutely clear, we refer back to the robots discussed in Chapter 2 (Simmons et al., 2002), where the representations of planning and execution correspond to the linguistic representations (concerned with implementation) and the dialogue models (concerned with planning). Such robots can (at least in theory) communicate directly (e.g. via wireless devices) at the

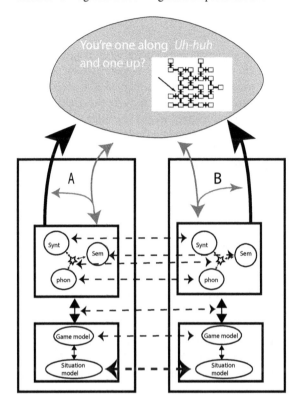

Figure 6.5 Channels of alignment (dotted lines) between interlocutors' representations.

planning or execution level. People of course cannot do this (assuming no telepathy) and so the channels do not correspond to processes of information transfer. Instead, they describe the alignment between (private) representations – an alignment that is a result of the workings of the dialogue system (described in Chapters 4 and 5). The way in which such alignment happens is the subject of the rest of this chapter and Chapter 7.

6.3   Alignment of Linguistic Representations

We now consider linguistic alignment, as captured by the dotted arrows between A and B's dialogue implementers; Chapter 7 considers alignment of A and B's dialogue models. We begin by distinguishing what we term *focal alignment* from *global alignment*.

6.3.1   Focal Alignment

Focal alignment refers to alignment at the point when *A* produces an utterance (and *B* attends to it). The interlocutors are aligned if they activate the same representations at this point. Thus they are aligned if *A* refers to a particular person as *the chef* and *B* understands what *A* says (i.e. he does not mishear or not know the meaning of *chef*) and realizes who *A* is calling *the chef*. At this point, both *A* and *B* activate the same representations (such as the lexical entry for *chef*). Obviously, there will be a slight 'lag' in focal alignment (perhaps hundreds of milliseconds), while the addressee processes the speaker's utterance (and this lag might be different for linguistic alignment from dialogue model alignment).[14]

But there are many ways in which *A* and *B* could be misaligned. One possibility is that *A* uses *chef* to refer to the person doing the cooking (CHEF1) but *B* interprets *A*'s utterance as referring to the head chef who is wandering around the restaurant (CHEF2). Such misalignment can lead to serious confusion. In this case, it is due to *A* and *B* having different links between their linguistic representations (specifically, their binding nodes for [DEF-PERSON-WHO-COOKS$_1$, N$_1$, /ʃef/$_1$]) and the tokens in their situation models. If, on the other hand, *B* simply misheard *A* (e.g. hearing *ref* rather than *chef*), then *A* and *B* would be misaligned with respect to both linguistic representations and situation models (rather than with respect to any link between the representations). Another possibility is that *B* has just started learning English and erroneously believes that *chef* means waiter. If so, *A* would activate [DEF-PERSON-WHO-COOKS$_1$, N$_1$, /ʃef/$_1$] and *B* would activate [DEF-PERSON-WHO-WAITS$_1$, N$_1$, /ʃef/$_1$], so they would be semantically misaligned. Interlocutors can therefore be focally well aligned with respect to some channels but focally misaligned with respect to others.

These examples also demonstrate how alignment (or misalignment) can percolate between representations. When *B* interprets *chef* as meaning referee or waiter, it is very likely that *B* will assume that it does not refer to the person that *A* intended to refer to. In these cases, the linguistic misalignment percolated down to misalignment of the situation model. It is in fact possible for misalignment to percolate in the other direction as well, for example if *B* could

---

[14] Neural evidence for alignment at different levels of abstraction between narrator and listener comes from Lerner et al. (2011). They compared changes in the narrator and listener's BOLD responses when listeners heard intact stories or stories that were scrambled at the level of words, sentences or paragraphs. They found that the changes were more strongly correlated when hearing intact than scrambled stories and that the cortical areas reflecting these correlations became more extensive as the stories became more intact. In other words, if the listener heard only the words, alignment with the narrator was less widespread than when hearing the sentences (i.e. allowing for syntactic alignment) and the whole paragraphs (allowing for alignment at higher levels of meaning).

not see a chef and therefore assumed that *A* must have uttered *ref* or meant waiter. (In practice, *B* might of course assume that *A* was mistaken about the identity of a person that she thought was a chef – in which case, percolation to linguistic representations would not occur.)

6.3.2   Global Alignment

Informally, *A* and *B* are globally aligned if they have similar patterns of activation of conversationally relevant linguistic representations and are therefore likely to make similar linguistic choices – that is, to produce similar utterances under similar conditions and to interpret such utterances in similar ways. (Global alignment depends on timing, but over the timescale of an interaction; whereas focal alignment depends on timing of an individual utterance.) As with focal alignment, global alignment can refer to individual levels of representation or to links between representations. At the lexical level, two interlocutors are aligned to the extent that the same conversationally relevant words (or other lexical entries; see Section 6.1.2) have high levels of resting activation. Each word in *A*'s lexicon has a resting level of activation (e.g. based on the frequency with which *A* has encountered that word), with that resting activation indicating how easy it is for *A* to access the word (in production or comprehension; cf. Forster, 1976). Thus, *A* has a distribution of levels of activation for these words. More specifically, *A* and *B* can have different levels of activation for words themselves (e.g. *funicular*) or for interpretations of the words (e.g. *powder* as snow vs talcum). Then *B* is lexically aligned with *A* if his distribution is similar to *A*'s (and indeed in principle this degree of global alignment could be quantified). The degree of global alignment between interlocutors of course varies over time and differs from the degree of alignment between other interlocutors.

Now consider links between levels. For example, two globally aligned diners would both be likely to refer to a person who cooks in a restaurant as a *chef* or both be likely to refer to such a person as a *cook*; whereas two misaligned diners would be more likely to use different words from each other. The tendency to align would occur because *A* and *B* have similar resting levels of activation for the associations between specific referring expressions and entities in particular types of situation – for example, using *chef* to refer to formally dressed people who cook in expensive restaurants. In other words, they would both have high activation for [PERSON-WHO-COOKS-IN-EXPENSIVE-RESTAURANT$_1$, N$_1$, /ʃef/$_1$] (and low resting activation for [PERSON-WHO-COOKS-IN-EXPENSIVE-RESTAURANT$_1$, N$_1$, /kuːk/$_1$]). Such alignment is global because it relates to persistent patterns of activation during the interaction, rather than the momentary activation that occurs across the speaker and the listener at a specific point of an utterance.

Global alignment also applies to syntax. Interlocutors have activation levels for particular constructions, for example actives and passives. So *A* and *B* are well aligned if their activation levels for both constructions are similar to each other, and badly aligned otherwise. Now consider links between levels, such as syntax and semantics. In general, people are more likely to use a passive when the patient is emphasized, but it might be that *A* has a stronger tendency to do so than *B*. If so, *A* and *B* would be less well aligned in this respect. The notion of global alignment also applies to other linguistic levels (and applies to gesture as well).

6.3.3   The Relationship between Focal and Global Linguistic Alignment

Global alignment changes through the dialogue, and of course interaction (in general) enhances global alignment. It is a consequence of focal alignment, which decays but does not (always) entirely disappear. When *A* utters *chef*, the momentary activation of *chef* for both *A* and *B* is raised well above its resting activation level and then it decays in both *A* and *B* to a similar extent.

The rate or extent of decay depends greatly on the specific representation or link between representations in question. For example, a single use of a frequent unambiguous word has little effect on its resting activation level. In contrast, *A*'s choice of *chef* to refer to a person cooking in an expensive restaurant, when *B* would previously have used *cook*, quite dramatically changes *B*'s subsequent use of *chef* (and indeed *cook*). In this case, the degree of global alignment of *A* and *B* increases substantially. For example, Brennan and Clark (1996) found that interlocutors often adopted a dispreferred term (e.g. *pennyloafer*) to refer to a familiar object (a shoe) after hearing their partner use that term. Similarly, *A*'s use of a passive to describe a transitive event leads to focal syntactic alignment between *A* and *B*. Activation decays slowly and hence both *A* and *B*'s resting activation for the passive is enhanced (see Pickering & Ferreira, 2008).

Thus, focal alignment can alter global alignment at one or more representational levels (as reflected in the channels of alignment in Figure 6.5). Note that global alignment also alters focal alignment. If *A* and *B* have more similar patterns of activation, then they are more likely to produce the same utterances or to interpret utterances in the same way.

One aspect of the global-focal relationship concerns routinization. If *A* introduces a complex expression with a novel interpretation (e.g. *right indicator*), and *B* understands what *A* says, then *A* and *B* are focally aligned (in this respect). If *A* and *B* both store this expression (i.e. by binding its semantics, syntax and phonology), then their global alignment increases. Because complex expressions can be lexicalized but need not be (Jackendoff, 2002), this process of routinization means that interlocutors' lexica are extremely flexible and may change during a conversation, and so lexical alignment may change as well. We discuss focal and global alignment (and misalignment) of dialogue models in Chapter 7.

6.4   Processes of Alignment

We now sketch some of the processes that can lead to interactive alignment of linguistic representations. Moreover, we focus on the automatic alignment of linguistic representations and situation models. As we have noted, one manifestation of alignment is linguistic repetition (i.e. behaviour matching). When *A* and *B* enter a restaurant, *A* might prefer to refer to the person cooking as a *cook* but *B* might prefer to refer to that person as a *chef*. Their resting activation levels for *cook* and *chef* are therefore very different and so they are not aligned. When *B* hears *A* say *cook*, *B* focally aligns with *A* on the referent, so long as *B* recognizes that *A* is referring to that person. This process raises the activation level of *cook* relative to *chef*, and so *A* and *B*'s global alignment increases.

Such alignment does not require any conscious or deliberate processing by either interlocutor – it is primarily the result of automatic activation of linguistic representations, and whether they are aware it is happening does not matter. And a consequence of such global alignment is that *B* is now more likely to utter *cook* than before. In fact, interlocutors show a strong tendency to repeat each other's choice of words (e.g. Brennan & Clark, 1996) and syntax (e.g. Branigan et al., 2000). This process is due to repetition priming between interlocutors, with such priming taking place at different linguistic levels, not merely the word (Pickering & Garrod, 2004). But importantly, there can be a strategic component to alignment – interlocutors can decide to align to a greater or lesser extent. In one study, they repeated unusual word choices more often if they believed they were made by a computer than by another person (Branigan et al., 2011). Our account does not require alignment to be entirely automatic.

Automatic alignment is not limited to repetition and can reflect associative priming rather than repetition priming. For example, the word *chef* is linked to (upmarket) restaurants and all of their characteristics, such as waiters, menus, and expensive dishes (e.g. caviar) or drinks (e.g. champagne) – characteristics that are represented in long-term memory and constitute part of the situation model associated with the chef. Importantly, these links are likely to hold for both interlocutors, at least when they are from similar cultural backgrounds. In other words, they are already fairly well aligned. We can regard them as having similar networks of links, so that the word *chef* (including its semantics and phonology) is strongly linked to the words *waiter, menu, ordering, caviar*, and *champagne*. These connections are highly structured, and correspond to something like a restaurant 'script' (Schank & Abelson, 1977).[15] These knowledge structures are represented in long-term memory (and they help provide it

---

[15] Hence we refer to these connections as links rather than associations, which are often regarded as unstructured (e.g. Meyer & Schvaneveldt, 1971).

with organization). So when interlocutor *A* utters *chef*, both *A* and *B* activate *chef* (i.e. alignment via repetition), but also they both activate the network of words, concepts, and relationships associated with upmarket restaurants (i.e. alignment via links). This parallel activation across the interlocutors constitutes alignment, and so the alignment percolates from *chef* to other aspects of the network.

Such alignment is therefore not limited to the representation of a word or utterance itself – informally, it is 'broad' rather than 'narrow'. It cuts across both levels of linguistic representation and background knowledge. So the use of *chef* leads to alignment of the semantics, syntax and phonology of *chef* and on background knowledge about chefs, which in turn can lead to alignment of other background knowledge relating to restaurants. Hence it can also lead to alignment of other words such as *waiter* or *menu*. Such alignment is of course captured in the channels of alignment in Figure 6.5.

We have noted that such 'broad' alignment requires the interlocutors to have similar linguistic and non-linguistic knowledge. The more similar the interlocutors already are, the more likely it is that they will achieve alignment with respect to the topic of discussion. For example, if *B* is from a more humble background than *A*, then *A*'s use of *chef* might trigger activation of *menu* and *ordering* but not of *caviar* or *champagne*. In some cases, the topic of discussion will be similarly understood by all interlocutors. But sometimes interlocutors from different countries, social backgrounds or professions will either align badly, or align well only after substantial effort. An important aspect of the linguistic knowledge underlying alignment is the existence of a communal lexicon (Clark, 1996, p. 107), which is a set of expressions and their interpretations that are used by members of a community. Of course, interlocutors who have more knowledge in common have more potential for focal and global alignment. For example, if *A* and *B* know the same words as each other, then they can align on their activation; if *A* knows many words that *B* does not, then alignment is not possible (unless *B* learns those words).

Percolation can also occur across linguistic levels of representation. In Branigan et al. (2000), a (naïve) participant and a confederate sat on opposite sides of a table with a divider between them. They took turns to describe cards to each other and to select the appropriate card from an array. For example, the confederate described a card as *The chef giving the jug to the swimmer* (a *prepositional-object* construction or *PO*). After the participant selected the matching card, she tended to describe her next card (which included the verb *hand*) as *The cowboy handing the banana to the burglar*. But if the confederate described his card as *The chef giving the swimmer the jug* (a *double-object construction* or *DO*), the participant tended to say *The cowboy handing the burglar the banana*. Such syntactic repetition often occurred when the confederate and the participant had to use different verbs. But when they had to use the same verb (e.g. *handing*), repetition was even more frequent (with the participant aligning with the confederate over 80 per cent of the time). In this case, there was percolation from (required) alignment on the verb to syntactic alignment. In the literature on syntactic priming, this phenomenon is called the lexical boost between interlocutors (Pickering & Ferreira, 2008).

In Cleland and Pickering (2003), a confederate described a coloured object using an adjective-noun structure (e.g. *the red sheep*) or an unusual noun-relative clause structure (*the sheep that's red*). Participants tended to repeat the structure just used by the confederate, thereby demonstrating syntactic alignment of noun phrases. In addition, participants were more likely to repeat the noun-relative clause structure when the confederate's utterance used a semantically related noun (e.g. *the goat that is red*) than an unrelated noun (*the knife that is red*). This study showed percolation from semantic alignment (in this case, farm animal) to syntax (and is called the semantic boost between interlocutors).

Alignment can be disrupted when interlocutors persist with misaligned expressions, for example when one negotiator refers to a person as a *terrorist* and the other refers to the same person as a *freedom fighter*, or when opposing lawyers use *foetus* and *unborn child* (see Danet, 1980). Such misalignment is typically strategic (and takes considerable effort to maintain). The alternative terms are linked to different networks of connections in both interlocutors – for example, *foetus* is linked to biological and mechanistic concepts (e.g. fertilized egg, placenta), whereas *unborn child* is linked to agentive and ethical concepts (e.g. feelings, human rights). In a debate, use of the opponent's choice of expression will activate the linked concepts (and may suggest some tacit acceptance of the opponent's stance).

Therefore, alignment is not always due to automatic processing. Interlocutors can explicitly agree to use a particular expression to refer to a particular entity (or event), in which case they show intentional focal alignment. But such discussion (or negotiation) is rare (e.g. Garrod & Anderson, 1987). In the following 'embedded repair' reported by Jefferson (1982, p. 63 see Example 6.1) the salesman invites the customer to align on a new expression (see Chapter 8 and also Chouinard & Clark, 2003, in which a parent repairs a child's utterance): importantly, the salesman did not start a discussion about whether *threads* was more appropriate than *wales*; instead, he simply

---

Example 6.1

CUSTOMER: *Mm, the wales are wider apart than that.*
SALESMAN: *Okay, let me see if I can find one with wider threads.* [Looks through stock] *How's this?*
CUSTOMER: *Nope, the threads are even wider than that.*

replaced *wales* with *threads*. Except in unusual (or highly complex) circumstances, speakers do not make suggestions about how to refer to something. In fact, they do not appear to engage in such intentional focal alignment even when it might resolve serious misalignment, and there is some evidence that it does not facilitate global alignment (Garrod & Doherty, 1994).

6.5   Consequences of Alignment

In accord with Pickering and Garrod (2004), we assume that linguistic alignment supports alignment of situation models. In other words, alignment percolates not only within linguistic levels but also from linguistic levels to levels associated more directly with communicative success. There is a complex (and not entirely clear) empirical literature on the relationship between the tendency for interlocutors to repeat each other's linguistic expressions and their communicative goals (see Garrod et al., 2018), which we briefly review.

Linguistic alignment affects the speed of situation model alignment. Ferreira et al. (2012) found that participants more rapidly matched a sentence produced by a confederate interlocutor (e.g. *the doctor is handing the apple to the ballerina*) to a picture when they had previously described a different picture using the same verb (*the cowboy handing the shoe to the pirate*) than using a different verb (*the cowboy giving the shoe to the pirate*), and using the same syntactic structure (a PO) than using a different syntactic structure (a DO). Fusaroli et al. (2012) had dyads discuss which of a set of stimuli was the oddball and compared their joint performance with their individual performances. Those dyads with relatively strong joint performance tended to align on confidence expressions (e.g. *quite sure*) better than those with relatively weak joint performance. In other words, focal linguistic alignment on task-relevant expressions led to communicative success. Ward and Litman (2007) found that lexical alignment with a computerized physics tutor was related to the students' learning outcomes. Lexically and syntactically aligned dyads who were instructing each other produced more accurate route descriptions on a map (Reitter & Moore, 2014; see also Carbary & Tanenhaus, 2011). Next, speakers' use of function words appears to be related to aspects of their personality, and Ireland et al. (2011) found that function word alignment is predictive of relationship success. Specifically, they showed that better aligned speed-daters were much more likely to indicate that they wished to meet again, and better aligned romantic partners were more likely to remain together. Finally, some studies suggest that linguistic alignment supports negotiation success (Sagi & Diermeier, 2017; Swaab et al., 2011). In sum, there is evidence of the relationship between alignment and communicative success, but much of the evidence is partial and correlational.

6.6   Conclusions

This chapter introduced different dimensions of alignment, one relating to its timescale (focal vs global), one relating to its content (linguistic vs dialogue model). It then sketched individual linguistic and non-linguistic representations relating to communication. It then considered the nature of linguistic alignment and how it comes about during dialogue, and discussed some of its non-linguistic effects. We now turn to the alignment of dialogue models and the meta-representation of alignment.

7   Alignment of Dialogue Models

Interlocutors construct representations concerned with both planning and implementation. In Chapter 6, we argued that they align both types of representation, but we concentrated on the linguistic representations associated with implementation. However, successful communication involves the alignment of situation models – in other words, when interlocutors interpret the world in similar ways to each other. In addition, interlocutors align on the games that underlie conversation – that is, with respect to their game models. Although Chapter 6 touched on the relationship between linguistic alignment and situation model alignment, we now consider alignment of dialogue models directly.

Figure 6.1 contrasted two dimensions of alignment – focal versus global alignment, and linguistic versus dialogue model alignment. When discussing linguistic alignment, we contrasted focal alignment (i.e. co-activation by both interlocutors as a result of one producing an utterance) with global alignment (i.e. converging on patterns of activation of linguistic representations). And alignment of dialogue models also occurs at two time-scales. For situation models, interlocutors represent a particular episode in the same way as each other, but they also 'build up' alignment over the course of an interaction. Interlocutors can therefore have situation models that are focally aligned, but they can also have situation models that are globally aligned. Informally, the former occurs momentarily, when two interlocutors have the same focus – they are both thinking about the same aspect of the world in the same way at the same time. The latter occurs when they have the same understanding of a situation as a whole. Successful communication relates to both aspects of situation model alignment.

With respect to game models, interlocutors align when they both represent and use the same game model, but misalign if they represent and use different models. Such misalignment occurs when *A* utters *Can you open the window?* as a move in an action-seeking game and *B* simply responds *Yes*, thereby offering a response that constitutes a move in an information-seeking game. But when *B* responds by opening the window, they align on an action-seeking game. Interlocutors of course typically play more than one game, and these

134

games can be organized sequentially or nested within each other. So the interlocutors can be focally aligned on the current game, but not globally aligned with respect to other games or their organization. Alignment of game models and alignment of situation models are of course closely related. Specifically, episodes in a situation model are defined by the content of dialogue games.

We consider the content of each interlocutor's representations (as do monadic theories), but this is not our ultimate concern. Instead, our concern is with the relationship between their representations. This relationship comes about as a result of the interlocutors putting information into the shared workspace and interpreting its contents. The first part of this chapter addresses the relationship between dialogue models themselves (that is, how they come to be aligned or not) and with the way in which individuals represent this alignment – in other words, the meta-representation of alignment. We then interpret alignment and its meta-representation in terms of the shared workspace and dialogue as a cooperative joint activity.

7.1 What Does It Mean to Align Dialogue Models?

We distinguish the elements of the situation model that are currently focused from those elements that are not focused, and so we begin by describing focal and global alignment. We then discuss what it means to align reference in the situation model and its relationship to background knowledge. Next, we characterize alignment in terms of the relationship between the individuals' short- and long-term working memories. We then link alignment of situation models and linguistic alignment via what we call dialogue routines. Finally, we consider what it means to align game models.

7.1.1   Focal and Global Alignment

We first consider the granularity of individual representations of situations, not in the context of alignment. To do this, we draw on Zwaan and Radvansky's (1998, pp. 165–167) distinction between current and integrated situation models in text comprehension, which is of course a form of monologue comprehension (see Chapter 10). Consider their example narrative (1):

(1)   *Peter took the elevator to the fifth floor. He went to talk to his professor. He was anxious to find out how the professor liked his draft. He walked up to the professor's office and knocked on the door. The professor looked up from his work.*

Using their terminology, the reader first constructs a current model for the first sentence, a model that includes a token representing a male individual named

Peter who rides an elevator. She then constructs a current model for the second sentence, one that involves the token for Peter (as she resolves the pronoun as referring to Peter), a new token for the professor, a goal of intentionality (as *went to* suggests intentionality), and so on. She then constructs what they call an integrated model that links the two models. The integrated model remains activated in long-term working memory, and the current model for each new sentence is constructed in short-term working memory. In this example, it may be that the interpretation of both sentences can be kept activated in short-term working memory (as it has sufficient capacity), and so they would both 'fit' into the current model. But an integrated model would be needed for the interpretation of the additional sentences.

Zwaan and Radvansky (1998) are concerned with individual representations in monologue comprehension.[1] In contrast, we are interested in dialogue rather than monologue (though we return to monologue in Chapter 10), with both interlocutors contributing to the development of the situation models. Moreover, we consider alignment between individuals' situation models and not merely the individual models by themselves. (We consider alignment of dialogue game models in Section 7.1.5.)

Our distinction between focal and global alignment of situation models relates to Zwaan and Radvansky's (1998) distinction between current and integrated models. We use the terms *focal situation model* (or *focal model*) rather than current model, and *global situation model* (or *global model*) rather than integrated model. In dialogue, the focal model is the result of a joint contribution (such as a statement and affirmation) or restricted set of contributions, and contains the principal elements referred to in the contributions (in the current context). The global model reflects the results of successive focal models and permits recall of aspects of those models. More fundamentally, we concentrate on alignment and not merely the content of model representations within individuals. Focal alignment occurs when interlocutors align on their focal models, and global alignment occurs when they align on their global models.

We illustrate focal and global alignment using a conversation in which one interlocutor narrates an event to the other. Crucially, the addressee affirms each contribution by the narrator (and so the conversation consists of a series of *instructing* dialogue games, see Section 6.2.1).[2] In our example, A narrates to B what their friends John and Mary did on their holidays. On the basis of his

---

[1] Note that Zwaan and Radvansky (1998) do not consider how such texts are written (i.e. with monologue production).

[2] In a different conversation, A and B might take turns to contribute (e.g. when they both know the story and are reminiscing). Our account does not require an asymmetric (narrator-addressee) conversation.

recollection, *A* first constructs a situation model in which John controls the car, Mary is transported towards London, and so on. *A* therefore utters (2) *John drove Mary to London*. At this point, *B* comprehends what *A* says, responds affirmatively (*OK*), and constructs an equivalent situation model to *A*. We can say that they are *focally aligned* – that is, with respect to this situation. (They of course linguistically align as well, but this is not our current concern.) Now *A* extends the situation model by adding the information that the car broke down outside York and then uttering (3) *They had just got to York when the car broke down*. *B* comprehends this utterance, produces an affirmation and extends his situation model as *A* has done, so that their situation models both contain John, Mary, a car, and an event (driving to London) with a sub-event (a breakdown near York).

At a later point, *A* describes another episode by turning to what they eventually did in London and says (4) *Mary took John to the theatre* and *B* affirms with *Yes*. *A* and *B* now focally align on this new event (Mary taking John to the theatre). The driving and breakdown episode is (presumably) no longer part of the focal situation model, though it is part of the global situation model (and *A* and *B* might not be globally aligned, for example if *B* had forgotten the breakdown event). However, Mary and John remain in the focal model.

We need to relate the focal and global situation models to background knowledge (i.e. knowledge that is not represented in the situation model). It may be part of *A*'s background knowledge that York has a famous cathedral, and this knowledge may be activated when *A* utters (2). But this knowledge does not figure in *A*'s focal situation model. Likewise, it may be part of *B*'s background knowledge that York has a railway museum, but again it does not figure in *B*'s focal situation model. Therefore, *A* and *B*'s focal situation model alignment is unaffected by whether they have the same background knowledge about York or not (indeed, whether they activate it or not). Having similar background knowledge enhances the potential for situation model alignment (e.g. with respect to other information about York), but alignment is not defined with respect to background knowledge.

7.1.2   Reference and Background Knowledge

So far, we have not considered what the entities (and events) refer to. Informally, *A* and *B* would not seem to be aligned in our example if they took *Mary* to refer to different women (or *John* to refer to different men). The word *Mary* is represented by a token in the model, and it is referentially individuated (i.e. it refers to a particular entity). For example, *A* might represent *Mary* by the MARY37-token. This token corresponds to the actual person MARY37 (Mary Smith, who lives at 10 Church Lane). In this case, *A* and *B* are aligned if *B* also represents *Mary* by the MARY37-token but are not aligned if *B* represents *Mary* by the MARY64-token).

A and *B* may have similar knowledge about the characters and relevant background events. For example, they may both know similar things about Mary (because they both know her from childhood). Alternatively, *A* might know Mary from childhood but *B* might know her as a work colleague. In both cases, they both set up the MARY37-token in their models. If they knew her from childhood, they can link the MARY37-token to a similar set of entities and events (school friends, birthday parties etc.) in their background knowledge (though they may also process the utterances without linking *Mary* to this knowledge). But if they knew her from different parts of their lives, they link the MARY37-token to a fairly different set of entities and events (though there presumably must be some overlap for them to talk about the same Mary).[3] Situation model alignment is unaffected by whether the interlocutors have similar background knowledge about Mary or not (though similar knowledge enhances the potential for subsequent alignment), but it is impaired if *A* and *B* refer to different Marys. Alignment is defined with respect to reference, but not with respect to background knowledge.

It is also possible to align (or misalign) on a fictional entity. If *A* and *B* are discussing the film *Mary Poppins*, then they can align on using *Mary* to refer to Mary Poppins (and introduce a corresponding token to their situation models). Although Mary Poppins is not real, the character is defined with respect to a particular causal history (which is public or conventional information). And *A* and *B* can refer to this character (even if they remember different details about her), just as if they referred to a real Mary. Interlocutors co-refer when they both represent the same referent and use *Mary* to refer to that referent – and (focal) alignment happens when *A* uses *Mary* to refer to that referent and *B* interprets *A*'s use of *Mary* as referring to that referent. Such alignment over reference holds in the same way for mythical creatures (e.g. unicorns) and real unobservable entities (e.g. quarks).[4]

Returning to our example (2)–(4), we note that background knowledge about Mary may not be very relevant to *A*'s or *B*'s understanding of the visit

---

[3] If *A* describes an event and utters *Mary* and *B* describes a different event and also utters *Mary*, and they both initially think they are referring to different people, they will both represent *A*'s event in relation to MARY37 and *B*'s event in relation to MARY64 (i.e. they are aligned on a situation involving two Marys). If they then both realize they are referring to the same person, they will both delete one token and will remain aligned.

[4] Our assumptions about the nature of reference (and hence what it means to align on reference) are based on Evans (1982). If I read *The Hound of the Baskervilles* and represent Sherlock Holmes on the basis of this novel, and then read *A Study in Scarlet*, I still represent the same Sherlock Holmes, because his identity is not defined by my experiences but rather by his role across all novels and perhaps other media. In the same way, you and I represent the same Sherlock Holmes even if we have read different Sherlock Holmes novels.

to London (though of course it could be relevant if it explained Mary's interest in London theatre), and so it need have no status in their situation models. But situation models can sometimes be augmented by inference. Consider the question of what vehicle John drives. If *B* believes that John usually drives his white van, but *A* believes that John usually drives a car, then they have different background knowledge that is potentially relevant. When *A* utters *John drove Mary to London*, both *A* and *B* may draw inferences about the vehicle so that they represent the vehicle in the situation model. If they draw different inferences, their (focal) situation models will differ, with *A* representing a car (as part of the driving event) and *B* representing a van. Hence *B* would be confused by *A*'s subsequent reference to the car. Such confusion would reflect misalignment. *B* might therefore utter *Do you mean his van?*, as an attempt to clear up the misalignment.

To take a different example, consider two interlocutors discussing a *James Bond* film (*Spectre*). They have both seen the film and therefore have similar representations relating to the characters, plot, settings and so on. So when they discuss a particular scene (e.g. when James Bond fights with the assassin Marco Sciarra), they are likely to be focally aligned (we assume that focal alignment relates to a particular scene) and globally aligned (with respect to other scenes in *Spectre*).

But now assume that their background knowledge about the James Bond character is fairly different. Specifically, *A* has seen the film *You Only Live Twice* but not *Goldfinger*, whereas *B* has seen *Goldfinger* but not *You Only Live Twice*. Therefore, *A* is familiar with the villain Blofeld (the cat-stroking head of the criminal organization Spectre) but not Oddjob (the hat-throwing sidekick of Auric Goldfinger), whereas *B* is familiar with Oddjob but not Blofeld. This means that *A* and *B* share some information about James Bond that is in the global (and therefore focal) situation model (e.g. that he fought Marco Sciarra in the film *Spectre*) but have some background information that is different from each other (e.g. how he overcame Oddjob vs Blofeld).

Importantly, they both represent the same character (James Bond) in their situation models. So when *A* mentions James Bond's fight with Marco Sciarra in *Spectre*, *A* and *B* construct focally aligned situation models (i.e. containing a JAMES-BOND-token).[5] They construct these aligned models because they can access the same relevant background information about *Spectre* (and it may be that *A*'s utterance triggers *B*'s memory of that scene). But of course their background knowledge about James Bond is different, and so they are focally aligned without having fully shared background knowledge (as might

---

[5] It is the same token because the fictional character has the same causal history (i.e. it is conventionally accepted that the same character appears in all *James Bond* films).

be the case for two enthusiasts who have seen all the films and remember similar details about the films).

However, interlocutors must share some relevant background knowledge to achieve focal alignment at this point. In our example, A and B's focal alignment comes about because they can access some of the same background information about *Spectre*. But if the conversation moves on and A notes differences between the Spectre organization in *Spectre* and in *You Only Live Twice*, then B (who has not seen this latter film) will not understand the comparison and hence not fully align with A. What has happened is that A has drawn on two aspects of background knowledge, whereas B has access to one of those but not the other. This discrepancy leads to a partial failure of focal alignment (which A might subsequently repair by describing the plot of *You Only Live Twice*). The example illustrates how focal (and indeed global) alignment and background knowledge are different constructs, but that they often interact. Our primary concern is with alignment of situation models but we are also concerned with its relationship to shared background knowledge.

Background knowledge relates to long-term memory. Long-term memory stores all the information that an individual knows, but the vast majority of this information is irrelevant for any particular conversation. In Chapter 6, we treated long-term memory as an enormous library from which a reader could retrieve a book successfully only with the support of a 'pointer' to the appropriate aisle, and now let us imagine a library of films. In this context, two individuals are focally aligned if they access the same films. But shared background knowledge about a topic has two different aspects to it. The individuals might or might not have the same set of films on that topic (i.e. James Bond). Alternatively, they might or might not have the same pointer (i.e. they might be directed to the same or different aisles). In our case, A and B's libraries have different films (apart from *Spectre*). Enthusiasts who have seen all *James Bond* films do have the same set of films, but still might not be aligned with respect to which film is being talked about. Importantly, when A says to B 'James Bond fought Marco Sciarra well' in the discussion of *Spectre* and B understands, A and B become focally aligned, even though they have different background knowledge about James Bond.[6]

---

[6] This example contrasts with a case of mistaken identity. In the *James Bond* films, Bond's boss is called M but in fact M is a role (each person appointed to this role is called M). So if A mentions M and intends to refer to one person and B takes M to refer to a different person, then A and B are focally misaligned. To make this possible, the situation model cannot just represent M but instead has to represent the (intended) referent of M. The difference between the two Ms can be seen as different pointers from the situation model to the background knowledge. But when A and B know different things about James Bond, they are still referring to the same character – roughly speaking, each of them realizes that there is some information that they lack but their partner does have.

7.1.3   Working Memory and Alignment of Situation Models

To understand alignment of situation models, we need to consider the relationship between the tokens in the focal and global models and how they are linked to the interlocutors' knowledge more generally. To do this, we expand on the notions of short- and long-term working memory. Ericsson and Kintsch (1995) noted that experts can construct complex memory representations to support domain-specific activities (e.g. chess players recalling board positions). These representations enable them to extend their working memory far beyond the capacity of short-term working memory (cf. Cowan, 1998). To do this, they use cues in short-term working memory to activate extensive areas of long-term memory, which constitute long-term working memory. In language comprehension (both text comprehension and narrative comprehension in dialogue), they assume that the comprehender represents entities and events that are mentioned in the current utterance, together with the protagonists of the text or narrative, in short-term working memory, and therefore they can be accessed directly (e.g. with a pronoun). In contrast, other entities and events from previous utterances are in long-term working memory, and can be accessed using a cue such as a definite description that is placed in short-term working memory.

Now let us briefly return to the perspective of individual representations in monologue comprehension. When the reader reaches the end of Zwaan and Radvansky's (1998) text (1), the representations of the professor and his work are in short-term working memory, as are key entities and events from earlier in the text, such as the protagonist Peter and his knocking on the door. The reader can therefore access representations corresponding to these entities and events directly. In contrast, the representations of Peter's draft and the event of his taking the elevator to the fifth floor are in long-term working memory but not short-term working memory. They can be accessed, but not accessed directly. For example, the reader could not (straightforwardly) interpret *it* in *He said he liked it* to refer to Peter's draft, and would experience some processing difficulty at this point. However, the reader could interpret *He said he liked the draft* without difficulty (with the assumption being that a pronoun needs a directly accessible antecedent).[7]

We can consider accessibility of information in working memory in terms of the distinction between explicit and implicit focus due to Sanford and Garrod (1981). Entities and events that are in explicit focus are immediately

---

[7] For example, Anderson et al. (1983) had participants read texts that sometimes involved a time-shift to a separate episode (e.g. *Five hours later* in relation to having a meal in a restaurant), and found that pronominal references to episode-dependent characters in the previous sentence (e.g. a waiter) became difficult to understand.

accessible – roughly speaking, it is possible to refer to them in English with pronouns. Entities and events that are in implicit focus require some foregrounding before they can be accessed – for example, by referring to them with a definite description. Explicit focus is limited to the focal situation model, which includes the protagonists that persist through the narrative. For example at the end of text (1), Peter and the professor are in explicit focus. Implicit focus involves entities and events that form part of the global but not focal model, such as the draft or elevator in (1), but also relevant background information, for instance that an office is where someone works, the professor's work is likely to be written documents lying in front of him on his desk and so on.

In comprehending a longer narrative, the reader's ability to access previously mentioned entities and events can be quite remarkable. Consider a long and complex novel with many characters whose names and qualities may be unfamiliar or confusing to many readers. For example, the novel *A Suitable Boy* (Seth, 1994) spends more than a thousand pages describing the lives of four extended Indian families, and the reader needs to be able to access considerable information about many different characters fluently in order to understand (and enjoy) the narrative. As the book unfolds, the reader accumulates information in long-term working memory and develops a complex situation model that reflects the key aspects of the text. This situation model is clearly well beyond the limited capacity of short-term working memory. To maintain this model, the reader therefore has to routinely access long-term working memory on the basis of an appropriate retrieval cue (e.g. a name or event description). It is of course possible to put down such a novel for a day or two and then resume without great difficulty, as a retrieval cue will typically still serve to access the relevant information from long-term working memory. Indeed, Ericsson and Kintsch (1995) discussed much research by Glanzer and colleagues (Fischer & Glanzer, 1986; Glanzer et al., 1981; Glanzer et al., 1984) in which participants experienced some but little difficulty when they resumed reading after a forced interruption (e.g. a time interval, or having to read something else). Ericsson and Kintsch noted that such difficulty was typically limited to the first sentence following resumption, and therefore interpreted the interruption as merely leading to a decay in the quality of the retrieval cue. In summary, long-term working memory may be extensive and long-lived.

Let us now return to dialogue. Imagine a shortlisting committee in which the members are discussing and building up extensive information about a set of candidates, before they make a decision about whom to shortlist. There is then a fire-drill and they all march out and stand making small talk with their colleagues, and return to the meeting 15 minutes later. They can of course straightforwardly resume where they left off, just as in Glanzer's experiments. This is because they are able to access long-term working memory in conversation.

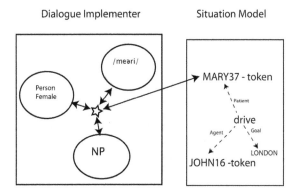

Figure 7.1 The linguistic representation underlying dialogue routines for MARY37 in the event described by *John drove Mary to London*. The nodes in the implementer correspond to semantics, syntax, phonology and the binding node that links to MARY37-token in a schematic of the focal situation model.

In relation to alignment, focal alignment of situation models occurs when interlocutors have the same representations in short-term working memory. These representations constantly change as the dialogue unfolds, and so the degree of focal alignment may also change. Global alignment of situation models occurs when the interlocutors have the same representations in long-term working memory. So if interlocutors have been discussing a complex situation, for example when a couple talks about a series of events involving their extended family that has comparable complexity to the plot of *A Suitable Boy*, they are globally aligned to the extent that they represent the same complex situation. Much of this information has been directly contributed by one or both interlocutors, but other information may have been inferred by both interlocutors – for example, they both make the same bridging inference to explain why a relative behaved as he did following a particular event.

7.1.4   Dialogue Routines

The process of linking language with the situation model takes place via dialogue routines (which we mentioned in Section 6.1.2). Let us introduce in relation to (2) (see Figure 7.1). The word *Mary* has semantics FEMALE-PERSON-CALLED-MARY, syntax Noun Phrase, and phonology /meəri/, but in this dialogue it refers to a specific person, say MARY37. As we have noted, interlocutors are linguistically aligned if they both use the word *Mary*, but are aligned with respect to the situation model only if they also use *Mary* to refer to the same person, such as MARY37. This means that the interlocutors treat the use of *Mary* as a retrieval cue for aspects of their long-term working memory that make reference to the same person. (They both access information about MARY37, but they do not necessarily access the same information, as we have discussed.)

The arrow connecting the implementer to the situation model in Figure 7.1 links the linguistic properties of the expression (here, *Mary*) and the entities in the model. The binding node in the implementer binds the linguistic representations and maps them 'as a bundle' to the corresponding token in the model. We use the term *dialogue routine* to refer to the composite of the linguistic representations and the token in the model – in this case, corresponding to the representations for *Mary* and MARY37-token. We call it a dialogue routine because the link emerges as a result of the dialogue itself. Moreover, it is defined in both linguistic and situational terms. We use *routinization* to refer to the process of establishing routines.

An interlocutor is likely to have a stable meaning for *Mary* (i.e. FEMALE-PERSON-CALLED-MARY), but can use *Mary* to refer to different female people. Therefore, two interlocutors are likely to already be aligned on the meaning of *Mary* but have to align on the reference for *Mary* in a particular dialogue. In other words, they develop the same link between the linguistic representations for *Mary* and MARY37-token. In our terms, routinization involves establishing alignment between the interlocutors.

In this example, the dialogue routine is a single word, but it is often a longer expression. In Pickering and Garrod (2004), we considered the example of people discussing politics and referring to *the previous administration* to refer to the last government of the UK. The interlocutors presumably begin with the same linguistic representations for the words *previous* and *administration* (with fairly similar levels of activation). But *A* now uses *the previous administration* to refer to the last government (which is represented as a token in her situation model). If her utterance is understood and accepted by the addressee, he establishes the same token in his situation model and their situation models become aligned. But more interestingly, they align on the relationship between the linguistic representation in the dialogue implementer (as indicated by the binding node) and the token in the situation model. In terms of Figure 7.1, the interlocutors align on a linguistic representation of *the previous administration* (i.e. with semantics GOVERNMENT-BEFORE-CURRENT-GOVERNMENT, syntax Noun Phrase, and phonology /ðə previɜːs ədmi-nistrəʃɜːn/) and its reference (which in 2004 was the John Major government). The linguistic representation is a multi-word lexicalization (Jackendoff, 2002) and its establishment may be part of the process of routinization (i.e. it need not have been lexicalized before the current dialogue); see Pickering and Garrod (2005).

Figure 7.2 The 'ice skater' tangram.

Now let us relate this account to studies of dialogue. Clark and Wilkes-Gibbs (1986) had a director describe tangram figures such as Figure 7.2 to a matcher. In their experiment, the director often started with long descriptions such as *The next one looks like a person who's ice skating, except they're sticking two arms out in front* and the matcher accepted such descriptions and found the appropriate tangram in an array. But the director subsequently started to refer to the same tangram with a much more succinct expression such as *The ice skater* and the matcher immediately understood that description. The interlocutors did not change their linguistic representations for *ice skater* (i.e. they were already aligned on its semantics, syntax and phonology) but they did align on the use of *The ice skater* to refer to a particular tangram. In other words, this example shows alignment of the link between linguistic representation and situation model. In this case, the process involves agreeing on the linguistic term to refer to a well-defined entity (the tangram). In Garrod and Anderson (1987), we can see examples when the linguistic term does not change but its reference has to be clarified. So when one interlocutor uses *I'm on the second row*, the other interlocutor has to determine that this refers to the row which is one off the bottom.

In sum, interlocutors establish dialogue routines when they use the same linguistic expressions to refer to the same things in a particular interchange (though sometimes the routine will of course persist). They may need to extend their lexica (to cover novel multi-word chunks) to make such links between linguistic representations and tokens in situation models. The alignment of situation models takes place over these links, and such alignment tends to be limited to a particular interchange (but need not be). Such alignment contrasts with potentially long-term (global) linguistic alignment – the contrast is between using *the chef* to refer to a particular chef (which is typically short-lived) and aligning on the use of *the chef* when meaning a particular sort of cook. One way to express this difference is that alignment of situation models is akin to alignment on episodic memory, whereas linguistic alignment (specifically, alignment on semantic representations) is more akin to alignment on semantic memory (e.g. Tulving, 1983).[8]

7.1.5   Alignment of Game Models

If *A* says *Where's John today?* and *B* replies *At home*, then they appear to be taking part in an information-seeking game with *A* being the seeker and *B* being the provider of the information. When they do this, they both represent the same game and represent both individuals' roles in the game. They are therefore aligned. However, they can also be misaligned. In Section 6.3.1, we used the example of two diners sitting in a restaurant when *A* asks *B*, *Can you speak to the chef?* If *B* now answers *Yes* and gets up to speak to the chef, then they are aligned on an action-seeking game. But if *B* answers *Yes* without getting up, then *B* treats *A*'s question as an information-seeking game, and so they are not aligned with respect the game model.

If *B* responds *No I won't*, then *B* is taking part in the action-seeking game in which *B* is the actor but refusing to act. There is no misalignment of game models. The failure to take part as requested is clearly a failure of dialogue as a cooperative joint activity (see Section 7.6) but is not a failure of alignment. But in successful cooperative joint activity, interlocutors accept each other's invitations to take part in dialogue games, and of course align on their dialogue game models. (Interlocutors also need to align on their role within a game, though this is much more of an issue in multi-party dialogue; see Section 10.2.5.)

Note also that dialogue games can be embedded (once or more than once; Levinson, 2013). For example if *B* responds *Do you mean the head chef?*, *A* says *Yes*, and *B* says *OK I'll try and find him*, then an information-seeking game (with *B* as information-seeker and *A* as provider) is embedded within an action-seeking game (with *A* as instructor and *B* as actor). Interlocutors can be aligned with respect to one game but not another, and we can therefore distinguish focal and global alignment of dialogue games, with focal alignment referring to the most-recently initiated game.

This example also highlights the relationship between focal situation models and focal game models. The active (i.e. most embedded) game corresponds to the focal situation model. When *A* utters *Can you speak to the chef?*, their focal

---

[8] We speculate that dialogue routines develop the characteristics of names (arguably, expressions with the same referent in all possible worlds; Kripke, 1980). When an interlocutor first uses the term *Our great leader*, it may refer to one person but could clearly refer to a different person if uttered at a different time. But when interlocutors fix on the term as a routine, they appear to treat it much more like a name – for example, any other use of *Our great leader* would simply be wrong. By doing so, interlocutors are of course reducing (or removing) ambiguity for the purposes of that conversation.

situation models represent this information (and so *A* and *B* are focally misaligned with respect to the reference of *the chef*). When *B* introduces the embedded information-checking game, this information leaves the focal situation model and is replaced by information about the head chef. *A*'s *Yes* completes the embedded game and *B*'s response leads to alignment on a focal situation model about speaking to the head chef (so that information 'pops back' from the global to the focal situation model). In sum, the focal game model defines the scope of the focal situation model.

7.2   Meta-representation of Alignment

Having considered what it means for individuals to align their dialogue models, we now turn to the question of what they represent about such alignment. We therefore introduce the notion of meta-representation of alignment (and misalignment). Alignment of dialogue model representations and alignment of linguistic representations underlies communicative success. We can think of these representations as *first-order* representations and their alignment as first-order alignment. Conversations also depend on *second-order* representations – representations that make reference to (first-order) alignment (but not alignment of meta-representations of alignment). We refer to these representations as meta-representations of alignment (which can themselves be aligned), and discuss some ways in which they can affect communication. These second-order representations are additional (and in some sense auxiliary) to the first-order representations that underlie alignment. The use of 'meta' is purely for clarity and emphasizes that we are considering a representation about alignment. Alignment is of course not a representation but the relationship between representations, and individuals can meta-represent this relationship.

With respect to reference, if *A* and *B* both refer to the same Mary, then *A* meta-represents alignment if she believes that this is the case (e.g. that *A* and *B* both represent MARY37-token), but (erroneously) meta-represents misalignment if she mistakenly believes that *B* refers to a different Mary (e.g. that *A* represents MARY37-token and *B* represents MARY64-token). Conversely, if *A* and *B* refer to different Marys, then *A* meta-represents misalignment if she believes this is the case, and (erroneously) meta-represents alignment if she mistakenly believes *B* refers to the same Mary as she does. This latter situation occurs when one interlocutor thinks the other has understood her but has not.

If *A* and *B* listen to the same speech (e.g. by a presidential candidate) in different rooms, and do not realize what each other is doing, then they may well align linguistically to some extent (e.g. raising the activation of *Medicare* to a similar level) and in terms of their situation models (e.g. with respect to health care policy). The process of achieving such alignment might differ from the process that occurs if *A* and *B* discuss the speech, but their (first-order) alignment may be the same. However, there is an important sense in which each individual's mental state is different in the former case of non-interactive alignment and the latter case of interactive alignment. We characterize this difference in terms of meta-representation of alignment – that is, whether they believe they are aligned or not.

Meta-representation of alignment is a 'social' representation about the relationship between two individuals' representations. In our interactive example, *A* can represent that *A* and *B* are aligned with respect to their understanding of the candidate's health care policy. In other words, *A* believes that *A*'s understanding equals *B*'s understanding. In principle, *A* might represent the candidate's policy and have a representation about *B*'s (presumed) representation without also representing that they are the same. But by default we assume that interlocutors meta-represent alignment when they have evidence for alignment. Of course, *B* can also represent that *A* and *B* are aligned with respect their understanding of the candidate's policy.[9] But if *A* and *B* each listen to the speech without realizing that the other is doing so, then there is no meta-representation of alignment: *A* does not represent that they are aligned, and neither does *B*.

Some experimental evidence suggests that misaligned interlocutors often mistakenly meta-represent alignment. Keysar and Henly (2002) had a speaker silently read a short text and then utter a (lexically or syntactically) ambiguous sentence to an addressee. Speakers believed that the addressees chose the intended interpretation (72 per cent of trials) more often than they actually did (61 per cent). In other words, they overestimated their effectiveness. In our terms, they sometimes meta-represented that they were aligned when they were not aligned.

Of course, an individual can also meta-represent misalignment, for example if *A* believes that *B* does not understand the candidate's policy in the way that *A* does. Informally, this means that *A* believes that *A* and *B* have different representations. In fact, meta-representation of misalignment is a major stimulus for pursuing (informational) conversations. So when *A* knows about the candidate's policy, believes *B* does not know, and would like *B* to have the same knowledge as *A*, then *A* is motivated to describe the policy to *B*. In other words, *A* seeks to remove the misalignment – to move from a meta-representation of misalignment to a meta-representation of alignment.

---

[9] Note that *A* and *B* are aligned on their meta-representation of alignment (i.e. they both believe the same thing about their alignment). They could in turn meta-represent that they are aligned on a meta-representation of alignment. Indeed, they could represent a mutual belief about alignment (cf. Lewis, 1969). But such higher-order representations are not central to our account.

Misalignment (particularly with respect to the focal situation model) is a driving force underlying control of conversation (see Chapter 8).

Individuals also meta-represent alignment of game models (i.e. represent that they have the same game model) or meta-represent their misalignment. When A asked B, *Can you speak to the chef?* and B responded *Yes* and spoke to the chef, then A and B aligned on the action-seeking game, and presumably also meta-represented their alignment (i.e. they both represented that they represented the same game). When B responded *Yes* and sat still, then A could meta-represent their alignment (if A thought B was just being awkward) or misalignment (if A thought that B had misunderstood). B may have believed he is in an action-seeking game and is just being awkward, and if so he could have meta-represented their alignment. But if he believed he is in an information-seeking game (and therefore responded what he thought was appropriate), then he could also have meta-represented alignment (even though he was mistaken about A's representation).

Our account of dialogue is framed in terms of *interactive* alignment (rather than just alignment). When A and B discuss the presidential candidate's speech, they of course align on their interpretation of the speech and on word choices (such as *Medicare*) but also meta-represent such alignment. This is because the speech is manifest to both interlocutors. It is also conceivable for individuals to meta-represent alignment without interacting – most obviously if some third party points out that the individuals have heard the same speech. And crucially, such non-interacting individuals cannot control the process of alignment. Of course, we focus on interactive alignment and its consequences.

7.3   Interactive Alignment and the Shared Workspace

So far, our discussion is in terms of the representations within the interlocutors. But our framework incorporates another key component – the shared workspace (and associated individual workspaces). The shared workspace relates to the individuals' joint plan for the action and its contents reflect the realization of that plan. When interlocutors converse, they place information in the shared workspace and manipulate that information. Importantly, the shared workspace is limited in scope – intuitively, at any instant it contains information that is in both interlocutors' attention.

We now provide a more precise discussion of the shared workspace and how it relates to the representations within the individuals. The shared workspace contains meaningful entities (i.e. signs and non-signs). The non-signs are objects and events that can be manipulated by the interacting individuals in pursuit of the goal of the cooperative joint activity. For instance, our furniture builders make use of a shared workspace that contains furniture components (such as legs or drawers), screws and tools, as well as events such as drilling holes. These entities are represented in the plan and can be manipulated in a manner that is relevant to the success of the activity. In other words, they jointly afford such manipulations. The workspace does not contain entities corresponding to the colour of the screws or the texture of the wood (or the event of radio playing in the background), assuming that they are not constituents of the plan (and in this context, the entities do not afford manipulations relating to colour or texture; Norman, 2013).[10]

The workspace for dialogue can contain such entities, which are the props associated with dialogue about 'matters at hand'. But it primarily contains *sign vehicles* – that is, physical entities with interpretations, such as spoken, written or signed words, gestures and demonstrations.

Our account is based on Pierce's (1931–1958) account of signification, which involves a three-way relationship between a *sign vehicle* (the physical realization of the sign), its *object* (what the sign stands for) and its *interpretant* (the understanding of the relationship between sign and object). Henceforth, we normally use *sign* as shorthand for Pierce's *sign vehicle* (as we did in Chapter 4). We use *referent* instead of *object*, as we use *object* for a particular kind of entity (i.e. contrasting with *event*). Pierce's *interpretant* relates to tokens in the situation model (though his use is not entirely clear). Our discussion is almost entirely in terms of linguistic signs, but much of our discussion can be applied to non-linguistic aspects of communication (see Section 11.1).

An object could be a particular person called Mary (e.g. Mary Smith from 10 Church Lane), and an event could be her breaking her leg (which occurred once, on 30 June 2017). So if interlocutors jointly observe this event, these

---

[10] Objects (and events) in the workspace are not patterns of light or colour, or components of the perceptual process such as edges or contours, and they have already been perceptually interpreted. Moreover, different perspectives on an ambiguous drawing can constitute different objects. So when *A* sees the duck in Wittgenstein's (1953/1958) 'duck-rabbit' and *B* sees the rabbit, *A* and *B* attend to different (meaningful) objects (even though the picture does not change) – and these objects have different affordances.

Figure 7.i The duck-rabbit.

If *A* and *B* both see the duck, then their shared workspace contains the duck; but if *A* sees the duck and *B* sees the rabbit, then *A*'s individual workspace contains the duck and *B*'s individual workspace contains the rabbit (and the shared workspace is empty). This example illustrates how the workspace is composed of entities of relevance to individuals – specifically, entities over which cognitive processes can operate.

entities (i.e. MARY37 and BREAK-LEG59) enter the shared workspace. If an interlocutor simultaneously says *Look, Mary broke her leg*, then *Mary-sign*[11] (together with signs for the other words) also enters the shared workspace. Both the signs and the props have representations in the interlocutors' situation models. Both *Mary-sign* and MARY37 correspond to the MARY37-token in each individual's situation model (i.e. reflecting Pierce's three-way relationship).

Importantly, words are signs and correspond to objects and events – specifically *Mary* corresponds to the object MARY37 and *Mary broke her leg* corresponds to the event BREAK-LEG59.[12] The signs are constituents of the workspace because they have interpretations (hence, the sound /m/ is not a constituent of the workspace, though obviously it is part of *Mary*). If A now utters *She couldn't get up*, the words are put into the workspace. The constituents of the workspace are the same whether *she* refers to MARY37 (i.e. *Mary* and *she* are co-referential) or not. To be meaningful, it is necessary for *she* (or indeed *Mary*) to have an interpretation but it does not matter what interpretation it has.[13] (But of course the situation model is affected by the interpretation: if *Mary* and *she* are co-referential, the model contains one token; if not, it contains two tokens which correspond to different referents.) Finally, if A utters *Mary broke her leg* while pointing to MARY37 (i.e. the real Mary Smith), then the shared workspace contains both *Mary-sign* and MARY37 herself.

Both signs and non-signs in the shared workspace are resources for the interlocutors (and signs and non-signs in A or B's individual workspace are resources available only to A or to B). Some of the non-signs correspond to props. When individuals are discussing matters at hand, they can add non-signs (by reaching for a tool) or signs (by uttering words). Note also that depictions such as gestures (e.g. pointing) or displays (e.g. holding up an item to be purchased) can also be signs in the workspace.

As the contents of the shared workspace are dependent on the plan, they can change if the plan changes. For example, if the furniture builders stop building and begin to admire their creation as a work of art, the colour or texture of the components might become important to their interpretation. If so, the workspace would reflect this change, for example now containing information about the legs' colour or the texture of the surface, as these properties have become meaningful entities. The workspace can therefore change dramatically rather

---

[11] Strictly, *Mary-sign₁*, with the subscript indicating the sign's position in the utterance (see Section 7.2.1). We also ignore the subscript indicating the speaker (see Section 4.5.1) and sometimes leave out *sign*.

[12] Note that we treat words rather than morphemes as the meaningful objects.

[13] The word *she* (or *Mary*) has a single perspective – it can be perceived only one way (cf. Chapter 7, footnote 9).

than incrementally, and such a change does not necessarily lead to any processing cost (because it is not a representation). Note also that components of an individual workspace can be moved to the shared workspace (e.g. when 'revealed' by one individual).

So far, we have assumed that the interlocutors' situation models are aligned. If *A* and *B* both interpret *Mary* as referring to MARY37, then both of their models contain MARY37-token, and the shared workspace contains *Mary-sign*. But if *A* interprets *Mary* as referring to MARY37 and *B* interprets *Mary* as referring to MARY64, then their models contain different tokens, but the shared workspace still contains *Mary-sign*. Under these circumstances, the interlocutors are linguistically aligned but not aligned with respect to the situation model.[14]

7.3.1   The Relationship between Alignment of Situation Models and the Workspace

We noted that each individual has an individual workspace, which contains entities that are not available to the other individual. For example, furniture builder *A* may be aware of a small component that is hidden from *B*'s view – a component that subsequently turns out to be important for the next joint action. In such cases, the component is (initially) manipulable by *A* but not *B*. And in the same way, the sign for a word can be in an individual workspace during dialogue. If *A* uttered *Mary* and *B* did not hear *A*'s utterance, then *Mary-sign* is in *A*'s individual workspace.

We illustrate the relationship between the workspace and alignment of situation models with examples. (Our examples involve single episodes and therefore relate to focal alignment.) We use simple examples involving a single episode that is represented in a focal situation model, and hence is related to the current state of the workspace. In the most straightforward case (Figure 7.3), *A* utters *John kicked Mary*, and *B* hears it correctly and interprets it as *A* intended. *A* constructs a situation model containing JOHN16-token, MARY37-token, and KICK-token, and *B* does the same – they both represent three tokens that correspond to the same entities or events (i.e. we ignore the representation of tense). Hence they are aligned (as illustrated by the dashed horizontal lines). The shared workspace contains signs corresponding to the words *John*, *kicked*, and *Mary*, and it also represents the order in which those words were spoken (e.g. *John-sign$_1$*, where the number indicates order). These signs are all in the shared workspace for *A* and *B*. The process by which *A* and

---

[14] Misalignment also occurs if *B* does not know which Mary *A* is referring to. A would represent *Mary* as MARY37-token, and *B* might represent *Mary* (imprecisely) as MARY37-token OR MARY64-token.

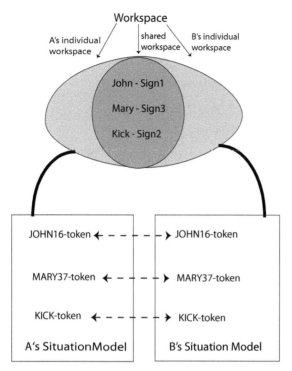

Figure 7.3 Referential alignment and the workspace. The shared workspace (dark grey) is flanked by A's and B's individual workspaces (light grey). The curved black lines represent links (in both directions) between the situation models and the workspace. In fact, A's situation model links to A's workspace and the shared workspace (but not B's workspace), and B's situation model links to B's workspace and the shared workspace (but not A's workspace). The dashed lines indicate channels of alignment. Note that Figures 7.3–7.5 leave out the dialogue implementer and dialogue game model.

B interpret *John-sign₁* as referring to JOHN16 (i.e. by placing JOHN16-token in the situation model) is a consequence of the sign itself combined with relevant background knowledge, which is similar for A and B.

Now consider a case of referential misalignment (Figure 7.4). B hears A correctly but interprets A as referring to a different Mary from B. A constructs a situation model containing JOHN16-token, MARY37-token, and KICK-token, and B constructs a model containing JOHN16-token, MARY64-token, and KICK-token. Hence they are misaligned with respect to interpretation of *Mary* (as illustrated by the cross-hatched dashed line between MARY37-token and MARY64-token). Just as in the case of referential alignment, the shared

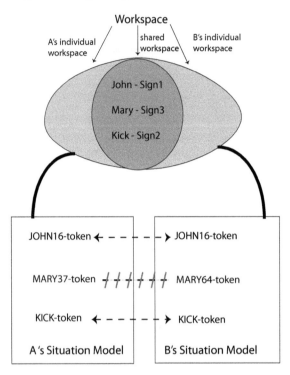

Figure 7.4 Referential misalignment and the workspace. As Figure 7.3, except that the cross-hatched dashed line indicates misalignment.

workspace contains sign vehicles corresponding to the words *John*, *kicked*, and *Mary* (and their order). In particular, the shared workspace contains the sign vehicle for *Mary* (i.e. *Mary-sign₃*), because it is shared by *A* and *B*. The sign vehicle *Mary* is interpreted differently by *A* and *B* on this occasion (presumably because of their different background knowledge), but the sign vehicle remains the same.

Next, consider a case of mishearing (Figure 7.5). *B* hears *A* incorrectly – *A* said *Mary* (referring to one object) but he heard *Martha* (referring to a different object). A constructs a situation model containing JOHN16-token (referring to JOHN16), MARY37-token (referring to MARY37), and KICK-token (referring to a kicking event), and *B* constructs a model containing JOHN16-token (referring to JOHN16), MARTHA12-token (referring to MARTHA12), and KICK-token (referring to a kicking event). Hence they are misaligned with respect to interpretation of what they heard as the last word (as illustrated by the cross-hatched dashed line between MARY37-token and MARTHA12-token). The shared workspace contains signs corresponding to the words

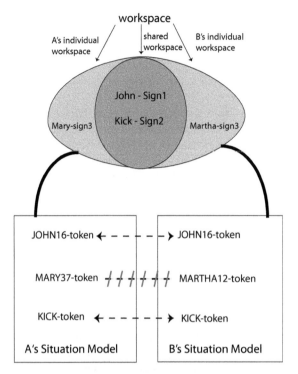

Figure 7.5 Misheard speech and the workspace.

John and *kicked* (and their order), but not *Mary* or *Martha*, because neither object is shared by *A* and *B*. Instead, *A* represents *Mary-sign₃* in her individual workspace, and *B* represents *Martha-sign₃* in his individual workspace. (This difference leads them to establish different situation models.)[15]

More briefly, let us consider examples involving definite descriptions rather than proper names. If *A* utters *John saw the shopkeeper* and *B* hears her correctly, then the shared workspace contains *shopkeeper-sign₄* (as well as *the-sign₃*). *A*'s and *B*'s situation models contain tokens referring to the shop-keeper – the same token if they are aligned on the shopkeeper's identity, and different tokens otherwise. We treat definite descriptions in the same way as

---

[15] If *A* said *Mary* but *B* (mis)heard *Martha* and they both referred to the same person (WOMAN257), then the sign vehicles *Mary* and *Martha* are distinct, and so *Mary-sign* is in *A*'s individual workspace and *Martha-sign* is in *B*'s individual workspace. Note that *A* and *B* have aligned situation models. The relevant tokens in the situation model are arbitrary (it only matters that they refer to WOMAN257). In this example, *A* and *B* would not be linguistically aligned, but this is not our focus here. A plausible scenario would be if *A* pointed someone out and referred to her as *Mary*, and *B* misheard *A* as saying *Martha*.

proper names. If *A* utters *John saw the bat*, then the shared workspace contains *bat-sign*$_4$. It does not matter whether *A* and *B* treat *the bat* as referring to the same entity (a particular piece of willow, say CRICKET-BAT23), or to different cricket bats, or whether *A* but not *B* treats *the bat* as referring to a flying creature. There is nothing in the workspace to distinguish any of these interpretations.

What is it that makes *Mary* and *Martha* distinct sign vehicles, but *Mary* uttered in a high pitch the same sign vehicle as *Mary* uttered in a low pitch? The answer is that all pronunciations of *Mary* cover the same range of interpretations (e.g. MARY1, MARY2 ...) whereas *Mary* and *Martha* cover different interpretations (e.g. MARY1, MARY2 ... vs MARTHA1, MARTHA2 ...). Similarly, any instance of *the bat* covers the same range of interpretations (an antique willow, a cheap piece of sports equipment, the creature flying around the attic). By 'covers', we mean the interpretations that could be given to the word in isolation – in many contexts, of course, some interpretations are ruled out. (In practice, different signs require a difference in an aspect of form that makes a meaningful distinction – typically one that is fixed for the language.)[16]

The workspace also contains props, which are meaningful objects themselves. The interlocutors align on representations of the props in their situation models. The shared workspace contains the actual person MARY37 (i.e. Mary Smith) if she is manifest to *A* and *B* (e.g. in front of both of them). This person is in the shared workspace when both *A* and *B* also represent the same person in their situation models (e.g. MARY37-token). But she is also in the shared workspace even if *A* believes the person is Mary Smith (hence represents MARY37-token) and *B* believes it is actually Martha Jones (hence represents MARTHA12-token). Similarly, a particular cricket bat is in the shared workspace if *A* and *B* both see it. It does not matter if *A* and *B* view the bat from different angles (in which case they have the same tokens in their situation models), or indeed if one of them believes it to be a hurley (in which case they have different tokens). Note that noises (e.g. the sound of a drill) can also be props. Props are not signs because they do not themselves have conventional signification, but they are physical entities (and can be of the same physical type as signs).[17]

---

[16] Interlocutors can also set up a contrast for a local purpose (i.e. as a kind of routine). Such contrasts can be seen as a kind of depiction, as when *A* refers to *Mary* spoken in an (intentionally) posh voice to refer to MARY64 (cf. Clark, 2016). In this case, *Mary* in a posh voice would constitute a different sign from *Mary* in *A*'s normal pronunciation.

[17] Note that we are concerned only with non-natural (conventional) meaning (cf. Grice, 1957), and ignore both natural non-linguistic meaning (e.g. lightning or spots) and natural linguistic meaning (e.g. sound symbolism).

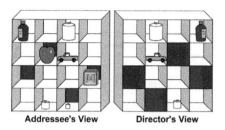

Addressee's View   Director's View

Figure 7.6 The director's and addressee's views of the opposite sides of the lattice when the director describes the bottom right candle (from the director's point of view) to the addressee who has a privileged view of an even smaller candle. From Keysar et al. (2000, Figure 1).

In many experimental studies of dialogue, the workspace contains both utterances and props. For example, in Keysar et al. (2000), a director and an addressee sat on opposite sides of a lattice and discussed candles that were visible to both of them ('shared' props). In some conditions, there were also 'privileged' props that were visible only to the addressee (see Figure 7.6). The participants' utterances were in the shared workspace, along with the shared props. But the privileged props were in the relevant participant's individual workspace (as they could not be seen by the other participant). Even when the addressee knew that the director could not see the candle, they incorrectly chose it 20 per cent of the time when asked to pick *the small candle*. On these trials, the participants' situation models were misaligned (see Figure 7.7). Determining the extent of the shared workspace can be challenging in situations in which interlocutors have a different perspective on a scene (though experimental results are complex; see Hanna et al., 2003).

Our framework is divided into the workspace (which is in the world) and representations (which are in each individual). The workspace contains those elements of the world that the individuals are attending to, and is made up of non-signs (i.e. objects and events) and signs (such as words and gestures) that correspond to entities – though interlocutors need not interpret signs in the same way. If both individuals attend to an entity, then it is in the shared workspace; if one individual (but not the other) attends to it, then it is in her individual workspace. Thus, if A and B both attend to a candle, then they the object (CANDLE24) enters the shared workspace. And if they have a conversation using the word *torch*, then the sign $torch_1$ enters the shared workspace.

The individuals represent the elements in their situation models. For the actual candle, both A and B represent the CANDLE24-token. And because they represent the same token (which in turn is the case because they attend to the same object in the shared workspace), they are aligned with respect to the

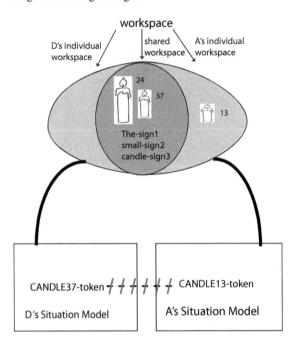

Figure 7.7 An illustration of a critical trial from Keysar et al. (2000) in terms of the workspace. The shared workspace contains props (CANDLE24 and CANDLE37, illustrated as pictures plus numbers) and signs. In addition, the addressee's workspace contains CANDLE13. On this trial, the director (D) uses *the small candle* to refer to CANDLE37, but the addressee (A) misinterprets it as referring to CANDLE13, and hence they become misaligned.

CANDLE24-token. In other words, if an entity is in the shared workspace, then the individuals are aligned with respect to that entity. They may perceive or think about different aspects of the entity (e.g. its colour versus its brightness) and so their alignment need not be complete, but they necessarily align with respect to the entity itself. For the word *torch*, both *A* and *B* represent its linguistic properties (e.g. /tɔ:tʃ/, Noun, and its meaning) and are therefore linguistically aligned. They may also be aligned with respect to its referent (if they refer to the same object).

In sum, the shared workspace is not representational but instead contains the elements over which representation is defined. In contrast, alignment is defined over representations (that is, in terms of the relationship between individuals' representations). In addition, the shared workspace is specified at a particular moment, and can change dramatically, for example when interlocutors move to a new topic of conversation.

7.4   The Shared Workspace, Meta-representation of Alignment and Manifestness

Now consider an example analogous to Keysar et al. (2000), in which there is a candle directly in front of the interlocutors. The candle is in their joint attention: it is in their parallel attention, and moreover it is manifest (i.e. both interlocutors assume that both interlocutors can see it). In contrast, the room also contains a lamp, which happens to be visible to both A and B, but A believes B cannot see it and B believes A cannot see it. Therefore, it is not manifest.[18] The candle can be jointly manipulated in the dialogue by either or both interlocutors. But the lamp cannot be jointly manipulated. For example, A can utter *the candle* and assume that B will align on the same object, but A cannot utter *the lamp* and assume that B will align on the same object.[19] However, both the candle and the lamp are in the shared workspace. Specifically, the lamp is in the shared workspace because it is in their parallel attention and they are interlocutors (i.e. engaged in cooperative joint activity).[20]

Objects have an affordance in relation to language use – a chair affords sitting in, but it also affords referring to. We have argued that objects that can be involved in joint activities have joint affordances (e.g. a heavy table affords joint lifting) as part of a cooperative joint activity. Reference to an object is part of a communicative act, and therefore the object jointly affords reference as part of dialogue. Therefore the candle jointly affords reference through the utterance *the candle* (whereas the lamp does not jointly afford reference through *the lamp*).

Now assume that A and B wish to act on the objects. A can straightforwardly utter *pick up the candle* and assume that B will do so (if B agrees to the action-seeking game). This is because A represents the candle in her situation model and believes that B represents the candle in his situation model. As B also represents the candle and believes that A represents the candle, the candle is manifest. But neither of them believes that the other represents the lamp, and so the lamp is not manifest.

A meta-represents that A and B are aligned with respect to the candle. But A cannot straightforwardly utter *pick up the lamp* and assume that B will do so, because A does not believe that B represents the lamp in his situation model

---

[18] If A believes A but not B can see the candle but B believes A and B can see the candle, then the candle is not manifest (see chapter 2).

[19] Of course, A's utterance may lead to B's alignment, but at this point the status of the lamp changes (i.e. it becomes manifest).

[20] A speaker can utter a disparaging remark under her breath and her partner actually hears what she says. If so, the remark is in parallel attention but is not manifest. It is in the shared workspace but is not jointly manipulable.

and A hence meta-represents that they are not aligned with respect to the lamp. Therefore, the meta-representation of non-alignment interferes with the action-seeking game and does so even though A and B are actually aligned with respect to the lamp.

Each interlocutor's situation model contains tokens corresponding to the candle and the lamp. But these objects are represented differently, and to capture the difference, we add a tag to each token – an *m-tag*, where *m* stands for meta-representation of alignment. Both interlocutors m-tag the candle token (e.g. as CANDLE51-token-m). But because A does not meta-represent alignment on the lamp, A does not m-tag the lamp token (e.g. it is LAMP19-token); and the same is the case for B. More precisely, m-tagging reflects confidence in meta-representation of alignment (i.e. on a continuous scale), so that what we call m-tagged tokens have an m-tag value approaching 1 (e.g. CANDLE-token-m$^{0.99}$), and other tokens have a much lower value (e.g. LAMP19-token-m$^{0.24}$, if confidence was fairly low).

Now let us return to the relationship between manifestness and the meta-representation of alignment. If both interlocutors perceive a manifest entity, then they necessarily meta-represent alignment with respect to that entity (and therefore m-tag it). For example, if an entity is in front of both interlocutors, then they will (typically) treat it as manifest and meta-represent alignment.

Interlocutors regularly attempt to make entities manifest. For example, if A utters *Can you see the lamp?* (when it is not salient), then she is likely to make it manifest to B. Her utterance initiates an information-checking game, in which an agreement by B (e.g. *yes*) leads both interlocutors to meta-represent alignment on the lamp – initially, A but not B represents LAMP19-token, and then both A and B represent LAMP19-token-m). Henceforth this lamp is jointly manipulable – either of them can now refer to it and presume alignment. In general, the absence of m-tagging motivates games concerned with establishing new entities, whereas the presence of m-tagging motivates games concerned with manipulating established entities.

Dialogue promotes the meta-representation of alignment because the interlocutors are aware of each other's presence and interpret their contributions in this light (e.g. the response *Got it*; see Chapter 8). In cases of misalignment (as in Figures 7.4 and 7.5), the interlocutors may subsequently discover that they are misaligned and hence meta-represent this misalignment. In contrast, meta-representation (of alignment or misalignment) does not normally occur without communication (i.e. in non-interactive alignment). In such cases, there is of course no workspace.

We have discussed m-tagging (and hence meta-representation) with respect to individual tokens in the situation model, but it can be inherited by the situation model as a whole. When A utters *John kicked Mary* (see Figure 7.3), A and B could m-tag John (e.g. if they assume they both have JOHN77-token) or Mary, or both. If they m-tag both John and Mary (and the kicking event) with high confidence, then they can also m-tag their focal situation model of the event with high confidence. In successful dialogue, such m-tagging of the situation model regularly occurs, and therefore they each need to represent one piece of information (cf. Galati & Brennan, 2010) in addition to the situation model itself.[21]

7.4.1   Our Framework in Relation to Common Ground

How do our proposals relate to the notion of common ground? According to Clark (1996, p. 12), people believe that they share a vast range of beliefs, and these beliefs make up their common ground. A proposition p is common ground (or common knowledge) for a community C if and only if (i) the members of C have information that p and that i (p. 95). For a dialogue, C refers to the interlocutors and p relates to the topic under discussion (Clark & Marshall, 1981; Stalnaker, 1978).[22] Grounding is the process by which interlocutors place information in common ground. When A and B stand in front of a lamp, they treat that object as part of common ground. And when A says *Do you remember the lamp?* and B replies *Yes*, then the interlocutors treat the lamp as part of common ground – that is, (i) both A and B have information that both A and B know about the lamp and that i.

Our framework does not rely on common ground. The central notion of alignment has a much more limited scope than common ground. Interlocutors have a great deal of common ground, most of which is not directly relevant to the dialogue. Only a limited number of entities are ever in the shared work-space – there are few entities that can be jointly manipulated. Common ground seems to relate much more closely to those aspects of long-term memory that interlocutors could potentially indicate were shared. In contrast, focal alignment relates to what is in parallel attention, and global alignment relates to the consequences of what has been in parallel attention. More importantly, alignment is defined (simply) as what is represented the same way across

---

[21] Similar concerns can arise with respect to complex speech situations. In a 'cocktail party', interlocutors A and B can converse while C and D also converse in the vicinity. It may be that A and B both overhear some of C's speech (e.g. *I nearly drowned!*). This speech is therefore in A and B's parallel attention. If A and B are both confident that both attended to it (e.g. because C spoke so stridently), then it is manifest (i.e. to A and B); if one or both is not confident that the other attended to it (e.g. because of the hubbub), it is not manifest. But in either case C's contribution is not part of A and B's conversation, and so is not part of their shared workspace for that conversation (i.e. it does not constitute part of their cooperative joint activity). If A and B start to discuss C's remark, then of course C's speech enters A and B's shared workspace.

[22] Common ground is related to earlier notions such as common knowledge (Lewis, 1969) and mutual knowledge or belief (Schiffer, 1972), but it does not require potentially infinite recursive models of interlocutors' beliefs.

interlocutors – A and B are aligned with respect to X if both of them represent X in the same way. Alignment makes no assumption about whether the interlocutors know that they know that they represent X.

So what about the meta-representation of alignment? A meta-represents that A and B are aligned with respect to X if A represents X and believes that B represents X. Much of the time, X would be in common ground. But X does not *need* to be in common ground. For example, if A perceives a secret document and B perceives the document, and A is spying on B and B is spying on A, and neither realizes what the other is doing, then both A and B can meta-represent alignment with respect to the document. But the document is not in common ground. In our terms, they are aligned on the document and they both meta-represent that they are aligned on the document. But the spies are not performing a cooperative joint activity and hence there is no shared workspace for the document to be in.

Manifestness does not require common ground, because it relates to perception rather than beliefs. The candle is in joint attention, and the interlocutors do not need to represent common ground with respect to perceptual knowledge. In other words, (i) A and B have information that both A and B perceive the lamp, but they do not also have to represent (i). And the same is the case for utterances themselves, which are also in joint attention. Our account accords with Peacocke (2005), who states that 'the openness of communication does not require the inferential structures in Schiffer's account of mutual knowledge. The openness of my communication consists rather in the fact that you and I have full joint awareness that I am saying that it's time for lunch. We equally have open knowledge that I said it's time for lunch' (p. 315; *Schiffer* refers to Schiffer, 1972, but Peacocke's comments relate to common ground as well).

Interlocutors can of course represent their interpretations of utterances (or indeed of objects). Such interpretations of course involve beliefs rather than perception. (These beliefs can involve semantics, but they can also simply be the belief that an utterance or object has been perceived.) We assume that interlocutors meta-represent alignment with respect to such beliefs.

If interlocutors wish to represent common ground with respect to such beliefs, they could do so by representing indefinitely higher-order meta-representations (presumably using a recursive formulation rather than infinite iteration). But interlocutors do not use such higher-order meta-representations during dialogue (except in highly unusual circumstances). So when A utters *Shall we go to the Kalpna?* and B responds *Where?*, B's response indicates that B meta-represents that A and B are misaligned. B's response leads to A's clarification (*The Indian restaurant*), which typically leads to alignment and meta-representation of alignment. This potentially iterative process is central to Chapter 8 and demonstrates how (first-order) alignment and (second-order) meta-representation relate to each other. Notice that they never construct higher-order representations. Even if *B* did not understand *A*'s clarification, *B* would query the clarification (*You mean the one with the buffet?*), but *B* would still meta-represent misalignment only of their beliefs about the restaurant's identity. *B* would not meta-represent that they are not aligned on their meta-representations (i.e. that *A* meta-represents that they are aligned about the restaurants' identity, and that *B* meta-represents that they are not aligned). There is no need for such third-order representation (any more than there would be if they were aligned). In fact, there is an iterative process, but this process is 'externalized' – it is the dialogue itself.

It is of course possible for a successful reference to require higher-order representations (in highly unusual circumstances), as pointed out by Clark and Marshall (1978). But the need for such representations is almost entirely removed by conversation. Interlocutors who suspect misalignment simply ask for clarification, and such clarification depends on exactly what the interlocutors believe (see Chapter 8). If they did not do so, they would rapidly exceed their processing abilities. In sum, interlocutors do not make regular use of representations incorporating common ground during conversations. But we should note that dialogue is affected by conventions – for example, what responses are appropriate in a given situation within a particular culture – and such conventions relate closely to common ground (see Chapter 11).

7.5   Cooperative Joint Activity and the Goal of Conversation

In Chapter 4, we noted that the interlocutors both have the goal that they both understand each other via communication – in other words, that they communicate successfully. In relation to our framework, *A* has the goal that *A* and *B* become aligned and believes that *B* also has this goal. Similarly, *B* has the goal that *A* and *B* become aligned and believes that *A* also has this goal. In other words, *A* meta-represents that *A* and *B* are aligned with respect to this goal, as does *B*. This *goal-to-communicate* is represented in each interlocutor's game model. During conversation, it has an m-tag. If *A* wishes to engage *B* in communication, then *A* represents *goal-to-communicate* without the tag. If *A* says *Can I ask you a question?* and *B* responds *OK*, then *A* adds the m-tag (and *B* establishes the same representation).

At the 'top' level, dialogue is a 'game of pure cooperation' (following Lewis, 1969), in which interlocutors are committing to the goal of successful communication. In a cooperative joint activity, each individual is committed to the success of the activity. In addition, each represents the roles that each individual plays. Roughly speaking, each individual has to act in particular ways and has to 'manage' their partner, for example instructing their partner on what they need to do at a particular point and re-directing them if they stray off course (see Bratman, 1992). In other words, the goal-to-communicate, when it is tagged, is a joint intention (Bratman, 1992; cf. Tuomela & Miller, 1988; Searle, 1990), and it involves commitment by both interlocutors.

The goal-to-communicate is reflected in interlocutors' commitment to dialogue games. So when *A* asks *Where are we going for lunch?*, she is instructing *B* that his role in the game is to provide an answer. If *B* answers appropriately, then he is fulfilling his role and supporting the game's success. If *B* does not provide an appropriate answer, then it is *A*'s responsibility to 'manage' *B*'s behaviour. For example, *B* might respond *eh?* if he does not hear correctly and it is then *A*'s responsibility to repeat the question. In this example, *A* initiates an information-seeking game and makes sure that *B* joins the game by acting appropriately. If an interlocutor wilfully fails to respond appropriately, then at some point the cooperative joint activity collapses.

We also claim that interlocutors have the goal of aligning situation models – more specifically, that they want both them and their partner to construct aligned situation models in which critical elements are m-tagged. This condition is obviously correct for straightforward conversations, where interlocutors wish to understand the topic of conversation in the same way. In rational arguments, interlocutors seek alignment but they compete over what the object of alignment is. For example, *A* claims that Jane is a spy, *B* insists that she was framed, *A* presents several pieces of evidence, and *B* tries to refute each of them in turn. Clearly, they initially misalign over whether their situation models represent 'Jane is a spy' versus 'Jane was framed', but it is *A*'s goal that *A* and *B* end up aligning on the former and *B*'s goal that they end up aligning on the latter. Note that *A* might know that Jane was framed but want to incriminate Jane (because she doesn't like her). In this case, we propose that *A* represents 'Jane is a spy' in her situation model (and uses this as the basis for her utterance), but also represents 'Jane was framed' as part of her background knowledge. (In other words, people do not need to believe the contents of their models.)[23]

So *A* has the intention of aligning *A* and *B*'s models and has the commitment to manage *B*'s intention of aligning *A* and *B*'s models. *A* seeks to align their models by making contributions that support alignment, for example providing contributions that *B* can understand and which are likely to lead to their models becoming more similar (such as providing information that *A* knows but *B* doesn't know, or helping *B* to clarify or disambiguate his situation model). In addition, *A* manages *B*'s attempts to align, in particular when *B* goes off track. For example, if *A* knows that *B* is misrepresenting something that *A* believes

---

[23] When teachers simplify complicated concepts for students, their situation models become aligned over the simplified concepts. The teachers also represent the more complicated aspects of the concepts as part of their background knowledge.

she is representing accurately (e.g. misinterpreting who *A* is talking about), then *A* attempts to bring *B* back on track (e.g. clarifying who she is talking about).

7.6   Conclusion

In this chapter we have discussed the alignment of dialogue models (situation models and game models) and related them to reference, background knowledge and linguistic alignment. We have also discussed the way that interlocutors meta-represent alignment and considered its role in developing the shared workspace and driving alignment. Our framework allows interlocutors to interact in a way that supports communicative success without requiring extensive higher-order representations.

Part III

Using the Shared Workspace Efficiently

8   Saying Just Enough

In the previous chapters, we interpreted conversational success in terms of alignment. But to explain the process of alignment, we must return to how interlocutors use the shared workspace. To do this, we must always remember that the shared workspace is a highly limited resource, and that this is a consequence of individuals' cognitive limitations. The shared workspace contains only those elements that the interlocutors can manipulate, monitor, and predict and be confident that their partners can also manipulate, monitor and predict at the same time.[1]

Given this limitation, interlocutors need to use the workspace efficiently. And because it is a shared resource the interlocutors must ration its use, portioning out the content of their contributions – giving feedback when it is needed, being as succinct as possible. To do this, they aim to say just enough between them to achieve alignment. But they also need to use the time available on the shared workspace efficiently – minimizing the gaps between each other's contributions, coordinating the timing of B's response with the timing of A's contribution. By efficiency, we mean joint efficiency, which corresponds to what Clark and Wilkes-Gibbs (1986) call least collaborative effort (see also Schober & Brennan, 2003 on 'least communicative effort'). Ideally, individuals engaged in cooperative joint activity seek to minimize overall effort (rather than their individual efforts). And interlocutors do the same, both with respect to the content of their contributions and their timing. In other words, interlocutors take on a commitment to efficiency as part of the cooperative joint activity.[2] We now discuss the efficient distribution of effort in relation to content, and turn to the efficient use of time in Chapter 9.

We ended Chapter 5 with a model of the dialogue system (see Figure 8.1). In successful dialogue, what goes on above the line mirrors what goes on

---

[1] When two people design a project using a real whiteboard, they can add words and diagrams only to the extent that each can attend to them and be confident that their partner could also attend to them. The number of elements is very limited, and the same is true of our shared workspace.

[2] What interlocutors commit to is related to Grice's (1975) maxims of conversation (most particularly, the maxim of quantity). However, they do so jointly as part of a cooperative joint activity – that is, they both intend that they jointly aim for least collaborative effort.

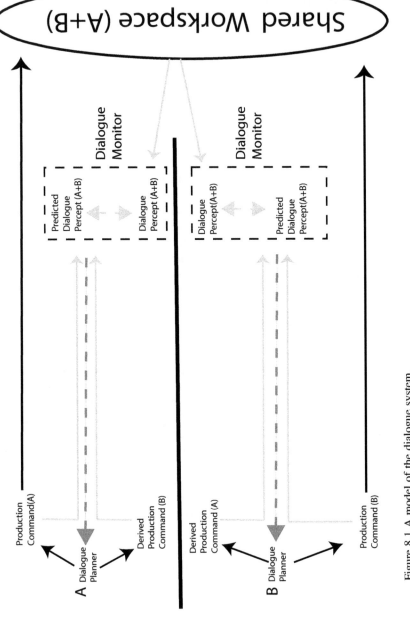

Figure 8.1 A model of the dialogue system.
Reproduced from Figure 5.5.

below the line. *A*'s dialogue models are captured by the dialogue planner and their links to the production commands and derived production commands, and therefore these components of the figure are aligned in successful dialogue. But in addition, aligned interlocutors predict (via simulation) and monitor similarly. So when the shared workspace contains *you're one along uh huh* (i.e. *A*'s contribution underlined), they both compute the same dialogue percept(A + B). After *B* utters *you're one along*, *A* prepares an affirmation and if *B* is sufficiently aligned with *A* then *B* predicts that *A* will prepare an affirmation. If so, *A*'s production command(A) will match *B*'s derived production command(A). Hence, they will be matched with respect the relevant pair of light grey arrows. Moreover, their predicted dialogue percepts will also be matched, as will be the discrepancy (prediction error) that feeds back to their dialogue planners (dashed dark grey arrow).

Of course, interlocutors are not always sufficiently aligned that they can make such accurate predictions. (And even if they can predict affirmation, they might predict *OK* rather than *uh-huh*.) But in general, interlocutors that are better aligned (with respect to dialogue models) will predict each other better and be less surprised by each other's contributions. A consequence is that good prediction (or indeed postdiction) provides evidence for alignment and therefore supports the meta-representation of alignment. Conversely, serious failure to predict leads to surprise and hence the potential meta-representation of misalignment.[3]

In Chapter 5, we discussed how interlocutors used the shared workspace to jointly control the dialogue, and we begin by relating this discussion to alignment. We then consider the way in which interlocutors distribute their contributions (because they both have to contribute to the process of alignment). We then show how they monitor joint contributions in the workspace, use it to provide what we term commentaries on the alignment process, and act on the basis of those commentaries. An important consequence of this process is succinctness, which minimizes the use of the workspace.

8.1   Cycles of Successful Alignment

Let us consider a simple, successful cycle of alignment and the mechanisms that underlie this process, in relation both to Figure 8.1 and to the meta-representation of alignment. In Example 8.1, we assume that it is lunch time

---

[3] As mentioned in relation to joint activity more generally (Section 3.5), meta-representation of alignment may lead to the feeling of joint agency. In most dialogue, the interlocutors do not simultaneously make the same contributions and therefore the lines emanating from the production commands are not matched, and so the feeling of joint agency may be weakened. Perhaps a stronger feeling of joint agency might occur when two addressees provide the same answer at the same time, or when two people speak chorically.

Example 8.1

A: *Where are we going for lunch?*
B: *Kalpna*
A: *Thanks for letting me know.*

---

and that *B* has decided on his own where *A* and *B* are going for lunch; *A* suspects that *B* has decided this but is not party to *B*'s decision. Thus, they both meta-represent misalignment of the situation model (with respect to the restaurant).

On the basis of her meta-representation, *A* plans an information-seeking game to determine where *A* and *B* are going to eat and thus places her question in the shared workspace(A + B). When *A* asks her question, she invites *B* to take part in an information-seeking game and predicts that *B* will accept this invitation. *B* does accept this invitation and therefore meta-represents dialogue game alignment.[4] This combination of dialogue game alignment and situation model misalignment leads *B* to utter *Kalpna* – a move which is consistent with the dialogue game but which should remove situation model misalignment. *B*'s response is triggered by the feedback from the dialogue monitor (we discuss its timing in Chapter 9). When *B*'s dialogue planner receives this feedback, it generates the production command which places *Kalpna* into the shared workspace.

In turn, *A* predicts that *B* would mention some restaurant or other, via the right-facing grey arrow from the derived production command(B). *A* might do no more than this, or she might predict a set of different restaurants (each with a probability). *A* performs dialogue monitoring and generates a prediction error that feeds back to her dialogue planner. This discrepancy can be managed covertly (not triggering a query) because it is consistent with the situation model (either because Kalpna is a restaurant, or because it is one of the predicted set of restaurants). Therefore *A*'s next production command simply leads to the final move in the information-seeking game, indicating its completion.

In our example, *A*'s meta-representation of misalignment motivates her to propose an information-seeking game. *A* now meta-represents alignment and this meta-representation motivates *A*'s conclusion of the game. In other words,

---

[4] *B* might not predict *A*'s question, and if so they would be temporarily misaligned with respect to the information-seeking game. If *A* regarded this misalignment as problematic, then *A* could use a pre-sequence such as *Can I ask you a question?* If *B* responded *Yes*, then *A* and *B* would be aligned on the upcoming game (and would both meta-represent this alignment).

meta-representation motivated both of *A*'s contributions. *A* and *B* have successfully enacted a cooperative joint activity via the shared workspace. The misalignment and its meta-representation do not imply any failure of communication – the game is offered and accepted, each contribution is straightforwardly understood, and the situation models become aligned with respect to new information. Thus, the interaction 'stayed on track' and involved no 'detours'.

Dialogue can also 'stay on track' when interlocutors are negotiating with each other. In Example 8.2, neither *A* nor *B* has determined where they should go for lunch. When *A* gets hungry, she instantiates 'lunch at X' in her situation model and assumes that *B* does not also instantiate 'lunch at X'. She thus represents 'lunch at X' without including an m-tag and therefore meta-

---

Example 8.2

A: *Where shall we go for lunch?*
B: *How about Kalpna?*
A: *Agreed.*

---

represents misalignment. To correct this misalignment, she initiates what we call a negotiation game. *B* accepts by contributing his move to the game, uttering *How about Kalpna?* *A* completes the game by accepting *B*'s proposal (a *confirmatory response*), and again there are no 'detours'.

To capture the distinction between proposals and their acceptances, we treat acceptances as m-tagged with very high confidence but proposals as m-tagged with low confidence (see Chapter 7). Until accepted, proposals remain 'under discussion' (see Ginzburg & Sag's, 2000, use of Questions Under Discussion or QUDs) and the interlocutors therefore do not meta-represent alignment over the proposal. At the end of this exchange, *A* and *B* both represent LUNCH-AT-KALPNA-token-m. Before *B*'s contribution, *B* represents LUNCH-AT-KALPNA-token (i.e. not m-tagged) and assumes that *A* does not represent LUNCH-AT-KALPNA-token (and note that we omit the m-tag when confidence is low). Immediately after *B*'s contribution, he still represents LUNCH-AT-KALPNA-token, as his move constitutes a proposal rather than a statement of belief. For it to become a shared belief, it must be accepted by *A* (as part of the game), at which point *A* and *B* simultaneously construct LUNCH-AT-KALPNA-token-m (and they become aligned and meta-represent alignment). Again, they have successfully executed a cooperative joint activity.[5]

---

[5] This process of moving from representations that are not m-tagged to one that are m-tagged relates to Clark's (1996) notion of grounding; see Section 7.4. If *A* and *B* have individually decided that they should go to the Kalpna without realizing that their partner has decided the

As we have noted, speakers vary in their confidence about m-tagging a representation. If *A* says *We are going to the Kalpna for lunch*, then *A* m-tags LUNCH-AT-KALPNA-token with high confidence if she assumes that *B* will obey without question (perhaps because they go there every week), but *A* m-tags it with low confidence if she thinks it quite likely that *B* will refuse to obey her. In dialogue, speakers often do not m-tag their contributions with high confidence until they have some evidence of acceptance. The same issues relate to the understanding of words and their interpretation – speakers may presume that their words are understood as intended immediately they are uttered, or they may require some evidence of acceptance. In a doctor-patient consultation, the doctor may assume that her advice will be taken, or may require some form of acceptance from the patient. In Keysar and Henly (2002), speakers meta-represented alignment with their addressee on 72 per cent of trials (and hence m-tagged at this point) – but note that their judgements were not spontaneous (i.e. they were elicited).[6]

In straightforward ('ideal') dialogue, both alignment and its meta-representation go through successful cycles. Interlocutors make new contributions that temporarily break alignment, but where the canonical use of dialogue games directly re-establishes alignment and its meta-representation. Focal alignment comes and goes, but global alignment grows (i.e. with respect to the aspects of long-term working memory that are linked to the situation model). The interlocutors' aim is to extend their global alignment and the temporary focal misalignment is a necessary 'cost' to achieve this aim. This process of managing misalignment is a standard component of successful dialogue as a form of cooperative joint activity. And in such 'ideal' dialogues, every utterance contributes to alignment – saying 'just enough' means contributing in an orderly manner.

8.2   The Role of Commentaries on Alignment

Our discussion so far is limited in two ways. First, we have considered dialogue only in terms of contributions whose primary role is to add

---

same thing, they both represent LUNCH-AT-KALPNA-token; if they subsequently discover that they have the same goal, then they both represent LUNCH-AT-KALPNA-token-m.

[6] We have discussed m-tagging in relation to the interpretation of interlocutors' utterances, as represented in their situation models. But we have noted that interlocutors may represent inferences within their models. For example, when *A* utters *John drove Mary to London* (Chapter 7, Example 7.2), we discussed whether *A* and *B* specify the vehicle (car, van, etc.) in their models. *A* might represent car and presume that *B* also represented car, in which case *A* would m-tag the car token; alternatively *A* might make no assumption about *B*'s representation of the vehicle, in which case *A* would not m-tag the car token. The more apparent it is to *A* that the information is known to both *A* and *B*, the more likely it is that *A* will m-tag the information. In general, information in explicit focus is likely to be m-tagged, and information in implicit focus is less likely to be m-tagged.

(informational) content – contributions that directly lead to the development of interlocutors' situation models. Second, we have not considered dialogue that involves detours. We therefore now consider contributions whose primary role is to comment on the progress of the dialogue, and then show how they apply to dialogue that 'stays on track' and dialogue that 'goes off track'.

Dialogue rarely involves long, uninterrupted contributions from each interlocutor in turn. Rather than simply listen in silence when it is not their turn to speak, addressees produce queries, interjections, acknowledgements of agreement or approval, and they also nod, raise their eyebrows and express disgust. These contributions are often concurrent with the speaker's turn – the addressee does not typically interrupt the speaker and does not 'take the floor'. Their purpose is to control the progress of the dialogue on the basis of the meta-representation of alignment. We refer to such contributions as *commentaries* and treat them as having a *commentary function*. This commentary function does not add content to situation models, but rather relates to the m-tagging of those models. Importantly, commentaries often have an *informational function* as well. For example, replying in an incredulous tone of voice (or extremely slowly) adds new information but at the same time reduces confidence in m-tagging.

Speakers are actively affected by such commentaries. In Section 7.1.4, we noted that Clark and Wilkes-Gibbs (1986) found that directors reduced the length of repeated descriptions of geometric figures, under conditions when matchers provided commentaries (see also Krauss & Weinheimer, 1966). But Hupet and Chantraine (1992) found no length reduction for tangrams when there was no matcher to provide commentary. Moreover, Bavelas et al. (2000) had narrators describe close-call stories to addressees who either provided commentaries or did not. In one study, addressees were instructed to count the number of *t*s produced by the narrator. This task required concentration and meant that they did not respond normally, for example not expressing surprise or excitement at moments of high drama. When the addressee did not provide commentaries, narrators told their stories less well, particularly at what should have been the dramatic ending.

Evidence that commentary helps the interlocutors to align globally comes from a study concerned primarily with iterative learning (Fay et al., 2018). An instructor described a route through a map to a route-follower in a dialogue condition (in which the follower could provide commentary) or a (non-interactive) monologue condition (in which no commentary was allowed). Followers reproduced the route more accurately in the dialogue than the monologue condition, and therefore we assume that their representation of the route on the map (i.e. their global situation model) was better aligned with the instructor's representation.

In contrast, it does not appear that commentaries affect (first-order) focal alignment. As we have discussed (Chapter 6), alignment is primarily driven by priming – a largely automatic tendency for interlocutors to repeat aspects of structure and interpretation. And priming occurs in monologue (when there is no commentary) to a similar extent to dialogue (e.g. Pickering & Ferreira, 2008). Of course, priming can decay over time, perhaps partly as a result of intervening language, but it can last for a long time, so that speakers tend to reuse a word, structure, or interpretation that they have heard some time before (e.g. Branigan et al., 2011; Garrod & Doherty, 1994; Hartsuiker et al., 2008). But also a commentary is not necessary for alignment, with most experimental studies showing alignment under conditions when the interlocutors produce no commentaries, and there is no evidence of commentaries enhancing alignment.

Commentaries (with respect to their commentary function) are therefore important to conversational success, and such success is of course defined in terms of alignment. But they do not *directly* contribute to alignment, by moderating priming effects – they do not act on the alignment channels. Instead, they act over meta-representations of alignment. Interlocutors use such meta-representations to drive their subsequent contributions by managing their contributions to the shared workspace and, more generally, facilitating distributed control of the dialogue. We now consider commentaries indicating high confidence in alignment and commentaries indicating low confidence.

8.2.1   Positive Commentaries and Alignment

A *positive commentary* indicates high confidence in alignment. The most straightforward example is an acknowledgement. We argue that positive commentaries such as acknowledgements influence dialogue control in two ways – by supporting efficient alignment, and by promoting succinctness. Together, these influences mean that acknowledgements facilitate the goal of least collaborative effort. We discuss alignment in this section, and return to succinctness in Section 8.3.

An addressee can use an acknowledgement to indicate that he believes he has achieved some degree of focal alignment with the speaker. He can utter short vocal contributions such as *yeah*, *OK*, and *mm* – contributions which comment on the speaker's current or immediately preceding utterance. He can produce a gesture of acknowledgement such as a nod. He can produce longer acknowledgements, for example by repeating part of the utterance being accepted, as in *A: I'm at a little place called Ellenthorpe. B: Ellenthorpe* (Fernández & Ginzburg, 2002). By repeating this constituent, the addressee is indicating meta-representation of alignment on *Ellenthorpe* (and therefore supporting its m-tagging). Such repetition of course involves repetition from speaker to addressee, which also has a direct effect on linguistic alignment (roughly, via the activation of the word *Ellenthorpe*). In general, acknowledgements are very common: in their analysis of part of the British National Corpus, Fernández and Ginzburg found that 55 per cent of non-sentential utterances were acknowledgements.

The addressee's acknowledgement indicates that he meta-represents some degree of alignment. This leads the speaker in turn to meta-represent some degree of alignment. And then these meta-representations of alignment guide both interlocutors' subsequent contributions. *A* typically does not initially m-tag her representation of her contribution with high confidence. *B* understands *A* and m-tags his representation (because understanding means that he believes he has the same understanding as *A*). When *B* produces his acknowledgement, *A* m-tags her representation (as she presumes alignment).

Such acknowledgements affect the way that dialogue is controlled. Informally, an acknowledgement indicates alignment and the interlocutors use this evidence to determine how the conversation should proceed. In terms of Figure 8.1, *B* monitors *A*'s contribution in relation to his prediction about *A*'s contribution, and feeds the prediction error back to his dialogue planner. If there is no need for *B* to modify his plan, then *B* constructs a production command corresponding to an acknowledgement such as *Yeah*. *A* predicts that *B* will understand her contribution, and when *A* hears *B* utter *Yeah*, *A* registers little prediction error. She therefore does not modify her dialogue planner and constructs her next production command as originally intended.

We have treated acknowledgements as indicating some degree of focal alignment. But exactly what aspects of focal alignment can vary. If *A* utters *John drove Mary to London*, and *B* says *Yeah*, then *B*'s acknowledgement might mean that he has m-tagged the complete (focal) situation model. This is probably the most common use of acknowledgement. However, addressees can also acknowledge components of a focal situation model. *B*'s *Yeah* might instead mean that he has m-tagged London (something that would be more likely if London were a little-known village). Note that *A* and *B* might m-tag different things – *A* interprets *B* as acknowledging the interpretation of the complete utterance, whereas *B* in fact intended to acknowledge *London* alone. (In such a case, both interlocutors would have mistakenly assigned m-tags.) Acknowledgements are therefore a potentially blunt instrument.

Notice that alignment does not necessarily mean agreement. For instance, a policeman could acknowledge a suspect's description of events without accepting its truth. However, through the process of understanding the suspect's story, the policeman's situation model becomes aligned with the suspect's (and the policeman and the suspect might meta-represent alignment). Likewise, I might make a dubious intellectual or political argument, and you might respond with *OK* after each assertion. In this case, you are perhaps indicating that you are following the argument and therefore aligning on its content, not that you agree with it.

Thus, successful alignment is indicated by acknowledgement rather than acceptance. In fact, many contributions (e.g. many uses of *Yeah* or *OK*) are acknowledgements but it is sometimes unclear whether they indicate acceptance as well (i.e. they have a clear commentary function but their informational function is not clear). So long as they are acknowledgements, they lead to meta-representations of alignment. But note that some contributions merely indicate hearing the speaker, and if so, they do not indicate alignment of situation models.

We have argued that acknowledgements indicate meta-representation of alignment and also control the dialogue. Some acknowledgements also provide additional information about the contribution. Thus, the response *brilliant* is an acknowledgement that also indicates that the addressee likes what was said. Some commentaries are simultaneously acknowledgements and continuers (which have an additional function) – for example, *Go on* might indicate that the addressee has aligned with the speaker but also strongly encourage elaboration. But on other occasions, the addressee might encourage elaboration without acknowledgement, as the addressee is not confident that he has aligned with the speaker. For example, *Please expand* is a request for more information, and does not necessarily imply confidence in alignment. The decision about which commentary (if any) to produce is driven by the addressee's plan and by conventions about what response is appropriate, and plays a more significant role in relation to negative commentaries.

8.2.2   Negative Commentaries and Recovery from Misalignment

An addressee can use a *negative commentary* to indicate low confidence in alignment. Simple examples are interjections such as *eh?*, *what?*, and *mm?* (where the interrogative intonation distinguishes it from *mm* as a positive commentary), as well as gestures such as a head-shake or a look of puzzlement. However, negative commentaries are often more extensive, in part because they are used to diagnose a source of misalignment. These negative commentaries affect the process of alignment in a different (and perhaps more complicated) way from positive commentaries and are typically used to bring the dialogue 'back on track'. Negative commentaries are typically interjections – that is, contributions that interrupt the speaker and often lead to reformulations (see Drew, 1997).

We illustrate with Example 8.3, taken from Horton and Gerrig (2005).

Example 8.3

A: and um it– you know it's rea– it's it was really good and of course she teaches
         theology that was another thing
B: mm
A: I– m– I– Isabelle
B: oh that's great.

B's use of *mm* appears to be a negative commentary, because *A* treats it as an indication of failure to align. *A* presumably infers the locus of difficulty as the underspecified reference *she*. Specifically, *A* constructs a situation model in which Isabelle teaches theology. *B* assumes that *A* has a person in mind – a situation model containing a particular person – but *B* cannot identify that person. Therefore *B* cannot construct a complete model (i.e. one containing all necessary components), assumes that *A*'s utterance is based on a complete model, and therefore meta-represents misalignment. That misalignment in turn triggers *B*'s production command that leads to *mm*. *A* is surprised by *mm* (because it creates a large prediction error, as *A* did not expect a negative commentary) and therefore modifies her dialogue planner, constructs a new production command, and produces the correction *I– m– I– Isabelle*.

But why does *A* produce this correction? In fact, *A* realizes that *A* and *B* are not aligned (probably because *B*'s model is incomplete or otherwise problematic). For *A* to communicate successfully and achieve alignment, she has to express her model in a different way. This is an example of how individuals performing a cooperative joint activity are committed to keeping it on track.

A has two concerns: to determine the locus of difficulty and to produce an appropriate correction. To determine the locus, *A* draws on two aspects of *B*'s negative commentary – its timing and its content – and on the context. In (3), *B* simply utters *mm*, which has little content (beyond being a negative commentary). But *A* can determine from its timing that it must refer to something about *A*'s immediately preceding contribution (i.e. because it is a commentary on focal alignment). In addition, *A* must pay attention to her own contribution, in order to determine where difficulty might lie.[7] In this case, *A* assumes that *B* cannot resolve *she* and therefore plans a correction.[8]

A needs to produce a correction that is likely to re-establish focal alignment. In this case, *A* wishes *B* to align on Isabelle teaching theology, has determined that *B* has not identified Isabelle, and therefore decides to name her. When *A* utters *I– m– I– Isabelle*, *B* produces an acknowledgement, and they meta-represent alignment (i.e. m-tag the focal situation model with high confidence). In Pickering and Garrod (2004), we suggested that such expansions are likely to be the first approach to resolving misalignment.

So far, we have considered simple negative commentaries that do little more than indicate failure to align (at a particular time). But negative commentaries

---

[7] *A* might consider potential loci in turn, for example going backwards from the point of interruption. *A* is in fact initiating self-repair, but where the trigger is caused by the addressee rather than the speaker herself (cf. Levelt, 1983).

[8] If *B* were a child, *A* might infer that *B* did not understand *theology* (and change it to *about God*). *B*'s identity is therefore a potentially relevant aspect of the context.

can of course be more diagnostic and give the speaker at least some clue to the specific problem. Consider Example 8.4 from Drew (1997):[9]

Example 8.4

HAL: an' Leslie 't was marv'lous (.) D'you know he had (.) **forty nine g'rillas**. .hh th-there. (b) (.) br[eeding in ( )

LESLEY: [pf– f– **Forty nine wha:t?**
HAL: **G'rillas.**
LESLEY: .hh Oh ye-s?

In this example, Hal utters something highly implausible (*g'rillas*) and Lesley responds with a negative commentary (*Forty nine wha:t?*). This commentary is longer and more informative than *mm* in (3), but it has (at least) two possible interpretations. Lesley could produce this commentary because she failed to linguistically align with Hal – that is, he represented a particular word (*g'rillas*) and she failed to align on this representation. Alternatively, she aligned on the word (i.e. its semantics, syntax and phonology) but could not use it to construct a situation model that she plausibly believed could correspond to Hal's situation model. It appears most likely that Hal interpreted Lesley in the former way and so restated the problematic word (though from Lesley's response it is not clear whether Hal's contribution led to alignment).

This example illustrates how negative commentaries can lead to complex processes of recovery. In fact, Lesley instigates an embedded information-seeking game (using *Forty nine wha:t?*) and Hal complies by providing what he assumes is the appropriate information (*g'rillas*). We can explicate this embedded game itself in terms of the control mechanism in Figure 8.2. Lesley predicts that Hal will mention something that *he* might have forty-nine of (e.g. a small common animal), so that her predicted dialogue percept has the associated semantics (small common animal). But then Hal puts *g'rillas* into the shared workspace so that Lesley's dialogue percept has an associated semantics (i.e. for gorillas) that is incompatible with the predicted semantics (small common animals). This leads to Lesley modifying her dialogue planner and constructing a negative commentary that focuses Hal on the problematic word *g'rillas*. (As noted, we do not know exactly what Lesley meant.) Hal does expect a negative commentary, processes Lesley's contribution to the shared workspace (i.e. *Forty nine wha:t?*), and feeds the discrepancy back to his planner, causing him to stop the main narrative and prepare an appropriate response (i.e. as part of the

---

[9] *(.)* indicates brief pause; *[* indicates overlap; *:* indicates lengthening; *.hh* indicates long inhalation. We have added bold font for illustrative purposes.

embedded game). Meanwhile, Lesley uses her derived production command to predict Hal's potential responses, one of which is presumably *G'rillas*. Lesley's final utterance appears to accept Hal's response, thereby ending the detour, and encouraging Hal to continue the narrative.

As with acknowledgements, negative commentaries (when successfully resolved) ultimately lead to alignment. But rather than simply providing an indication that the interlocutors can m-tag their situation models, they indicate that m-tagging is not possible and that the speaker needs to reformulate if she wishes to m-tag her contribution – that is, to be confident that she is understood. In this sense, the negative commentary leads to alignment, but in a less direct way than an acknowledgement. The decision about which negative commentary to make is driven both by communicative goals (as we have discussed) but also by conventions (see Chapter 11), for example in relation to politeness (and indeed it is sometimes regarded as inappropriate to comment at all, in which case misalignment may persist).

Finally, the negative commentary is also linguistically aligned with part of Hal's contribution. This linguistic alignment itself helps Hal identify the problem – *Forty nine wha:t?* must relate to *forty nine g'rillas* (whereas a simple *what?* might instead relate to *br[eeding]*). This example shows the tight interrelationship between alignment and commentary. In fact, the relationship between alignment and commentary can also occur for positive commentaries: In many languages (e.g. Mandarin), respondents can give an affirmative answer to a question by repeating part of the question (e.g. the verb).

8.3   Commentaries Promote Saying Just Enough

Successful dialogue requires alignment, but it also involves collaborative efficiency. The shared workspace is a highly limited resource, so the interlocutors need to carry out their business of aligning their dialogue models in a manner that is compatible with this limitation. In other words, they should jointly contribute in as efficient a manner as they can – as a pair, they should say just enough but no more. Each interlocutor should therefore aim for succinctness (so long as their partner can align without extensive elaboration). The role of commentaries is to control the dialogue so that it leads to efficient alignment. We illustrate how this comes about with respect to positive and negative commentaries in turn, and also consider commentaries with hybrid functions.

8.3.1   *Positive Commentaries Promote Succinctness*

In Chapter 7, we noted that Clark and Wilkes-Gibbs (1986) had pairs of people converse about the arrangement of complex figures (tangrams) such as

1. All right, the next one looks like a person who's ice skating, except they're sticking two arms out in front.
2. Um, the next one's the person ice skating that has two arms?
3. The fourth one is the person ice skating, with two arms.
4. The next one's the ice skater.
5. The fourth one's the ice skater.
6. The ice skater.

Figure 8.2 A sequence of descriptions of Figure 7.2 (from Clark & Wilkes-Gibbs, 1986, p. 12).

Figure 7.2. On six successive occasions, the director described these figures to the matcher (along with a set of other figures), and the matcher identified each figure and provided acknowledgement to the director. Over the trials (1–6), the director's descriptions became more and more succinct (see Figure 8.2). Following Hupet and Chantraine (1992) we infer that succinctness was due to acknowledgements, which we assume occurred at the end of each turn.

The fact that the matcher identified the appropriate tangram on each occasion indicated that the director and matcher were focally aligned – that is, aligned with respect to the description of the particular tangram (Figure 7.2). In other words, on each of the six trials, they were aligned with respect to the link between the description and the situation model.

By providing an acknowledgement at the end of each description, the matcher indicated meta-representation of focal alignment. In more detail, the director provides a description for the tangram (on each occasion). The shared workspace contains this description (as sign vehicle) and the tangram itself (as the referent of that description) – they are now in joint attention and can be jointly manipulated. By providing the description, the director proposes a situation model (e.g. in 1, containing tokens corresponding to a person, arms, act of skating etc.) that corresponds to Figure 7.2. The matcher then establishes the same situation model as the director and provides acknowledgement, which the director takes as an indication of alignment. At this point, both director and matcher m-tag their situation models – they meta-represent focal alignment over the contents of this model. This same process occurs on each subsequent trial, with focal alignment being re-established on each occasion.

So why do A's descriptions become shorter? Recall that the interlocutors attempt to minimize collaborative effort, and in this case A helps bring this about by producing descriptions that are as short as possible while allowing B to identify the referent without difficulty. A provides the long description in (1), gets an acknowledgement and meta-represents focal alignment. But (1) led to a complex situation model and an unwieldly associated description, with some components of the description being discriminatory (e.g. *ice skating*) and others not being discriminatory (e.g. *person*). More discriminatory components tend to be retained in the global situation model, as they have more activation in long-term working memory. On subsequent trials, the director finds it easier to recover discriminatory components and describes them first. If the matcher can align on the description at this point, then he may quickly acknowledge, and the director and matcher can assume successful focal alignment. The game is then complete and the director can move on. On subsequent trials, the director can predict alignment on the basis of a more succinct contribution, and the matcher is more likely to acknowledge earlier. This process demonstrates distributed control across the dialogue, with the director being concerned primarily with providing information and the matcher providing commentary.

Of course the referring expressions do not simply become more succinct – they retain aspects of linguistic form. For example, (1–3) in Figure 8.2 retain *arms*, and (1–6) retain *ice* (and *skating* and *skater* are of course linguistically related). As the director and matcher understand each other, we can assume that they are linguistically aligned. The process of simplification is therefore affected by the mechanisms of alignment (including within-speaker priming) as well as by mechanisms of its meta-representation.

In the later rounds, the director uses *the ice skater* as a routine that directly recovers the tangram in Figure 7.2, and the director and the matcher are aligned on this routine. This routine does not involve compositional analysis (e.g. there is no need to compose or decompose *person* and *ice skating*) but rather points directly to the referent (arguably as a rigid designator). Specifically, it is a dialogue routine because it refers in this way for the purposes of the current dialogue (i.e. the referential communication task) – it is established as discussed above and presumably eventually fades when the interlocutors have finished. Alignment on this routine is global – the interlocutors can use *the ice skater* to refer to this tangram at any point in the dialogue, and when they do so, their partner would also activate the tangram directly. Thus, one effect of acknowledgements is to promote dialogue routines (i.e. to establish, at least temporarily, new entries into the interlocutors' lexica). And because they point directly to the referent, they are efficient (in that they reduce communicative effort).

Clark and Wilkes-Gibbs (1986) pointed out that the sequence of descriptions in Figure 8.2 was atypical. More frequently, the director produced part of a description, the matcher acknowledged and the director continued with the remainder. In such cases, the director refers to part of a (potentially complex) situation model and the matcher acknowledges that part, so that they both m-tag that part of the model. The director then refers to another part of the model and so on. An example of this is *You're one along: uh huh: and one up?* (Garrod & Anderson, 1987). In many cases, the director pauses to elicit an acknowledgement (which of course makes the acknowledgement itself more predictable), but acknowledgements can also occur without being elicited and can of course occur concurrently with the speaker's contribution. These examples indicate that the location of the acknowledgement is informative – it indicates that the addressee is acknowledging a contribution that has imme-diately preceded the acknowledgement.

8.3.2   Negative Commentaries Lead Initially to Expansion

In Example 8.3, *A* responded to *B*'s negative commentary (*mm*) by expanding *she* to *I– m– I– Isabelle*, and such immediate expansions are a typical response to a negative commentary. The speaker realizes that it may be necessary to put more information into the shared workspace to achieve focal alignment.

In Example 1.1, *B* first asked *A* to describe her position in the maze, and *A* responded:

> 4———**A:** Right : two along from the bottom one up:
> 5———**B:** Two along from the bottom, which side?
> 6———**A:** The left : going from left to right in the second box.

In (4), *A* described her position in terms of her situation model of the maze. (It is unlikely that *A* regards her position as manifest.) On the basis of (4), *B* could not determine *A*'s position and therefore meta-represented that *A* and *B* were not aligned, and therefore produced the negative commentary in (5). This commentary is structurally similar to Lesley's use of *Forty nine wha:t?* above, with *two along from the bottom* involving repetition and providing context and *which side?* indicating the locus of misalignment.

For *A* to communicate successfully and achieve alignment, she has to express her situation model in a different way. Thus she has to expand on her contribution, because what she has said so far is insufficient. In (6), she directed her response to address the locus of misalignment. Her expansion is quite extensive – it does not merely involve the simple response *The left*, but involves an attempt to describe the model explicitly.

The conversation continued:

> 7———**B:** You're in the second box.
> 8———**A:** One up :(*1 sec.*) I take it we've got identical mazes?
> 9———**B:** Yeah well : right, starting from the left, you're one along:
> 10———**A:** Uh-huh:
> 11———**B:** and one up?
> 12———**A:** Yeah, and I'm trying to get to . . .

It now appears that *A*'s expansion did not immediately solve the problem and *B* ended up describing what he took to be *A*'s position in (9) and (11). His description appears to be more successful and led to two acknowledgements from *A*, at (10) and (12), together with an appropriate continuation. It seems that B's negative commentary (at 5) led immediately to expansion (and lack of m-tagging) but led eventually to positive commentary that resulted in contraction (and m-tagging). Negative commentary resulted in a detour (involving expansion). But the detour was justified because it led to alignment on a succinct description. It may be that the interlocutors continued to use this description scheme, as was the case for many pairs in Garrod and Anderson (1987).

This example illustrates the general point that negative commentary leads to a detour – the commentary causes the speaker to meta-represent misalignment and to reformulate in order to re-establish alignment. The detour involves some form of expansion and in this sense negative commentary has an opposite effect to positive commentary.

Negative commentaries initially appear to work against succinctness, but they can eventually combine with positive commentaries to support succinctness. In Example 1.1, the interlocutors changed from *two along from the bottom one up* (4) to *one along ... and one up?* (9, 11), and after further exchanges, they ended up using succinct 'coordinate' descriptions such as *one-one* and *two-four*. (In general, interlocutors shifted towards such 'coordinate' descriptions; Garrod & Anderson, 1987.) This eventual succinctness is likely to be a consequence of the interplay between negative and positive commentaries (such as *uh-huh*; 10). In this example, the negative commentary actually led to a form of reconceptualization, which promoted succinctness. Reconceptualization also occurs when a speaker re-describes a tangram from a new perspective (e.g. *the person standing on one leg with the tail* to *ice skater*; Clark & Wilkes-Gibbs, 1986, p. 25). In sum, the negative commentary is necessary to achieve appropriate alignment, but can eventually support greater efficiency with respect to the shared workspace.

8.3.3   Contributions with Multiple Functions

It is not only positive commentaries that lead to meta-representations of alignment. As Clark and Schaefer (1989) pointed out, an addressee can indicate understanding by making an additional relevant contribution. In our terms, such a contribution has an informational function (by extending the situation model). But at the same time it has a commentary function, by indicating that the addressee meta-represents alignment with the speaker. And it does so without the speaker producing an utterance (i.e. no utterance is implemented).

Such an utterance is not needed because the new contribution itself is enough to lead to high confidence in alignment. It simultaneously allows the speaker to meta-represent alignment with the addressee and licences her to continue (i.e. in accord with her dialogue plan). For example, if A asks B a question and receives an appropriate response, then *A* can assume the question (and response) are m-tagged, and can ask another relevant question (if her plan is to interrogate *B*).

Many contributions play an informative and a commentary function. A contribution's informative function refers to the way in which it directly leads to development of the dialogue models, for example by adding new content to the situation models. So if *A* utters *Did you go away at Easter?* and *B* responds *Yeah*, then *B*'s response changes both interlocutors' situation models: *A* first represents *B*'s going away as a Question Under Discussion, and *B*'s response establishes it. But it also licences m-tagging, and also indicates that *A* can make a fresh contribution. If *A* utters *I went away at Easter* and *B* responds *Yeah*, then *B*'s response has no informative function but it does have the commentary function of licensing m-tagging and promoting a continuation.

Now consider completions. Clark and Wilkes-Gibbs (1986) reported *A: This one has uh uh . . . B: Tentworms*, in which *A* appears to be inviting *B* to describe what they are both looking at. Let us assume that *A* has a referent in mind (and that the referent is manifest). By completing *A*'s utterance, *B* indicates that he is aligning with *A*'s dialogue plan, and that *A* and *B* therefore meta-represent alignment over the situation model. *B*'s contribution also promotes a continuation from *A*. Of course, *Tentworms* also has an informational function, as it contributes to the situation model.

On other occasions, the completion need not be part of the speaker's dialogue plan. An addressee can add a continuation to a speaker's contribution, perhaps with a modifier (*A: . . . they got men and women in the same dormitory. B: With the same showers!*) or with a connective (*A: Alistair [. . .] has made himself self coordinator. B: And section engineer.*); examples from Fernández and Ginzburg (2002). In these cases, *B*'s completion has a commentary function (by indicating that *B* meta-represents alignment over *A*'s contribution) but also provides new information.

Some informative contributions have a negative commentary function. For example, in *A: Joan had an eight hour car journey to get . . . B: Nine hours*, the addressee *B* realizes that *A* is wrong about the length of the car journey, and therefore corrects *A* (Fernández & Ginzburg, 2002). *B*'s response is informative but also indicates that *A*'s contribution (with respect to the time) should not be m-tagged. It may be that *A* and *B* now m-tag that Joan had a nine hour car journey, but this would require *A* to provide a contribution with a positive commentary function (i.e. an acceptance of *B*'s correction). A related type of contribution is an embedded repair (e.g. *A: I need a new bolt for my filter. B: What size bolt does your pan take?*, where *pan* is the correct term for *filter*; Jefferson, 1982), which combines a negative commentary at the level of linguistic alignment with new information (see also Example 6.1).

In sum, many contributions lead to meta-representations of alignment and thus support succinctness. In other words, they help control the dialogue in support of least collaborative effort, which of course means that they are more likely to be compatible with the limited capacity of the shared workspace.

8.4   Saying Just Enough Together

We have argued that interlocutors attempt to optimize the use of the shared workspace as a way of following least collaborative effort – as a pair, they should say just enough but no more. (The important point is that the joint contribution is minimized, rather than that one or other contribution is minimized.) To illustrate this relationship, we turn to Isaacs and Clark (1987), who contrasted dialogues between experts and non-experts about New York City landmarks. They noted that New Yorkers have names for particular landmarks (e.g. *The Citicorp Building*) and assume that these names are shared among New Yorkers. So they use these names when referring to the landmarks in conversations with other New Yorkers, but use longer descriptions (e.g. *one huge building pointed at the top, Citicorp Center*) when talking to out-of-towners. In an experiment, New Yorkers very quickly realized whether they were talking to other New Yorkers or out-of-towners, and this realization affected their referring expressions. We presume that they rapidly determined whether they meta-represented global linguistic alignment (can my partner refer to the same entities in the same way as me?).

In Example 8.5, the positive commentary *Yeup* indicates two things:

Example 8.5

DIRECTOR.   What's this. This is probably South Street Seaport.
MATCHER.   Yeup.
DIRECTOR.   You got it?
MATCHER.   Fulton Fish Market. Yeah.
DIRECTOR.   Right. Okay.

It first indicates that the matcher is focally aligned (with respect to both language and situation model) with the director and meta-represents that alignment. But it also suggests that the matcher can identify New York landmarks and provides some evidence that he is an expert. His subsequent *Fulton Fish Market* provides stronger evidence. At this point, the director can meta-represent global linguistic alignment – that is, the director and matcher are likely to know a similar set of referring expressions and their referents. The director can therefore use more succinct expressions in the expectation that they will lead to further focal alignment. For example, the director could subsequently use names such as *The Citicorp Building* and not need to use longer descriptions. And in fact pairs of experts together used fewer words than expert-novice pairs, who used fewer words than pairs of novices (Isaacs & Clark, 1987).

In Section 6.4, we pointed out that interlocutors who focally align on an expression (*chef*) align more broadly on everything associated with that expression (both linguistic expressions such as *waiter* and background knowledge such as what happens in expensive restaurants). A New Yorker who utters *The Chrysler Building* activates much information about New York City in another New Yorker, and this information extensively overlaps with her own activated information, such as names for other landmarks. The same degree of overlap would not happen with an out-of-towner. In contrast, if a New Yorker utters *The Chrysler Building* and gets a quizzical response, she suspects that she is conversing with an out-of-towner who has not activated much information about New York City and therefore meta-represents that they are not locally or globally aligned. To deal with such misalignment, the New Yorker uses a longer description based on clearly identifiable characteristics of the landmark, and continues to do so.

8.5   Conclusion

Interactive language therefore involves both automatic alignment and commentary on that alignment, with the commentary specifically functioning to promote meta-representation of alignment. These two processes iterate, with *A* and *B* alternating in their contributions, but with *B* providing commentaries on *A*'s contributions and *A* providing commentaries on *B*'s contributions. When one interlocutor speaks, the addressee's response provides a commentary on the speaker's contribution in a way that indicates whether the interlocutors are aligned or not.

Dialogue involves the iteration of automatic (first-order) alignment and commentaries on such alignment. But we have argued that they are two independent processes. Alignment is driven by encountering appropriate primes from one's interlocutor, modulated by factors such as the time between prime and target (Hartsuiker et al., 2008) and whether the prime was addressed to the participant (Branigan et al., 2007). The main role of commentary is to indicate whether the addressee has aligned her situation model with the speaker's, through the processes discussed above (indicating successful alignment, indicating failure to align). So if the maze game players go from *one along ... and one up?* (9, 11 in Example 1.1) to *one-one* and *two-four*, they have aligned their descriptions via automatic priming and have shortened them using (positive) commentaries, so that they achieve alignment with least collaborative effort (i.e. optimal use of the shared workspace). Commentaries typically do not involve extensive linguistic alignment (though note our examples of repetition in Section 8.2.2) – and any such alignment is not central to their commentary function.

In conclusion, interlocutors make optimal use of the shared workspace by crafting their contributions so that they say 'just enough'. They extensively comment on each other's contributions in a way that confirms alignment or indicates failure to align. If alignment is confirmed, their partners can move on to the next contribution, and can often use more succinct expressions successfully. If alignment fails, they can reformulate and bring the dialogue back on track. Conversation is an iterative process in which new contributions are added to the workspace and confirmed by the interlocutors, via alignment and meta-representation of alignment in turn.

9   Speaking in Good Time

People find it very difficult to perform two unrelated cognitively challenging activities at once, whether these are collaborative joint activities or not. And this is largely because they cannot maintain two complex independent plans simultaneously. In the same way, interlocutors cannot hold two conversations (or two parts of the same conversation) at once. They cannot construct and maintain two dialogue models. Instead, interlocutors engage in a single dialogue, and to do this they collaborate on a single plan for the dialogue (see Chapter 4).[1]

Within a dialogue, the interlocutors develop their own contributions. But they each mesh their own contributions with their partner's expected contributions to construct their dialogue plans (and in successful dialogue these plans become aligned). For such meshing to occur, each interlocutor must represent the order of each step in the plan – for example, a step corresponding to an answer must come after the step corresponding to the relevant question. But it is also necessary for each interlocutor to time their contributions correctly – for example, without extensive overlap or long silences. Such timing relates to the process of implementation and each interlocutor must link their planner and implementer appropriately. This chapter therefore discusses the shared workspace framework in terms of order and timing.

The shared workspace not only contains a limited amount of information but it is also ephemeral. In particular, it contains sign vehicles (from speech and gestures) that fade rapidly. So interlocutors have to time their contributions efficiently, only speaking when it is appropriate for them to do so but not leaving unnecessary periods of silence. In other words, they speak in good time, in a way that seeks to minimize collaborative effort. To do this, they contribute in the right order and thereby give the dialogue an appropriate

---

[1] If they do not collaborate on a single plan, then they are not engaged in dialogue – they are simply talking over each other (see Chapter 4, p. 69).

structure. And they then produce those contributions at a rate which develops the shared workspace in an efficient manner.

9.1 Sequentiality and Timing

We contrast steps and timing. The dialogue planner makes use of steps – that is, sequential components of the plan. In contrast, the implementer operates in (real) time and therefore at specific rates. In the plan, step 1 is ordered before step 2; the implementation of step 1 must begin before step 2. Such relationships occur over large- or small-scale components.

A relatively large-scale component is a dialogue game and its implementation. Interlocutors plan the order of contributions using their dialogue planners. For example, an information-seeking game specifies that the request is ordered before the response. The implementer reflects the same sequentiality, with the answer having to begin after the question begins. In practice, the answer normally depends on most of the question, and the respondent will begin the answer only when he is able to identify the question and formulate what to say.

A smaller-scale component is a pair of words. The utterance *two-four* (e.g. in relation to the maze game; Section 8.3.2) means something different the utterance *four-two*, and moreover an utterance in which *A* says *two* and *B* says *four* at the same time has no meaning. If *A* and *B* plan to utter *two-four*, then they both represent that the plan for *two* is ordered before the plan for *four*; and to implement this plan, *A* must begin uttering *two* before *B* begins uttering *four*.

Sequentiality feeds into timing, but timing and sequentiality are distinct. A question is ordered before its answer, and *two* is ordered before *four*, but the specific timing does not matter. The contributions can be produced at fast or slow rates, and they can be separated by a long or short gap or may overlap to a limited extent. So far, our analysis of dialogue has taken sequentiality into account, but has largely ignored timing. In a sequence, one event may precede or follow the other (i.e. they are ordered), or the two events may occur in parallel; in terms of timing, one event may begin or end at some specific time relative to another (and therefore they may overlap). As in Section 5.3, we refer to steps in a sequence using s; at step s, two sequential upcoming steps occur at $s + 1$ and $s + 2$, whereas two parallel upcoming steps both occur at $s + 1$. If two people answer the same question together, their responses occur at the same step (i.e. they are in parallel), and are in time with each other (i.e. they are choric; see Section 10.2.4).

Steps occur in the context of planning, and most of our discussion relates to steps that correspond to moves in dialogue games, for example information-seeking followed by its response. But the steps are realized in the context of implementation, so we can also discuss steps that correspond to linguistic expressions such as words or syllables. And these steps are implemented in real time at a certain rate that depends on the interlocutor's speech rate. Our concern is with particular aspects of speech rate – perhaps syllable rate or perhaps the rate at which dialogue games take place. A recurring behaviour such as syllable articulation occurs at a particular rate, for example every 200 ms (i.e. at 5 Hz), and this rate determines the rate at which the steps in the plan are realized in the shared workspace. The interlocutors put contributions into the shared workspace at that rate and must predict, comprehend and monitor them at that rate.[2]

As we have discussed, the timing of dialogue involves some concurrency – interlocutors may contribute at the same time, with overlap at turn-ends and commentaries (including gestures) during each other's contributions. But interlocutors do not speak at the same time as each other, as a consequence of the sequentiality of their plans. In the information-seeking game, the sequentiality of the game moves is reflected in the timing of the contributions – the answer must largely follow the question. When B completes A's utterance, the sequence is A's contribution then B's contribution, and their relative timing reflects this order. When A comments part-way through B's contribution (e.g. *one along* <u>*uh-huh*</u> *and one up?*), the sequence is that the commentary is ordered after its source (*one along*). Of course, the timing of the commentary might not exactly reflect this order – for example, it might overlap with the rest of B's contribution (though not in this case).

So we assume cooperative joint activity requires meshing of plans in terms of sequencing and meshing of behaviours in terms of timing. When ballroom dancers A and B perform a successful twirl, this occurs because A and B's plans mesh. That is, B plans a sequence in which B holds up his hand at step $s + 1$ and A twirls at $s + 2$, and A plans the same sequence (where s refers to a place in the sequence). If so, their plans are aligned. In addition, both A and B predict that B will hold his hand up in x ms and A will twirl in (approximately) $x + 400$ ms, and B actually holds his hand up in x ms and A actually twirls in $x + 400$ ms. If so, their behaviours are synchronized. Of course the synchronization occurs because A and B are dancing at the same rate and in phase with each other.

In dialogue, alignment depends on both interlocutors representing the same sequence of steps relating to communication. Informally, both interlocutors think about the same relevant aspects of the world in the same sequence as each other. On the other hand, synchrony reflects the relative timing of each interlocutor's contributions to the shared workspace. When interlocutors' plans

---

[2] Note that we did not distinguish steps and timing in Pickering and Garrod (2013).

are aligned and their behaviours are synchronized, we can say that the dialogue flows well.[3]

Synchrony can be regarded as a component of behaviour matching (with respect to timing). Matching of the content of a behaviour (e.g. producing a particular word) corresponds to aligned representations (activation of the appropriate lexical entry). Matching timing, in contrast, corresponds to underlying synchrony. We now suggest that speech rate is controlled by neural oscillations, and that synchronizing speech rate will lead to synchronizing such oscillations. This relationship appears similar to the relationship between behaviour matching of content (e.g. words) and underlying cognitive representations (lexical entries). But we propose that there is an important difference, because mechanisms such as oscillations (as opposed, say, to a representation of 180 ms) are not representations of cognitive states (they are not 'about' entities such as words or syntax).[4] As noted in Section 4.5.4, there is some evidence that interlocutors' speech rates converge during conversation. This convergence does not reflect alignment and therefore cannot be captured by the channels of alignment in Figure 6.2. Instead, the convergence relates to timing, so that interlocutors who are in sync have similar speech rates.

We have argued that interlocutors (and cooperative joint actors in general) seek efficiency by minimizing their collaborative effort (Clark & Wilkes-Gibbs, 1986). To do this, they seek to optimally distribute their contributions, in terms of both sequencing (who performs which step) and timing (when they do so). Below, we interpret sequencing and timing with respect to dialogue, and discuss plan meshing in Section 9.2 and behaviour meshing in Section 9.3.

9.2   Planning and Sequentiality

For many cooperative joint activities, it would be most efficient for both actors to contribute in parallel – that is, they should plan their contributions to occur at the same step. Thus, two actors moving a heavy table plan 'wait, lift, walk' as three parallel steps (which lead to synchronized behaviour; see Section 9.3). That is, 'wait' is step s, 'lift' is step $s + 1$, and 'walk' is step $s + 2$. In this case, parallelism across actors is necessary – they can move the table only by combining their efforts. In other activities, parallelism increases efficiency –

---

[3] And we could say that the interlocutors are coordinated (as are the ballroom dancers). However, we use 'coordination' sparingly because it is used in different ways in the literature. In our examples, both the joint actors themselves and observers of the action would presumably report that they experience fluency. They might also have the experience of joint agency (Bolt & Loehr, 2017), which would be an illusion (see Chapter 2).

[4] In Pickering and Garrod (2013), we regard time as (typically) instantiated rather than represented.

for example, two actors paint a room more quickly if they paint walls in parallel (rather than one after the other). And in fact, parallel contribution is a major reason for rejecting the simple 'transfer' Figure 2.1 as a model of joint activity and instead proposing the shared workspace model in which contributions can be planned whenever appropriate. However, parallelism is not always possible. In some joint activities, B's step $s + 1$ depends on A's previous step s, so B cannot plan $s + 1$ until he has processed s. If different screwdrivers are appropriate for different furniture components, then B cannot plan which screwdriver to use until A has selected a particular component.

Dialogue is an almost entirely sequential form of cooperative joint activity. A response depends on a previous request, and so the request occurs at step s and the response occurs at step $s + 1$ (or later). If another game is embedded within the first game, then the respondent's embedded completion is also sequential. This occurs when the initiator of an instructing game has word-finding difficulty (as in *A: This one has uh uh … B: Tentworms*; see Section 8.3.3), or in an embedded information-checking game (as in *one along uh-huh and one up?*). Commentaries are also sequential on their sources, as for example when A produces an ambiguous word and B indicates misalignment with *eh?* or alignment with *Yes* or a nod. A's utterance is an implementation of step s and B's commentary refers to step s and is an implementation of step $s + 1$. (As these steps reflect sequentiality and not timing, it is possible for contributions at $s + 1$ to overlap with those at s.)

Now let us explain how the sequentiality of dialogue is compatible with our shared workspace framework, specifically with respect to distributed control. We return to Figure 5.5 (repeated as Figure 9.1 below). In our account, monitoring does not merely promote self-repair (which is its main role in monological theories of monitoring such as Levelt, 1983). Instead, it serves to maintain the flow of dialogue. It focuses on the comparison between the actual and predicted joint contribution. It then feeds the result back to the dialogue planner and any resulting prediction error leads to corrections, interjections or pauses, but also to decisions to take the floor from the interlocutor (e.g. to complete his utterance or simply shout over him). Such feedback can even lead the speaker to completely update her dialogue planner, as when she embeds a new dialogue game (e.g. when her interlocutor responds to her question with *why did you ask that?*).

In Chapters 5 and 8, our focus was on the process of joint monitoring and how it enabled distributed control. Now our concern is with the way that the speakers make new contributions to the dialogue – that is, how they construct a new production command and use it to put a new contribution into the shared workspace (i.e. via the thick black arrows), a contribution that is appropriate both in terms of content and sequentiality.

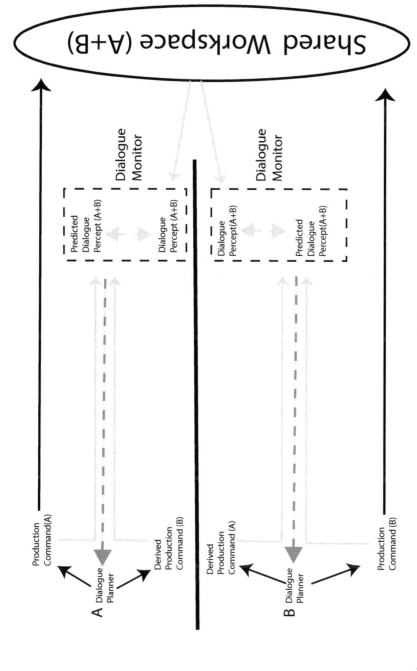

Figure 9.1 A model of the dialogue system. *A*'s dialogue planner bidirectionally feeds into *A*'s production command and derived production command for *B*, and *B*'s dialogue planner bidirectionally feeds into *B*'s production command and derived production command for *A*. Reproduced from Figure 5.5.

Of course, Figure 9.1 is compatible with either sequential or parallel contributions, and is therefore appropriate for well-flowing dialogue in which one interlocutor produces the primary contribution at any given time (e.g. that John fell over) and the other is able to supply commentary (e.g. *aargh*, indicating concern). When this happens, the shared workspace is updated from two directions at once (so to speak). Each interlocutor can then compare the dialogue percept (that refers both the primary contribution and the commentary) with their prediction and can act accordingly. Sometimes each of them will detect a significant discrepancy which will be fed back to update their dialogue planners and lead to new production commands for themselves and derived production commands for their partner. If they choose, they can both then contribute again. Thus, information passes through different arrows in Figure 9.1 at the same time.

Let us consider some very simple (artificial) exchanges. In our framework, we assume that the dialogue planner (i.e. both the situation model and the game model) for both *A* and *B* bidirectionally feed into the production and derived production commands. We assume (Chapters 6 and 7) that the interlocutors *A* and *B* are (to some extent) aligned and assume that the planning sequence maps directly onto timing (as discussed in Section 9.3). In our examples, *A* and *B* regularly eat lunch at one of two restaurants (*Kalpna* and *Nile Valley*) and are deciding between them. Hence they are aligned both with respect to the situation model (which contains those two restaurants and no others) and the dialogue game (information-seeking).

In (1), *A* produces a disfluent primary contribution by failing to utter a restaurant name and *B* produces an appropriate commentary by querying (dots indicate disfluent speech, left brackets indicate overlap):

1.   *A* Let's go to the ... [today
       B   [where?

A produces *Let's go to the* and this contribution enters the shared workspace. (Ignoring previous utterances and context, the shared workspace simply contains *A*'s utterance.) At this point (step *s*), *B*'s dialogue percept is the content of *let's go to the* (i.e. its semantics, syntax and phonology, but also its game move). This percept matches *B*'s predicted dialogue percept sufficiently well (because *A* is saying what *B* would expect *A* to say at lunch time), and therefore leads to minimal prediction error feedback to her dialogue planner. *B* predicts on the basis of the utterance so far that what will enter the shared workspace (i.e. the predicted dialogue percept) at step $s + 1$ will have the semantics RESTAURANT, syntax Noun, and phonology **/kælpnɜ:/** or **/naɪlvæli:/**. But *A* then mumbles and so nothing relating to *B*'s prediction enters the shared workspace. Hence *B*'s dialogue percept at $s + 1$ does not sufficiently match *B*'s predicted dialogue percept, and so a large prediction error feeds back to *B*'s dialogue planner.

B then decides whether to produce a commentary or not (making use of meta-representations of misalignment; see Chapter 8). At this point ($s + 2$), *B*'s dialogue planner draws on the fact that there is a missing goal (a restaurant) and a set of conventions for dealing with an incomplete dialogue move. To bring the dialogue back on track, the convention is that *B* should step in under such conditions and update the shared workspace with a query that is likely to in turn lead to *A* updating the shared workspace with an appropriate restaurant name. *B* follows this convention by uttering the query *Where?* (We focus on *B*'s component of Figure 9.1, as *A* does not respond.)

In (2), *B* does not respond to *A*'s disfluency and *A* self-corrects:

2.   A Let's go to the ... today – I mean, Kalpna

Again, *Let's go to the* enters the shared workspace at step *s*. *A* plans to say *Kalpna* at $s + 1$ and hence predicts that it will enter the shared workspace at this point, but in fact produces indistinct sound (such as a cough, represented by dots). Thus, *A*'s predicted dialogue percept has the semantics KALPNA (which would include features such as RESTAURANT and INDIAN), syntax Noun, and phonology /**kælpnɜ**:/ as well as a complete dialogue move. But this prediction does not sufficiently match the actual dialogue percept, and so feedback (i.e. the discrepancy between /**kælpnɜ**:/ and the indistinct sound) goes back to *A*'s dialogue planner.

On the basis of this feedback, *A* decides to self-correct at $s + 2$. *A*'s dialogue planner draws on the fact that there is a missing goal and on conventions for dealing with an incomplete dialogue move and concludes that *A* should complete the dialogue move by correcting the utterance. Thus, *A* acted on feedback to *A*'s planner. It may well be that *A*'s derived production command for *B* remained null when *A* produced the disfluency; in other words, *A* predicted that *B* would not respond to the disfluency with a query. Alternatively, *A* may have predicted that *B* would interject, but *A* decided to correct as quickly as possible and therefore remove the need for *B* to interject (cf. Schegloff et al., 1977). Note that we have ignored *B*'s component of Figure 9.1, as *B* did not respond.[5]

---

[5] It seems appropriate to analyse this self-correction (*I mean, Kalpna*) as a form of commentary on oneself. Sometimes, both interlocutors try to correct at the same time, as shown in this example from Turnbull (2003), with ↑ indicating rising intonation:

A: they were talkin to her (.) she was was general (.) general anesthetic [oh sorry local]
B: [or a (.) oh local] anesthetic↑ that's (.) was it really↑
A: yeah

When *A* said *general anesthetic*, both interlocutors realized that the utterance is implausible (as *they* would not talk to someone under such circumstances). We assume that *A* made an error of word selection (i.e. always planned to describe someone under a local anaesthetic) and that *B*

The control structure of our model can also deal with question-answering (i.e. where there is no disfluency or overlapping speech):

A: Where do you want to go for lunch?
B: Kalpna.

A puts *Where do you want to go for* into the shared workspace at step *s*. *A* plans to say *lunch* at *s* + 1 and hence predicts that *A* will put *lunch* into the shared workspace at this point, that *A*'s dialogue move will be complete, and that *B* should make the next move at *s* + 2. When *lunch* enters the shared workspace, the dialogue percept matches the predicted dialogue percept and the dialogue move is complete. As a result, *A* predicts that *B* will respond with appropriate information (one of the two restaurant choices) at *s* + 2.

Meanwhile, *B* perceives *Where do you want to go for* from the shared workspace at *s*. Based on *A*'s utterance and the context (in particular, that it is lunch time and it is *A* and *B*'s habit to go to a restaurant), B constructs the predicted dialogue percept *lunch* at *s* + 1. *A*'s uttering *lunch* confirms that *A*'s dialogue move is complete and *B* should respond appropriately. *B* therefore utters *Kalpna* and it enters the shared workspace at *s* + 2. Meanwhile, *A* predicts that the next contribution to the shared workspace will have the semantics RESTAURANT, syntax Noun Phrase, and phonology /ˈkælpnɜ:/ or /ˈnaɪlvæli:/ – that is, *Kalpna* or *Nile Valley*. *A* can then compare the predicted dialogue percept (*Where do you want to go for lunch? Kalpna* or *Nile Valley*; with *A*'s contribution underlined) with the actual dialogue percept (*Where do you want to go for lunch? Kalpna*). This minor discrepancy feeds back to *A*'s dialogue planner, and *A* may confirm (with a 'closing' commentary such as *OK*) as it satisfies her dialogue plan. Importantly, this example shows how the framework can explain the control underlying turn-taking (and not merely self- and other-repair), and provides an example of a joint dialogue percept (i.e. shared across the interlocutors' contributions).

These examples illustrate how dialogue flows in the context of Figure 9.1, and in particular how control is distributed. At the same time, they illustrate how the process that corresponds to acts of monitoring (self- or other-monitoring) in isolated language processing does not merely detect errors

---

believed that *A* made an error of word selection (and so *B*'s interjection did not involve querying the situation model). So *A* constructed a predicted dialogue percept containing the meaning *local* and then uttered *general*. The discrepancy fed back to *A*'s production command and led to *A*'s correction *oh sorry local*. (As the error relates to implementation, *A* did not update the situation model.) At the same time, *B* postdicted the dialogue percept *local anesthetic* and detected the discrepancy with *general anesthetic*, and this discrepancy led to *B*'s attempt to correct *A*'s utterance (using the critical word *local*). Of course, *B*'s postdiction actually occurred after *A* produces *anesthetic* – it is unlikely that *B* predicted *local* earlier. This example emphasizes that processes involved in the monitoring and control of dialogue do not always involve prediction.

and promote repair. It also underlies the way in which interlocutors take turns, which are of course sequential. Thus, the mechanisms used for external monitoring are the same mechanisms that are used for turn-taking – a relationship that is not at all apparent in discussions of monitoring that focus on monologue (e.g. Levelt, 1983; Nozari et al., 2011; Postma, 2000).

Decisions about whether to produce a simple commentary or to take the floor (perhaps by interrupting) depend on choices arising from feedback to the interlocutors' dialogue planners. They involve the same mechanism, and the interlocutor can make a choice about how to apply the mechanism. The choice depends on the value and cost of producing a simple interjection at that point versus taking the floor as part of a new embedded game (see Chapter 8).

9.3   Mapping Sequences to Rates

When interlocutors use the implementer to convert plans into behaviours, they have to instantiate sequences in real time. And given the harsh limitations on the shared workspace, they (generally) seek to maximize the rate of instantiation – both by minimizing the time it takes to instantiate each step and by minimizing the time between each instantiation (i.e. reducing gaps and increasing overlap). Given that dialogue involves sequential steps, the timing of dialogue approaches optimality – each contribution and any commentary are added to the shared workspace as soon as possible.[6] For example, intervals between turns are very short (e.g. Stivers et al., 2009) and in-turn contributions (such as *tentworms*; Clark & Wilkes-Gibbs, 1986) tend to occur at approximately the same rate that they would if produced by one speaker – something that is a consequence of comprehenders activating production-based representations via simulation. Thus interlocutors speak in good time.

Speech rate in dialogue faces two pressures. First, a speaker attempts to contribute at the fastest rate that is comfortable for both herself and her addressee. She is usually limited by her own production abilities (which tend to be more constrained than comprehension abilities) but her addressee needs to be able to understand and provide appropriate commentaries (which the speaker can if necessary respond to). This pressure relates directly to the shared workspace – by contributing rapidly, the speaker allows the addressee to process the contents of the workspace rapidly.

---

[6] It might be possible to regard such dialogue as 'ideal' (perhaps a kind of 'citation dialogue'), with each step being implemented in a way that follows the previous step without overlap or gap (no-gap/no-overlap ideal; Heldner & Edlund, 2010). Alternatively 'ideal' dialogue might involve whatever overlap the interlocutors can accommodate.

Second, there is an additional pressure, which leads towards speech rate synchronization – that is, convergence. Synchronization is one of the four characteristics of cooperative joint action systems that allow them to succeed (see Sections 2.6 and 4.6.4); we discuss evidence in Section 9.4.2. It is in some sense the counterpoint to alignment, with alignment being defined in terms of content and synchronization being defined in terms of rate. Synchronization is motivated by the control structure of dialogue and in particular the fact that both interlocutors need to contribute to the success of the joint plan at a time that is appropriate for both of them. Interlocutors need to compute their own and their partner's appropriate timings and it is more straightforward to do so if they can combine these computations (see Section 9.4).

Our discussion of rate involves two components which interface at the level of the syllable (which we treat as the basic unit of rate in language; e.g. MacNeilage, 1998). The first component is the number of syllables at each step. As we have noted, utterances involve steps at different levels (relating to planning and implementation). In our example, *you're one along: uh huh and one up*, the planning sequence is information, check, information (in information-checking games), with alternating contributors (i.e. *B A B*). This sequence is mapped to the linguistic representations, with each word-grouping [*you're one along:*] [*uh huh*] [*and one up*] having a semantics, syntax and phonology. But we are concerned with the mapping to the number of syllables at each step (4, 2 and 3). The second component is the speech rate – that is, the number of syllables per second. To determine the timing of an utterance, we divide its number of syllables by its rate. If *B* utters *you're one along:* at five syllables per second (5 Hz), then it takes 0.8 s.

As we have noted, steps take place sequentially or occasionally in parallel, and the sequence of steps can cross speakers. But when they are mapped to actual timings (i.e. implemented), steps can overlap across speakers or can be separated by gaps. Such timing is a major issue in relation to who should speak when ('turn-taking'; e.g. Heldner & Edlund, 2010). Moreover, commentaries (which are sequential in terms of steps) often overlap with the main contribution. In order to minimize the complexity of the shared workspace, steps tend to be implemented without extensive gaps (so that they can enter the workspace as quickly as possible). The main reason for limited overlap is computational – interlocutors cannot typically process two complex contributions simultaneously.

9.4   Timing and the Flow of Dialogue

A joint activity flows well when the actors' behaviours are compatible with each other in a way that facilitates that activity. For example, a ballroom dance flows well if the dancers' behaviours have the appropriate timing and content for each other (which of course means that their plans and implementation mesh). Importantly, the dancers need not be doing the same things: the male might hold his hand out for the female to twirl.

Similarly, a dialogue flows well when the interlocutors contribute at the right time, and in the right way. For example, a conversation in which there is almost no gap between contributions flows better than an otherwise similar conversation in which contributions are separated by a second or longer and where the effect of such gaps is to delay the conversation reaching its goal. Conversely, a conversation in which interlocutors overlap to the extent that they fail to understand each other does not flow well. Such situations occur when technology interferes with communication (e.g. old-fashioned telephony), with some conversations involving non-native speakers, or when very argumentative interlocutors are unable to compromise on who should hold the floor (see Section 10.2.5).

A conversation flows best if the interlocutors get their timing right – specifically, that their timing is appropriate for each other. And fluency is clearly a consequence of synchrony. Synchrony occurs when participants engage in a joint activity at the same rate (with respect to their contributions), so that their contributions mesh with respect to the activity as a whole. So successful ballroom dancers perform their own actions at time points that are synchronized with their partner's actions. For example, A's foot forward starts and finishes at the same time as B's foot back, or B puts his arm up when A starts a twirl and puts it down when A finishes.

Dialogue flows best when the interlocutors speak at the same rate (which we assume is syllable rate; see Section 9.4.2). Information flows through A's arrows in Figure 9.1 at the same rate as through B's equivalent arrows (i.e. they are time-locked to each other). A produces utterances at the same rate as B (thick black arrows) but also A predicts A and B's joint contributions at the same rate that B predicts those joint contributions. Moreover, A and B monitor at the same rate and draw on their dialogue planners (i.e. mapping between steps and timing) at the same rate. And of course A prepares her production command at the same time as B prepares his derived production command, and B prepares his production command at the same time as A prepares her derived production command. When their mechanisms are synchronized, the effect is the same as it would be if they were both controlled by a single timing mechanism. Just as speakers cannot maintain two dialogue models, so they cannot maintain two timers.[7]

In reality the amount of synchronization is limited, but we argue that the more synchronized they are, the more successful the conversation is likely to

---

[7] The evidence for the difficulty of maintaining two timers goes back to early studies on maintaining more than one rhythm for finger tapping (Klapp, 1979).

be. In this section, we first describe the role of timing in the model of the dialogue system, and then sketch its likely basis in synchronized neural oscillations.

9.4.1   Modelling Timing in Dialogue

We consider the importance of synchrony by first addressing the effects of asynchrony (in relation to Figure 9.2). Let us consider the simple case of a dialogue in which A and B initially speak at different rates. A produces an utterance *Can I go outside to fly my kite?* at her standard slow syllable rate, say 4 Hz, whereas B has a standard faster rate of 5 Hz. A therefore places *Can I go outside to fly my* into the shared workspace at $R_A = 4$ Hz, and then predicts that she will utter *kite* after 250 ms using $A\text{-}PR_A = 4$ Hz (i.e. assuming A accurately predicts her own rate). The dialogue percept will match the predicted dialogue percept and lead to no modification of the production command (and note at this point B has not contributed).

Now consider it from B's point of view. B predicts the content of A's completion (*kite*) and we assume that he does so accurately. But what prediction does he make about its timing? He can use his own speech timing (i.e. $B\text{-}PR_A = 5$ Hz), but then the predicted dialogue percept will not match the actual dialogue percept (e.g. B would predict that /t/ would occur when A actually utters /k/). Alternatively, B could use A's speech rate (i.e. $B\text{-}PR_A = 4$ Hz), but we argue that this would be difficult because it would require B to use two different timing mechanisms (i.e. one for R_B and $B\text{-}PR_B$, and the other for $B\text{-}PR_A$): it would require switching mechanisms when responding to the question. Such switching would presumably incur a switch cost (and hence additional difficulty when the contributor changes). In practice, interlocutors need to perform such switches whenever they have different speech rates.

When we consider fluent dialogue involving concurrent contributions (i.e. primary contribution plus commentary), the value of synchrony becomes even more apparent. Assume that A utters *Let's go to the … today* and B responds *eh?* during the disfluency. If A and B have roughly similar rates, B produces *eh?* at about the time that is compatible with B encountering the discrepancy after *the*. In our terms, B would construct a predicted dialogue percept of an intelligible word after *the* (perhaps a noun referring to a restaurant) but this predicted percept would mismatch the actual dialogue percept (noise), and the feedback from this discrepancy would lead to rapid production of *eh?* But if their rates were very different, then problems are more likely to emerge. If B sticks to his own timing, then he would not make appropriate predictions throughout the utterance and would not be surprised by A's pause. Moreover, B's response might suggest that B was actually querying something

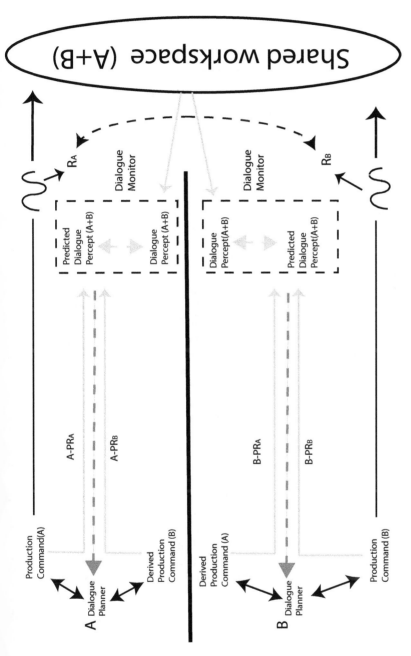

Figure 9.2 A model of the dialogue system that incorporates timing. *A*'s and *B*'s speech rates (e.g. syllables per second) are indicated by arrows (R_A and R_B) emanating from the speech waves that are integrated into the thick black arrows. In addition, *A* and *B* both predict their own rates and their partners' rates, as indicated by the labels *A-PR*$_A$ (i.e. *A*'s prediction of *A*'s rate), *A-PR*$_B$, *B-PR*$_B$ and *B-PR*$_A$. The double-headed dashed arrow between R_A and R_B reflects synchronization (and is comparable to a channel of alignment).

about *Let's go to the* rather than the noise (so that *A* would misunderstand *B*). And if *B* switches to *A*'s timing, then *B* will correctly detect *A*'s disfluency but would then have to switch back to his own rate before commenting.[8] This example shows how asynchrony may destabilize the dialogue system.

Now consider Figure 9.2 when the interlocutors are synchronized. Under these conditions, $R_A = R_B$. As interlocutors predict their own rates, $R_A = A\text{-}PR_A = R_B = B\text{-}PR_B$. As all of these reflect the same underlying speech rate, the remaining predictions of rates 'across interlocutors' (i.e. $A\text{-}PR_B$ and $B\text{-}PR_A$) are the same as well, and a single timing mechanism suffices (i.e. both interlocutors use the same rate and predict that both of them use that rate). So when *A* produces *Can I go outside and fly my ...*, *B* predicts *A*'s completion (*kite*) will take the time that *A* would actually take to produce that completion. It should be clear that the model in Figure 9.2 when synchronized works like the equivalent model in Figure 9.1 (i.e. without timing), as we had implicitly assumed appropriate timing. Thus, synchronized interlocutors tend to achieve communicative success and the dialogue flows – specifically, there is no switch cost. Conversely, asynchronized interlocutors are less likely to achieve communicative success.[9]

Moreover, asynchronized interlocutors may misinterpret each other's game moves. For example, *B* asks a question speaking at his own fast rate and predicts a rapid answer, but *A* being a much slower speaker takes her time replying. As a result *B* assumes that *A* is failing to perform the appropriate move in the information-seeking game (e.g. that *A* is evading making a response), whereas *A* assumes the slower response was compatible with the game. In fact, timing of such responses influences how people interpret them. In an event-related potential study, Bögels et al. (2015) found that, when listening to questions and answers, participants showed surprise (as indicated by an enhanced N400) when hearing an unexpected 'no' as compared to an expected 'yes' response if it came immediately after the question (within 300 ms). However, when the response was delayed by 1 s, the pattern reversed with an N400 for a delayed 'yes' but not for a delayed 'no' response. In other words, overhearers monitor responses both in terms of their content and their timing (as reflected in different surprise reactions according to when the response occurs) and we assume that interlocutors do so too.

In summary, synchronized interlocutors distribute control efficiently, because they time when they speak and when they predict their partner will speak appropriately. But when synchronization does not occur, interlocutors

---

[8] Of course, such disfluencies might actually trigger convergence.
[9] We hypothesize that more synchronized interlocutors will tend to make shorter contributions (with minimal gaps), because they will not incur major switch costs.

need to maintain two timers to avoid a clash when they switch from producing their own speech to predicting their partner's speech. Synchrony therefore supports appropriate patterns of timing of contributions and commentaries in accord with Chapter 8.

9.4.2   The Mechanisms of Synchronization

There is evidence that speech rates between dialogue partners tend to converge. For example, Schultz et al. (2016) measured speech rates when participants recited their part in a play alongside a confederate. A participant's speech rate increased with a fast speaking confederate as compared to a slower one and *vice versa*. Similarly, Himberg et al. (2015) showed that when two speakers alternated to produce a story one word at a time their speech timing became synchronized.[10] Although there was no stability in speech timing overall, with both long and short inter-word intervals occurring throughout the story, the inter-word intervals across the two speakers were highly correlated. In other words, when one speaker took a long time producing a word, the other speaker took a long time producing the next word. And in a study using the *Switchboard* corpus of telephone conversations between strangers (Godfrey & Holliman, 1993), Cohen Priva et al. (2017) found that the speech rates of conversational partners converged. The second-best predictor of a speaker's speech rate was the baseline speech rate of their interlocutor (the best predictor unsurprisingly was that of the speaker's own rate).

We argue that conversational partners track each other's speech rates via the double-headed dashed arrow in Figure 9.2, such that A's rate (R_A) affects B's rate (R_B) and *vice versa* (as in Schultz et al., 2016). This arrow reflects a causal relationship between the interlocutors (unlike channels of alignment; see Figure 6.5). If the interlocutors fully synchronize, their predictions will be appropriately timed without the need for two timers. And just as with predictions of content, the system is presumably robust enough to allow small discrepancies.

We propose that interlocutors' speech rates synchronize because the neural oscillations also become synchronized. Such synchrony occurs predominantly in the *theta* range (roughly, 4–7 Hz). These *theta* oscillations in speech correspond to the frequency of the speaker opening and closing her mouth and hence the rate of her syllabic articulation (Chandrasekaran et al., 2009). Both auditory and pre-motor cortices reveal ambient (background) oscillations in this range (Giraud et al., 2007) and when people listen to speech,

---

[10] In accord with footnote 9, we propose that highly interactive dialogue with short contributions may be particular effective in promoting synchrony.

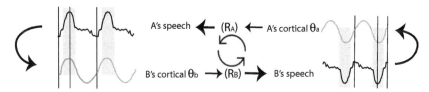

Figure 9.3 Neural mechanisms of speech rate convergence. Speaker A's speech rate R_A governs A's speech oscillations (upper left waveform in black). These speech oscillations drive B's neural oscillations in auditory cortex and hence pre-motor cortex (both represented by lower left waveform in grey). B's pre-motor neural oscillations drive B's speech rate R_B, which governs B's speech oscillations (lower right waveform in black), which in turn drives A's neural oscillations in auditory cortex and hence pre-motor cortex (both represented by upper right waveform in grey). Speech rate synchrony between R_A and R_B is indicated by the rotating arrows, which correspond to the double-headed dashed arrow in Figure 9.2.

oscillations in auditory cortex synchronize with *theta* oscillations in speech (see Zion Golumbic et al., 2013; Gross et al., 2013).[11] *Theta* synchronization to speech in auditory cortex is related to *theta* synchronization in pre-motor cortex (Park et al., 2015; see also Assaneo & Poeppel, 2018; Onojima et al., 2017). Finally, we assume that syllabic speech rate is governed by oscillatory rate in cortical speech motor systems such as pre-motor cortex – an assumption that is consistent with MacNeilage's (1998) frame-content mechanism of speech production.

These three stages of *theta* synchronization (speech to auditory cortex, auditory to pre-motor cortex, pre-motor cortex to speech) are illustrated in Figure 9.3, which is an expansion of the double-headed dashed arrow in Figure 9.2. Speaker A's speech rate R_A governs A's speech oscillations. These speech oscillations drive B's neural oscillations in auditory cortex and hence pre-motor cortex. B's pre-motor neural oscillations drive B's speech rate R_B, which governs B's speech oscillations, which in turn drives A's neural oscillations in auditory cortex and hence pre-motor cortex, and so on.[12]

---

[11] According to Arnal and Giraud (2012), timing predictions come from this neural entrainment. In the presence of a fast speaker, auditory cortex first adapts by increasing the rate of oscillations. These entrained oscillations then enable the listener to predict when the information that allows speech recognition will occur. In other words, cortical oscillations come to reflect the timing of critical speech events (at the beginning and end of syllables).

[12] Zion Golumbic et al. (2013) also found that neural synchronization depended on attending to the speaker. This finding suggests that synchronization between speakers may depend on parallel attention.

9.5   Integrating Content and Timing

We have argued that interlocutors synchronize their speech rates based on acoustic information largely associated with syllables. This process appears to be independent of the process associated with predicting the content of the speech, which is based on linguistic representations. But content and timing are of course eventually combined. In Figure 9.2, the process of synchronization via the double-headed dotted arrow affects the rate at which interlocutors put information into the shared workspace. The interlocutors are therefore also able to extract information from the workspace at this rate (via the left-facing light grey arrows). In turn, the rate at which they can perform dialogue monitoring is affected. In conclusion, synchronization affects the whole process of dialogue control.

More specifically, the addressee can combine the results of synchronization (i.e. prediction of syllable rate) with those of linguistic prediction (i.e. prediction of content) to determine the appropriate timing for turn transitions. We have discussed how timing of an utterance is a consequence of its number of syllables and syllable rate. Such calculations also apply to predictions of utterance timing. Garrod and Pickering (2015) argued that predictions of content and predictions of timing are initially separate. Interlocutors predict what their partner is going to say and their partner's speech rate. If they predict that their partner will say a specific word (e.g. *elephant*), know its number of syllables (3), and also determine their partner's syllabic rate (e.g. 200 ms per syllable, or 5 Hz), then they can predict how long their partner will take to speak (here, 600 ms to say *elephant*).

Such predictions are of course useful for turn-taking. For example, the addressee could predict the speaker's final word (e.g. *At the zoo did you see the enormous elephant?*). In such cases, the addressee can prepare a response (e.g. *Yes*) that is timed to begin rapidly after the speaker finishes. Such prediction can help explain why gaps between turns tend to be so short. Moreover such predictions can help the addressee to determine when to make a commentary.

9.6   Conclusion: Saying Just Enough in Good Time

Efficient control of dialogue occurs when the interlocutors work together to build up the workspace in a manner that promotes alignment – quickly, accurately and with least collaborative effort. In Chapter 8, we showed how interlocutors use commentary to help control the dialogue in way that promotes global alignment. In this chapter, we showed how they mesh their joint planning with the process of implementation, and in particular how the steps involved in plans are turned into the timing of speech. The consequence is that the interlocutors contribute efficiently to the shared workspace so that dialogue becomes fluent.

Part IV

Extending the Shared Workspace Framework

10   Communication beyond the Minimal Dyad

The goal of this book is to develop a theory of dialogue in all its diversity. But we have so far developed the shared workspace framework for two interlocutors having a face-to-face, informal conversation (and typically one which is cooperative and incorporating relatively equal contributions). We refer to this as *minimal dyadic conversation* (and the interlocutors as a *minimal dyad*). It is developmentally and evolutionarily primary, does not require special training, and is typically not cognitively taxing (Garrod & Pickering, 2004). We therefore regard it as the basic setting for language use and also treat it as the model for dialogue in general. Dialogue takes place in an enormous space of settings, from symmetric three-party conversations to discussions among large groups to broadcast interviews directed at a range of audiences. And of course many of these settings are far more difficult for the participants than minimal dyadic conversation. In this chapter, we show how our theory can explain dialogue in these diverse settings, and also how it can apply to monologue.

We start the chapter by extending the shared workspace framework (i.e. using Figure 4.2) to three individuals in a successful symmetric conversation, in terms of the shared workspace, alignment and control. We then illustrate it using an extract from dinner-party conversation among friends. We then address the structure of more complex multi-party dialogues, and in particular consider the effects of individuals having different conversational roles. We next consider restricted dyadic dialogue, as in half-duplex telecommunication. The final part of the chapter sketches how the shared workspace framework can be applied to monologue. In Chapter 11, we consider dialogue (and monologue) in relation to social structure, and to cultural artefacts and technologies (e.g. writing, social media).

10.1   Straightforward Three-Way Conversations

Our systems-based analysis applies to individuals participating in cooperative joint activity. In other words, they must commit to the success of the activity and all other individuals must accept their commitment. So when *A*, *B* and *C*

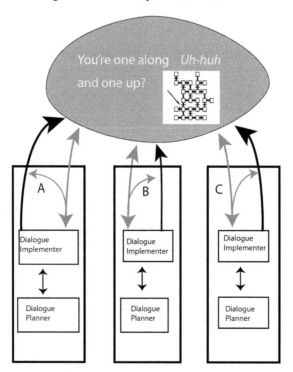

Figure 10.1 The shared workspace framework for triadic dialogue about the maze game (assuming the presence of *C*, who is not contributing at this point).

have a conversation that tries to resolve a problem they face together, they all commit and accept that their partners commit to this goal. Thus, they all seek to align with each other with respect to the solution to the problem. And as they communicate successfully, they build up situation models that are aligned across all of them, and meta-represent that they do so. Moreover, they jointly attend to the same entities (signs and non-signs) which form the shared workspace that they can all draw on when contributing. In this section, all individuals have the same status in the dialogue.

We can easily extend the shared workspace framework from two to three interlocutors. Informally, all we need to do is to add an additional interlocutor into Figure 4.2 to produce Figure 10.1 for any triadic dialogue. Here, A, B, and C can all contribute to the shared workspace via their own thick black arrows and perceive or predict the shared workspace via the grey arrows. This figure represents the workspace that is shared among all interlocutors. In other words, this shared workspace contains the entities that A, B and C attend to. If A but not B or C attends to an entity, then it is in A's individual workspace. If A and B but not C attends to an entity, then it is in a partly shared workspace. (With more interlocutors, the structure of the workspace becomes increasingly complex.)

When *A*, *B* and *C* represent an entity in the same way, then they are all aligned with respect to that entity. For example, if *B* utters *You're one along* and *A* and *C* attend, they all align with respect to an aspect of language. If they interpret *one along* as referring to the same column in the maze, then all align with respect to the situation model. Alternatively, *C* might align with *A* and *B* with respect to language but not the situation model. Additionally, they might all meta-represent alignment with each other, or *B* might meta-represent alignment with *A* (as a consequence of *A*'s positive commentary *uh-huh*) but not with *C*. (We discuss the distribution of control in Section 10.2.6.)

10.1.1   A Dinner-Party Conversation

In Example 10.1, three diners (*A*, *B* and *D*) are discussing the pianist Rubinstein's hands (Tannen, 1989). A fourth diner (*C*) is silent.

Example 10.1

     1—**A:** they were like *(0.5)* putty. *(0.5)*
     2—**D:** [really?
     3—**A:** [just completely soft and [limp
     4—**B:**   [mush
     5—**A:** just mush. it was as though there was [no bone
     6—**B:**   [and warm.
     7—**D:** and short stubby fingers?
     8—**A:** short stubby fingers but just (0.5) totally covered with –
     9—**B:** fat.
    10—**A:** fat

Note: The brackets indicate overlapping speech; the numbers indicate noticeable pauses in seconds.

This conversation shows many of the same characteristics as minimal dyadic conversation. It is tightly interwoven (often with overlapping utterances), brief contributions (2), utterance completions (4, 6, and 9), and linguistic behaviour matching (4–5, 7–8, and 9–10). Clearly, the conversation appears to 'flow' as well as many dyadic conversations. The diners are committed to the success of the dialogue as a cooperative joint activity – they seek to align, and keep each other on track.

Now let us interpret Example 10.1 in the shared workspace framework. At (3), *A* described Rubenstein's hands as *just completely soft and limp*, and *B* uttered *mush* simultaneously with *limp*. It appears that *B* predicted the meaning of what *A* was about to say (but not the exact word). Thus *A* and *B* were aligned semantically but not lexically. *A* added (3) to the shared workspace via *A*'s black arrow. Before *A* completed the utterance, *B* predicted the meaning of *A*'s completion (flaccidity) via the upward grey arrowhead and used this prediction to produce a compatible interjection (4), so that *A* and *B* used their black arrows to contribute to the shared workspace simultaneously and without delay, in a way that reflects alignment.

We can be confident that *A* lexically aligned with *B* because *A* produced *just mush*. *A* and then *B* contributed further to the shared workspace (though *B* was not fully aligned with *A* as *B*'s contribution is syntactically inappropriate after *was*). *D* (as well as *A* and *B*) interpreted the shared workspace via the downward grey arrowhead, but we know only that *A* linguistically aligned with *D* (i.e. with respect to *short stubby fingers*). When *A* later said *short stubby fingers but just totally covered with* and *B* completed with *fat* (8–9), *A* repeated *B*'s completion (10), and so *A* and *B* were presumably lexically aligned (i.e. with similar patterns of activation for particular lexical items) at the point when *B* spoke (though it is also possible that *A* had not accessed *fat* until after *B* spoke).

Our analysis leaves out the silent diner *C*. This individual never used the black arrow, but comprehended using the downward vertical grey arrowhead (and may have predicted using its upward counterpart). It is likely that *C* was attending to the conversation and hence linguistically aligning, but we have no direct evidence for this.

The interlocutors also appear to have aligned with respect to their situation models. They discussed the same person and his attributes and so built up situation models containing the same referential token (RUBENSTEIN1) in the same relation to various properties (e.g. having short stubby fingers). The contributions with a positive commentary function (e.g. 4 and 6) support the meta-representation of alignment (though note that they all have additional functions such as requesting expansion or providing completion). Interestingly, the meta-representation in (4) occurs (in part) because *mush* is semantically compatible with *limp*, and therefore the interlocutors realized that *A* and *B* had aligned situation models. *D*'s response (7) also provides evidence of situation model alignment and hence supports meta-representation of alignment. As noted, such responses primarily indicate that that respondent has aligned with the speaker (as a result of their commentary function). Interlocutors can then use that evidence to meta-represent alignment – for example, the silent diner is likely to have meta-represented alignment with both speaker and respondent.[1]

---

[1] If the respondent had provided a stronger negative commentary to the speaker (e.g. *D* uttered *What?* in response to *A* at (2)), then the others (i.e. *B* and *C*) might have meta-represented

We can represent the extent to which the interlocutors align their representations by extending Figure 6.5 – that is, by incorporating representations and channels of alignment into Figure 10.1. In particular, there are channels of alignment between any pair of interlocutors, and so they can be more or less aligned at any level of representation within the dialogue implementer or planner. For example, it appears as though A and B are well aligned semantically after (4), but it is unclear whether C and D are aligned semantically with A and B to the same extent. In addition, A, B and D appear to be aligned throughout with respect to their situation models (as their contributions indicate understanding) – and C is presumably aligned as well (assuming C is paying attention). Their game models appear well aligned as well, because they query, respond and contribute appropriately. Of course, all of this alignment is the consequence of the interlocutors' contributions to the shared workspace, just as in dyadic conversation.

10.2   Playing Different Roles in Multi-party Dialogue

Conversational theorists have proposed that individuals around a conversation play different roles. If A directs a question or command to B and not C, then B has a different role from C. Thus, Goffman (1976) and Clark (1996) distinguished individuals who participate in the conversation from those who do not. These are (ratified) participants, and they contrast with overhearers. Clark distinguished three roles (which he calls *participant roles*) – the speaker, the addressee, and the side-participant (who is not addressed at a given point). To Clark, a side-participant may speak or be addressed elsewhere in the interchange. In contrast, overhearers do not participate in the conversation (and he divides them into bystanders and eavesdroppers, depending on whether the speaker is aware of their presence or not).

We classify conversational roles differently. Conversational roles relate to dialogue as a cooperative joint activity and therefore to the dialogue planner. In particular they arise from dialogue games. So far, we have treated a dialogue game as involving an initiator and a respondent, but in multi-party dialogue there are other ways in which people can relate to the game, both as individuals and (on occasion) as collectives – active and passive audience members, and overhearers. These roles affect the way in which individuals use their dialogue

---

misalignment between A and D. More generally, they might all have meta-represented low confidence in alignment with each other. To do this, they could m-tag the situation model corresponding to Rubenstein having flaccid hands with low confidence. Here, they applied the m-tag to the set of diners rather than any particular pair – and we suspect that an interlocutor can m-tag with respect to an individual or a group but not to both at the same time.

implementers in relation to the shared workspace – how they put information into it and how they monitor it.

10.2.1   Types of Conversation Role

Players play dialogue games. Each game is dyadic and involves an *initiator* and a *respondent*. Of course, different individuals can play games at different stages in multi-party dialogue. The initiator uses the dialogue planner to begin the game by performing the first move – a move which typically involves language but can involve a communicative gesture (e.g. beckoning with an arm movement). By beginning the game, the initiator also specifies (and therefore licences) the respondent. The respondent can complete the game by an appropriate move, such as linguistic or non-linguistic acceptance or an action (e.g. approaching the initiator). Of course, the respondent can also perform a different move, for example initiating an embedded game (as part of a commentary). In successful conversations, players align their situation models (both focally and globally) and of course also align their dialogue game models.

Active audience members (or the *active audience*) do not play the current dialogue game, but are licensed to play subsequent games. When the current game is complete, they can use their dialogue planner to initiate a new game (and thereby become a player). Under certain circumstances, they can comment on the current game, for example querying the initiator's contribution. Such a comment leads to an embedded game (in which they become a player) but does not complete the current game (which they are not licensed to do).

The active audience includes individuals who are closely associated with the current game, for example by participating in a triad with the players (e.g. at a party). Such individuals correspond quite closely to what Clark (1996) calls side-participants. In the dinner-party conversation (Example 10.1), the diners are either players or active audience members. But the active audience also includes groups of individuals in an auditorium who on occasion contribute to a conversation with a query or clap. We refer to the players and the active audience as *contributors*: people who take part in the cooperative joint activity of dialogue and thereby contribute to its success. In successful multi-party conversations, active audience members align their situation models with the players. They also align their dialogue game models (i.e. they agree with the players about their respective roles).

Multi-party conversations may also involve two kinds of *non-contributor*. First, *passive audience members* cannot use their dialogue planners to take part in the dialogue but are relevant to its success. Success depends on alignment among players, active audience members and passive audience members, and the players and active audience members have the goal of achieving this alignment. This is because the players and the audience are all part of a cooperative joint activity in which the contributors have the responsibility to keep players and audience on track. This task is most straightforward in relation to other players (who produce extensive commentary), less straightforward in relation to the active audience (who produce limited commentary), and most challenging in relation to the passive audience (who produce no commentary). Thus, the contributors use their planners to direct the dialogue towards the players and audience – they realize that cooperative joint activity relates to all of them and act accordingly. The contributors interactively align with the other contributors; they align with passive audience members but do not interactively align with them. In other words, contributors interactively align with each other and plan to (noninteractively) align with the passive audience. And they do this because they want to make sure that they do not leave any of the audience behind.

Overhearers are not part of the cooperative joint activity – the success of the dialogue is unaffected by their alignment with the contributors and audience members (and of course they cannot contribute). Contributors have no responsibility towards overhearers. However, overhearers can incidentally align with the contributors (and the audience). Under some circumstances (e.g. on a crowded tube) it is quite apparent to the contributors that some overhearers will attend (quite closely) to their conversation. But they are not part of the cooperative joint activity, as its success is not determined by the extent to which they align with the contributors.

10.2.2 Meta-representation of Alignment across Roles

As already discussed, players meta-represent alignment between themselves, for example by interpreting positive commentaries as indicators of alignment. They meta-represent alignment over the contents of the games, and do so by m-tagging situation models (e.g. the answer to a question). They also meta-represent alignment over their conversational roles (i.e. who is the initiator and who is the respondent). Such meta-representations are straightforward in dyadic conversation, because there is only one alignment relationship.

But in multi-party conversation, a player could meta-represent alignment over different individuals – between herself and the other player, among contributors or across the whole of an audience. What is impossible is for the player to meta-represent many different aspects of alignment at the same time – she does not have sufficient cognitive capacity. Just as we assume that players typically do not construct multiple situation models (corresponding to their own beliefs and their interlocutors' beliefs), so we assume that they typically do not meta-represent differential alignment with different people. In other words, a player might m-tag a component of their situation model in relation to the other player with a high degree of confidence, but would not then simultaneously m-tag that component with the audience. We propose that a player does not construct m-tags across different subsets of the players and audience at the same time. Instead, we propose that she typically m-tags with one subset.

To illustrate, we consider A's meta-representations of alignment in the dinner-party conversation (Example 10.1). When D produces the negative commentary *really?* (2), A m-tags across A and D the element that Rubenstein's hands are like putty with low confidence. This representation leads to A's expansion *Just completely soft and limp* (3). When B interjects with *mush* (4), which has a positive commentary function, A m-tags across A and B that Rubenstein's hands are flaccid with high confidence. This representation leads to A's restatement and then new contribution in (5). B's contribution in (6) leads to a further m-tagging across A and B with high confidence. And when D adds *and short stubby fingers* in (7), A treats this continuation as having a positive commentary function and now m-tags across A, B and D – presumably assuming that B aligns on (7) as well.

In practice, it is often impossible to know whether an interlocutor m-tags across one individual or many. For example, A may m-tag across C as well as B and D, even though C is a passive audience member throughout this exchange. More generally, an interlocutor can treat a commentary as evidence for alignment by the contributor or as evidence for alignment across some or all of the audience. And although we have illustrated meta-representations from A's point of view, all the other diners m-tag their representations as well.

In radio interviews, an experienced interviewer (A) often clarifies responses by the interviewee (B), and does so for the benefit of the passive audience rather than B. For example, B may use an acronym that A knows but judges will not be known to much of the audience. Therefore, A meta-represents misalignment across A and the audience. It is possible that A simultaneously meta-represents alignment across A and B – something that is possible for a highly skilled interviewer such as A. In contrast, B may not pay attention to the audience and so m-tags alignment across A and B. Therefore, A's meta-representation of misalignment drives A's contribution (i.e. expansion of B's response for the benefit of the audience). Notice that A's task is harder than B's, because B determines what to say on the basis of A's contributions, whereas A has to act on the basis of both B's contribution and inferences about alignment with the passive audience.

Contributors typically do not meta-represent alignment with overhearers. But even if they do so, they do not act on any such meta-representation – if they did, then the overhearers would become part of the audience.[2] Both

---

[2] Contributors can of course take into account overhearers, for example avoiding or disguising private topics on the crowded tube (see Clark & Schaefer, 1987). Such cases make it clear that overhearers can affect the conversation, even though they are not relevant to its success (as a cooperative joint activity). (A contributor would not want a malevolent overhearer to record

passive audiences and overhearers can meta-represent alignment between themselves and the contributors, but neither of them can use such meta-representations to drive contributions.

These contrasts relate to Schober and Clark's (1989) finding that over-hearers were consistently poorer than matchers at identifying a director's description of a tangram. The director and matcher are contributors to a set of games that enable them to align on a referent. Overhearers were accurate when they selected the tangram before the matcher. Presumably, they selected early because they were confident that they were aligned with the director's situation model – that is, they meta-represented alignment with the director. And this meta-representation is typically accurate. However, they were highly inaccurate if they did not select the tangram before the matcher. In other words, they were not confident about alignment with the director – they do not meta-represent alignment with confidence. And again, their meta-representation is typically accurate.

Schober and Clark's (1989) explanation of the matcher's advantage is that the matcher's responses lead to the contributions being grounded between the contributors (but not with the overhearer). In our terms, a matcher who meta-represents misalignment is able to provide a negative commentary that leads to the director revising in a way that promotes alignment. But an overhearer cannot provide such a commentary, and so cannot trigger the director into revising. Sometimes the overhearer is in a similar state to the matcher and so the matcher's negative commentary and director's revision aid the overhearer as well as the matcher. But this simply occurs by chance (unlike the radio presenter who provides a commentary for the benefit of the passive audience) and so the process is often unsuccessful. However, our account also provides another explanation of the matcher advantage (relating to implementation): matchers simulate more than overhearers, as they are engaging their produc-tion mechanisms more than overhearers. In other words, the preparation of responses enhances comprehension (and hence alignment).

10.2.3   *Realizing Conversational Roles in Implementation and Behaviour*

Our discussion of conversational roles relates to dialogue planning. But roles affect implementation – how people interact with the shared workspace using production, comprehension, prediction and monitoring. One way to appreciate the distinction between conversational role and what we call implementational status is to consider situations in which the game players use other people as proxies (see Goffman, 1981). When two politicians negotiate using

personal details, but whether this happened or not would be irrelevant to the success of the conversation.)

interpreters, the politicians are the players (i.e. use their dialogue planners) but their interpreters are the producers and comprehenders – they implement the politicians' intentions and manipulate the shared workspace.[3] The politicians have the contributor roles, but the interpreters have the implementational status of producers and comprehenders.

One important distinction in implementational status is between producers and non-producers – contributors (i.e. players and active audience members) can produce, whereas passive audience members and overhearers cannot. Of course, everyone can comprehend and predict. But only contributors can monitor – that is, comprehend and predict in a way that feeds into an act of production. Monitoring requires the process of comparison (i.e. comparing the predicted and actual utterance) and the potential to act on that comparison at that point – that is, to be able to use the feedback from the comparison to construct a new production command. Thus, passive audience members or overhearers cannot monitor. They can compare predicted with actual utterance, but can only cognize (rather than act) 'internally'. In other words, they can think about any discrepancy and try to resolve it in their minds. Faced with an ambiguity (e.g. *my friend*), a contributor can query the current speaker (*which one?*), but all that the non-contributor can do is try to work out which meaning the speaker is likely to have intended (and perhaps make different predictions in future).

Comprehension is affected by the comprehender's role, as discussed above (Schober & Clark, 1989); more generally, we assume it is harder for an overhearer than any of the other roles, because the utterances are not designed with them in mind. Comprehension by a contributor (i.e. a potential actor) is different from comprehension by a non-contributor, because the contributor always has the option of using a commentary to elicit clarification whereas a non-contributor does not. A contributor can decide between acting (*which one?*) or cognizing (I wonder who she's referring to), but a non-contributor can only do the latter. Finally, the comprehender's role affects production, because the initiator directs contributions towards respondents and takes into account audiences but not overhearers.

Consider the effects of conversational roles in terms of Figure 10.1. Contributors can contribute to the shared workspace, via the thick black arrows. The initiator starts the game by planning a contribution that reflects her first move – and therefore the initiator in the dialogue planner corresponds to the first speaker in the dialogue implementer. The respondent makes the next move by planning and implementing another contribution. The response move logically follows the initial move (i.e. in terms of the plan), but the

---

[3] Hence the politicians but not the interpreters (should) take responsibility for the outcome of the negotiation.

second utterance may overlap with the first (and reflects control; see Section 10.2.5). Both players comprehend, predict, and monitor contributions (via the grey arrows) – and in fact they can do so in dyadic as well as multi-party conversation. Prediction and simulation are particularly important for the contributors. Most importantly, prediction makes it likely that the respondent can react both quickly and appropriately (see Levinson, 2016), though it also allows the initiator to fluently continue a conversation. If synchronization depends on parallel attention (see Chapter 9, footnote 12), and contributors are more likely to maintain parallel attention than non-contributors, we speculate that synchronization is particularly important for contributors.

An active audience member can contribute to the shared workspace, via the thick black arrows. But his access is restricted, because players have priority during a game. For example, the initiator begins a game that the respondent is expected to complete, and so the initiator produces an utterance that is directed to the respondent. An audience member cannot answer the initiator's question appropriately – if he does so, he changes the game. The audience member has a much higher bar before contributing (or at least making a substantial contribution) – in other words, using the planner to initiate a production command. This reluctance reflects monitoring – the audience member may comprehend in a similar way to the players, but is less likely to use that comprehension to trigger a production command. Active audience members can contribute and therefore use prediction and simulation (and synchronization) to facilitate appropriate interjections. However, we propose that active audience members simulate (and synchronize) less than players – they are less likely to convert the comprehension-based representations into production-based representations. Indeed, active audience members align less than contributors in a three-party communication game: in one study, an experimental participant tended to repeat syntactic structure more after being addressed than after hearing a description addressed to another participant (Branigan et al., 2007).

A passive audience member cannot contribute to the shared workspace and does not have a thick black arrow. But he is still relevant to the conversation – for example, a contributor might utter *all of you* and use it to refer to the passive audience. They share the workspace with the contributors and active audience members – the shared workspace depends on parallel attention among the contributors and all of the audience. And the contributors and active audience jointly manipulate the shared workspace for the benefit of the passive audience member as well as themselves. The passive audience member can comprehend and predict, but cannot monitor, because he cannot use his comprehension and prediction to drive subsequent production. We propose that passive audience members simulate less than active audience members, as they cannot use production-based representations in actual production.

Like a passive audience member, an overhearer cannot contribute to the shared workspace and has no thick black arrow. Unlike the audience, an overhearer is not relevant to the conversation and his attention is not relevant to the shared workspace (so a contributor's *all of you* cannot refer to overhearers). Thus, he can comprehend and predict (and indeed simulate), but his ability to do so is limited because the workspace is not designed with his needs in mind (see discussion of Schober & Clark, 1989; Section 10.2.2). This reflects the fact that overhearers are not part of the system captured by the shared workspace framework.

Conversational roles of course relate to commentary. Obviously, only players and active audience members can provide commentaries. Players are in general more likely to provide commentaries than active audience members. And commentators can provide commentaries for their own benefit or for the audience (but not for overhearers). The consequences of such commentaries relate to the meta-representation of alignment (as discussed above).

Finally, note that roles can be fluid and be negotiated as part of the dialogue. Put another way, roles affect planning and implementation, but planning and implementation in turn affect roles. An initiator can designate a player (e.g. *What do you think, John?*) and in some circumstances can indicate that another individual is 'relegated' to the passive audience (e.g. saying *Sit still and listen!* to children).

10.2.4   Collectives

People can play games as collectives rather than as individuals, and dialogue games are no exception. Members of a collective all have the same role. For example, a performer can initiate an information-seeking game by addressing a crowd (*Can you hear me London?*) and the crowd can complete the game with a choric response (*Yes*). There are only two players (as in any dialogue game) but there are many comprehenders (who become speakers). Figure 4.2 involves two individuals, so it cannot capture collectives. But it is also not possible to capture collectives using Figure 10.1 (or a multi-party extension of it) because the collective puts a single contribution into the shared workspace – it has one black arrow rather than many. Instead, we treat the individuals that form a collective as feeding into a single black arrow. In Figure 10.2, we illustrate collectives in a dialogue between an individual and a collective of two, but of course the collective can be a crowd involving many people, or the dialogue can involve two collectives (e.g. two sets of sports fans taunting each other).

All three interlocutors take part in a collaborative joint activity in which there are two actors – an individual actor A and a collective actor $B + C$. In their game models, A, B and C represent an information-checking game with A

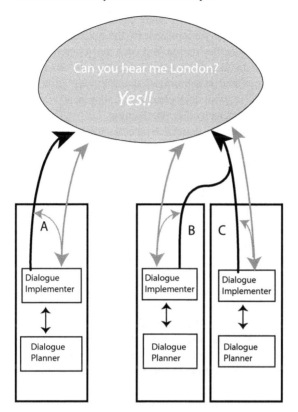

Figure 10.2 The shared workspace framework for a dialogue between an individual (*A*) and a collective of two individuals (*B* and *C*).

as initiator and the collective (*B* + *C*) as respondent. The dialogue planners for *A* and *B* + *C* are aligned in the normal way. However, there is a different sense in which *B* and *C* have aligned planners – they must plan to act in the same way as each other, so that they make the same moves in the same order (see Section 9.2).

Members of a collective plan to implement an utterance at the same step and typically all implement it at (approximately) the same time – that is, they speak in chorus (Cummins, 2003). To do this, they need to be very well aligned (with very similar patterns of linguistic activation), and they also need to be synchronized (so that they speak at the same rate). In this way, they make a single choric contribution to the workspace. In Figure 10.2, *B* and *C* have black arrows that merge into one before it enters the shared workspace. They remain individuals (of course) and so can both monitor and predict the shared workspace via the vertical grey arrows. They can also comprehend and predict their own contributions, which we represent by the horizontal grey arrows that meet the black arrows before they merge. But what they comprehend and predict and when exactly they do so will be very similar to each other. Alignment of linguistic representations and synchronization occur very strongly within the members of a collective (i.e. with thick channels of alignment) – and typically do so to a greater extent than across other interlocutors.

When speaking as a chorus the collective takes a single player role (initiator or respondent) and the members yoke their implementers, thus implementing the same utterance at the same time. When two interlocutors make the same move but they implement different parts of the utterance (e.g. one starts and the other finishes a response to a question), then they may also act as a collective but do not yoke their implementers. In Example 10.1, we might regard *A* and *B* as a collective that approaches (but does not quite reach) a chorus – when *A* says *limp* and *B* says *mush* concurrently (3/4), their implementers are yoked semantically and temporally but not phonologically. And when *A* echoes *B*'s *fat* (9/10), their implementers are yoked semantically and phonologically but not temporally.

When we consider alignment between the individual and the collective, we treat the collective as having a single set of representations that may or may not correspond to those of the individual. And all interlocutors can meta-represent alignment across the individual and the collective. So when *B* and *C* say *Yes!!* in Figure 10.2, *A* treats the collective as providing a single positive commentary and m-tags the representation of the fact that London can hear *A* with respect to *A* and *B* + *C*.

An important reason to represent several individuals as a collective is that it reduces complexity (both for the individual player and for the members of the collective). We have noted that a contributor cannot differentially m-tag across players, active audiences and passive audiences simultaneously. One solution is to treat sets of individuals as a collective – so long, of course, as they behave collectively. Individuals can therefore decide whether to treat certain multi-party interactions as involving a collective or just individuals.

Fay et al. (2000) contrasted discussions on the same topic in small (5 member) and large (10 member) groups. In small groups, members typically interacted dyadically – they contributed in *ABA* sequences (i.e. they alternated) and used extensive commentary (i.e. with short, overlapping utterances). Group members tended to align their situation models (i.e. their opinions) with the model of the speaker that they most often followed, not with the model of the dominant speaker. As discussed in Section 8.2, an utterance and commentary on that utterance ultimately tend to alignment over the contributors, and alignment over non-contributors is weaker (see Section 10.2.3). But in large groups, members typically did not interact dyadically – they contributed in *ABC* sequences (i.e. they did not alternate) and used much less commentary (that is, they made longer contributions, with fewer interruptions). Informally, speakers broadcasted to the group. Group members tended to align their situation models with the model of dominant speaker, and did not align with the speaker that they most often followed.

We argue that a small-group member interpreted the dialogue as dyadic between herself and the individual she was interacting with. Therefore any small group member tended to align with that individual rather than other members of the group. In contrast, a large-group member interpreted the dialogue as dyadic between an individual speaker (or broadcaster) and the other group members as a collective (active) audience (whether she was the individual speaker or a member of the collective). The broadcaster of course changed during the conversation, but one large-group member contributed over a quarter of the time. We argue that the collective aligned with the individual speaker, and so each member aligned predominantly with the dominant speaker.

10.2.5 Role Complexity and Distributed Control

Roles can change throughout conversations. The contributors of course alternate: an active audience member may become a contributor, a passive audience member may become active, or an overhearer can be accepted as a passive audience member. And an embedded game can have different contributors from the parent game (as when A asks B a question, and B seeks clarification from C in order to respond to A). Note also that active audience members can provide commentaries without attempting to become players (Example 10.1, 2).

Roles are part of the dialogue game model. As well as representing the game, each individual represents who is assigned to the player roles (initiator and respondent) and non-player roles. We have assumed that everyone's role is clear. That is, if one individual assumes that someone has a particular role, then all other individuals assume it as well. In other words, everyone is aligned with respect to roles. And these representations correspond to 'God's-eye' role assignments – that is, the players and non-players are defined objectively. But this is an idealization. If two individuals are contributing to a conversation and another individual walks up to them, then they may treat this new individual as an overhearer, whereas the new arrival may assume he is an active audience member. Or A can initiate a game and intends B to be respondent but B and C believes C has been selected. When there is role misalignment, roles are not defined objectively. It can be hard for an analyst to determine roles. For example, in Example 10.1, D appears to address A at (7), and B and C are audience members, but in fact D might actually address a collective consisting of A, B and C.

Potential contributors face challenges deciding who should speak and when, and can believe different things about who has which role. Quite often, the initiator selects the respondent (see Sacks et al., 1974) but on other occasions the respondent self-selects, and when a game is complete, there is typically more freedom about who initiates the next game. Importantly, potential contributors can compete. For example, two individuals can briefly adopt a respondent role, as when their responses overlap (as happens in Example 10.1 at 3/4 and 5/6; see Schegloff, 2000); for the conversation to succeed, one or other must yield. In fact, such conflicts can also occur in dyadic conversation – for example, two interlocutors may both decide to initiate a new game and therefore instigate production commands that lead to conflict and a temporary disruption of distributed control.

Multi-party dialogues present challenges with respect to timing and control – both for the interlocutors and the theorists. We illustrate multi-party control using Example 10.2 (from Schegloff, 2000, p. 25), in which Deb is querying Anne's claim that she used to buy many pairs of shoes before she was married, and her husband Dick keeps attempting to make a joke about it:[4]

This interaction is much more confusing than Example 10.1. There is no alignment with respect to conversational roles among the interlocutors (and so there is no 'God's eye' role assignment). Our interpretation is that Anne initiates an instructing game (1) without selecting a respondent. Then Deb completes the instructing game (with *Really mother*) and initiates an information-seeking game (2 and 4) with Anne as respondent, therefore claiming the respondent role and next initiator role. Dick interrupts Deb and himself initiates an instructing game (3 and 5), but this time with Deb as respondent and Anne as audience. Dick appears to abandon that game but

---

[4] For the details of the transcription, see Schegloff's paper. A more straightforward rendition of this exchange is:

ANNE:	Every six months I went in for shoes. and I had– must have had about, a hundred pairs a shoes.
DEB:	Really mother you spent–
DICK:	You know what -
DEB:	Boy were you wasted
DICK:	you know she exaggerated slightly.
DICK:	You know what– you know–
DEB:	What a waster you were
ANNE:	Don't say that I'm exa– just say I'm a liar.
DICK:	You know what your –
DEB:	It's not a question of lying it's a question of being–
DICK:	Your grandmother is a centipede that's why she has to have a hundred pairs of shoes.

Example 10.2

1—Anne: Every six months I wen' in fih shoes.'n I had– must'v
           had about, (0.5) a hundred pairs a shoes.
           (2.0)
2—Deb: Really mother = you spent–
           (1.0)
3—Dick: You know [wha : t,]
4—Deb: [Boy we]re you:: w– [w a s t e d]
5—Dick: [(you know) sh–] exaggerated
           slightly.
           (0.8)
6—Dick: Y' [know what– y'know– [( )]
7—Deb: [w h a t a w a s [ter you] w e r e]
8—Anne: [DON'T S]AY that I'm exa– just say
           I'm a liar.
9—Dick: Y'know what, yer [grandmother –] =
10—Deb: [>'ts nota question<] of =
           =[<ly:ing't's a question of being– >]
11—Dick: =[yer GRANDMOTHER IS A CENTI]PE:DE,
           that's why– sh[e esstuh hev a khundred pairs of shoes.

---

initiate a new instructing game (6), again with Deb as respondent and Anne as audience; this game involves a joke, as becomes clear. Meanwhile Deb continues (perhaps completes) her earlier game (7) with Anne as respondent. However, Anne selects Dick's game (8) rather than Deb's, and uses it to initiate a new instructing game (8) with Dick as respondent. Dick does not respond to Anne, but instead continues his instructing game (9) and (11), while Deb completes Anne's game and initiates a new instructing game (10), presumably with Anne as respondent.

This example illustrates the problems of distributed control in multi-party dialogue. To see this, let us imagine an extension of Figure 9.2 in which control is shared across more than two interlocutors (but we do not attempt to draw such a complex control structure). The interlocutors' interpretations of their roles affects the process of control – most importantly, the way in which feedback leads interlocutors to instigate a new production command. In Example 10.1, the diners largely agree on their roles. We assume A's utterance *they were like putty* (1) is directed at D – that is, A acts as initiator and selects D as respondent. Thus, D combines feedback and dialogue plan to instigate a command and put *really?* (2) into the shared workspace. The other diners are audience rather than respondents and therefore are less likely to instigate a command. In contrast, *D*'s negative commentary *really?* leads *A* and *B* to respond by expansion – they appear to play a collective role and have partly yoked implementers. And the lack of long pauses and the temporally yoked contributions (*limp* and *mush*, 3/4) indicates distributed control over timing with underlying synchronicity. Because the diners appreciate each other's roles, the control flows without disruption.

But in Example 10.2, the interlocutors do not align on their roles. At (6–8), they all speak concurrently, with Dick selecting Deb as respondent and Anne as audience, Deb selecting Anne as respondent, and Anne selecting Dick as respondent. And they are implementing concurrently and presumably making confused predictions, with apparent lack of synchronicity. This leads to failure to use distributed control appropriately.[5]

In Example 10.2, the interlocutors therefore show misalignment of their dialogue game models. But they also show misalignment of their situation models – it appears that Dick, Deb and Anne are all taking about different things and therefore construct different situation models. These two forms of misalignment are of course linked and show how focal alignment of game models leads to focal alignment of situation models. In addition, they presumably have difficulty synchronizing – for example, it is not clear whether an initiator (e.g. Deb at 4) is more likely to synchronize with the previous contributor (Dick at 3) or with the intended respondent (Anne, who last spoke at 1).

10.2.6   Summary

In summary, we have interpreted multi-party dialogue in terms of a framework of conversational roles, illustrated in Figure 10.3. It is divided into an inner region containing the contributors (players and active audience) and an outer region containing the non-contributors. Those in the inner region can post contributions to the shared workspace and those in the outer region cannot. The inner region contains the active audience and, in the centre, the players of the current dialogue game (the initiator and respondent). The outer region contains the passive audience – those individuals who the contributors communicate with – and, on the periphery, any overhearers to the dialogue. The more peripheral the role, the less engaged the role-holder. Any one of these roles can be filled by a collective rather than an individual. We have used these roles to interpret multi-party dialogue in terms of the shared workspace framework (Figures 10.1 and 10.2).

---

[5] Note that when there is a conflict caused by the breakdown of control, the interlocutors raise their voices (Anne at 8 and Dick at 11, indicated by capitalization). They are competing for control.

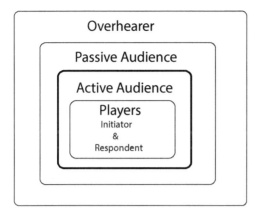

Figure 10.3 Conversational roles in multi-party dialogue. Those within the heavily weighted box are contributors to the dialogue. Central roles are more engaged in the dialogue than peripheral roles.

10.3   Monologue

We argue that the basic form of language use is minimal dyadic conversation. We have just extended our discussion to multi-party dialogue. We now extend our discussion in another direction – to monologue. Monologue occurs when the contributor can receive no response from an audience. In other words, monologue involves a complete block from the audience to the contributor. We first discuss a restricted form of dialogue with some of the characteristics of monologue, and then present monologue in relation the shared workspace framework and in representational terms. We then consider how it is produced and comprehended in turn.

10.3.1   Alternating One-Way Dialogue

To 'lead up' to monologue, we discuss an unusual but theoretically important type of dialogue involving half-duplex walkie-talkies (or equivalent technology), as introduced in Section 4.2. Such devices allow only one interlocutor (*A*) to contribute (i.e. speak and be heard) at any time. When *A* has finished, she releases the speech button, and *B* can then press his speech button to contribute. We call this *alternating one-way dialogue*, and it goes beyond minimal dyadic conversation.

In our framework, the current speaker (*A*) can post contributions to the shared workspace, but the addressee (*B*) cannot. Thus, simultaneous commentary is not possible. Instead, *A* is expected to utter *Over* when releasing the button (thus explicitly indicating the end of her turn), and *Over and out* at the end of the dialogue. We expect A's contributions to be affected by this restriction (though we know of no relevant study), in the same way that lack of feedback affects contributions (Hupet & Chantraine, 1992; Krauss & Weinheimer, 1966). Control of turn-taking is not distributed, but is (literally) in the hands of the speaker. She can relinquish control to her partner (but her partner cannot 'snatch' control) and when she does so, their roles reverse.

The interlocutors therefore have restricted ability to manipulate the shared workspace – they cannot both act on it at once. For example, if A adds too much information to the workspace, B cannot respond by commentary or by taking control. All that B can do is try to comprehend what A has contributed, and hope that A will either explain complexities and ambiguities or relinquish control. In other words, B cannot immediately produce commentary, though B can prepare a commentary for when A relinquishes control.[6] And A is presumably likely to produce contributions that she believes B will understand, given that B produces no commentaries that she can check. When A relinquishes control, then B can produce a deferred commentary (e.g. *Say again*). In general, such delayed commentary is likely to be less efficient and effective than a commentary produced as soon as possible (e.g. when the first word of A's contribution is unclear).[7]

Commentaries lead to the meta-representation of alignment and misalignment. In this form of dialogue, B cannot produce a commentary when appropriate, so A cannot determine whether B is likely to have aligned situation models with her. Thus, A cannot m-tag with certainty – she probably assumes a fairly consistent level of confidence for most elements in her situation model, but does not change that level of confidence during her utterance. Because alignment may be so important (e.g. in aviation traffic control), conventions emerge, for example procedure words such as *Mayday* or *Pan-pan*, or named letters (*Charlie*, *Foxtrot* etc.), that remove acoustic or linguistic ambiguity. When A releases the button, B can produce a positive or negative commentary, again using highly conventionalized expressions (e.g. *Say Again*, *Wilco*, *Negative*; Civil Aviation Authority, 2015). At this point, A can m-tag with confidence – and can construct a new production command if B releases the button.

The inability to provide timely commentary and hence to meta-represent alignment with confidence and in good time interferes with the progress of the dialogue (perhaps alongside concerns about intelligibility and avoiding ambiguity) and changes the nature of contributions from those that occur in minimal

---

[6] In a sense, B is temporarily a passive audience, but because B realizes he is likely to be able to contribute later, it may be better to regard B as a temporarily 'blocked' contributor.

[7] In the equivalent situation in minimal dyadic conversation, if B does not interrupt A but eventually utters *What did you mean?*, then A's contribution may be wasted and A may also be unclear where the problem lies.

dyadic conversation. Note that many of these contributions have novel meanings and sometimes forms – they resemble the routines that emerge in minimal dyadic conversation, but are more conventionalized (i.e. they are part of an established and indeed official lexicon).

10.3.2   The Shared Workspace Framework for Monologue

Monologue is (in effect) non-alternating one-way dialogue. The individuals do not change roles. In fact, there are only two roles, which we call the *designer* and the audience. The audience cannot contribute (and is therefore a passive audience) and the designer cannot relinquish control. Typically, the designer is an individual (though can be a collective); the audience is often a collective. Monologue contains no commentary, as a contributor has to comment on another person's contribution.[8] The designer is unlike a player (or a contributor) in a dialogue, because dialogue games require two players (and at least two contributors). In most multi-party dialogue, players are primarily concerned with alignment among themselves, but in all monologue, the designer can be concerned about alignment only with the audience. Because there is only one contributor (the designer), monologue does not involve games (the audience is not a player). Finally, dialogue roles are fluid, as an interlocutor may change roles repeatedly (i.e. dialogue is locally asymmetric but globally symmetric; see Section 4.1). In monologue, the two roles are fixed (i.e. monologue is globally asymmetric). Note that the designer communicates with the audience, and hence the audience is not an overhearer. All of these points hold whether the audience hears the designer as she speaks, or whether the designer is recording a podcast, or indeed writing, so long as the audience cannot respond in any way.

In Figure 10.4, the designer (A) puts contributions into the shared workspace via the thick black arrow, but the audience member (B) does not – he has no thick black arrow. The shared workspace contains elements that the designer and the audience both attend to (i.e. in parallel), even though they have been contributed by the designer alone. In our example, the designer delivers a news report but the framework holds for any form of monologue. The designer can predict, comprehend and monitor the shared workspace using the vertical grey arrow, and can also predict, comprehend and monitor her production processes using the horizontal grey arrow. In other words, the designer both produces and comprehends (using the monologue implementer). The processes represented

---

[8] So if a radio broadcaster says 'sorry, that might not have been clear' (and restates her point), she has not produced a commentary. Instead she has produced a self-correction (something that can also occur in dialogue; see Schegloff et al., 1977).

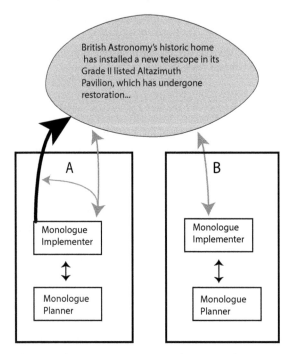

Figure 10.4 The shared workspace framework for monologue (with *A* as designer and *B* as audience), when *A* is giving a radio news broadcast and *B* is listening.

by the designer's grey arrows can help her to develop her contributions – for example, she may decide that one of her words was unclear or obscure, and therefore revise it. In contrast, the audience member is able to predict and comprehend the workspace but cannot use these processes to revise the workspace. He cannot monitor the workspace because monitoring requires both detecting a discrepancy between predicted and actual utterance percept and being able to act on that discrepancy. Moreover, the designer controls the workspace (just like the broadcaster in Section 4.4.1).

In monologue, it is not necessary for the audience member to comprehend an utterance at the time at which the designer produces it. Comprehension occurs when the audience member aligns with the designer, irrespective of when it takes place: I can understand you by listening to your speech or listening to a recording of your speech. Understanding corresponds to alignment of situation models, and situation models do not instantiate time (that is, time is not relevant to the model itself). Therefore alignment does not require (near-)simultaneity, because alignment is defined over orderings rather than timings.

A recording includes the components of the designer's utterance in order. For an audience member to align with the designer of the utterance she must encounter the elements of the utterance (e.g. syllables, words, phrases) in the sequence that the designer produced but not necessarily at the same time. Similarly, the workspace contains signs that are ordered (see Section 7.2.1) but not indexed for time. The designer and the audience have access to the shared workspace whether or not they attend to it at the same time. Parallel attention requires both individuals to attend to the same signs (including their order, as indicated by their subscript) but not to their (absolute) timing. Importantly, parallel attention does *not* require simultaneous attention. When delays occur in dialogue (e.g. in old-fashioned long-distance telephony), it can interfere with alignment – but the reason is that it interferes with commentary rather than because it prevents the establishment of a shared workspace via parallel attention. In other words, simultaneity is a constraint on dialogue, not the shared workspace.

How does the shared workspace framework differ in monologue from dialogue? In Figure 4.2, the shared workspace for dialogue contains contributions from both interlocutors – and so they can act on an individual contribution or a joint contribution (e.g. monitor compatibility between utterance and commentary). In monologue, it contains a contribution from the designer alone, so either individual can act only on an individual contribution. In dialogue, both the interlocutors can manipulate the workspace in a variety of ways – by utterances, by pointing at props and by moving them around. In monologue, such manipulations are all restricted to the designer (as when a TV weather forecaster highlights a region of a map), though the audience can interpret the whole of the workspace and not merely the utterance itself. In addition, a designer in monologue can have an individual workspace (e.g. the contents of a short autocue during a speech), as its contents can subsequently enter the shared workspace, whereas the audience has no individual workspace.[9] In recorded monologue, the designer has an individual workspace before the audience listens (see Section 11.3.2).

---

[9] A novice cook might learn how to cook a stir-fry by playing an (audio) podcast and following the instructions as they occur using real objects (a wok, ingredients, etc.). In this monologue, the podcaster sets up a shared workspace, for example by uttering *chop the spring onions*, and the cook follows the instructions. But the cook's objects are not props, as they do not form part of a shared workspace. The podcaster can monitor her own contribution, but cannot monitor the cook's response (and cannot respond if the cook cuts up the wrong vegetable). The cook's actions therefore do not enter the shared workspace. But in addition, they also do not constitute an individual workspace, because there is no route by which they could enter the shared workspace. The podcaster contrasts with a TV chef, who can demonstrate the chopping in the shared workspace, and can also introduce new ingredients from his individual workspace ('below the table'). The TV chef's ingredients are therefore props.

10.3.3   Representations and Processes in the Designer and the Audience

In monologue, the audience can of course align with the designer. When a designer writes (or reads aloud) a story, she establishes a situation model – and if the audience understands the story as the designer intended, then the audience develops the same situation model (at the focal and global level). In fact, we introduced situation model alignment using examples from monologue (Section 7.1.1). And the audience aligns with the designer at linguistic levels as well (e.g. via structural priming which occurs in isolated participants; see Pickering & Ferreira, 2008). Of course, the designer and audience do not align game models, because there are no monologue games that they can represent.

Note that we have already pointed out that speech acts are a rough monological equivalent to dialogue games (though recall that monologue does not involve games). Speech acts are typically framed in terms of the initiator's move, without reference to the respondent's move. So a declarative illocutionary act corresponds to an initiation move of an instructing game, an interrogative illocutionary act corresponds to an initiation move of an information-seeking game, and so on. In dialogue, the response to an instructing game can be either a minimal positive commentary or no commentary at all. In a monologue, it is straightforward for designers to use a declarative. In contrast, an interrogative game typically requires an informative move (i.e. the answer to a *wh*-question) and so it is difficult for designers to use an interrogative. There are of course 'rhetorical' exceptions to this, as when a designer asks a question for her audience to ponder, when the answer is obvious, or when she provides the answer herself. The audience has to determine the designer's speech act (e.g. Clark & Lucy, 1975), as one part of the process of alignment.

In Section 10.2.3, we proposed that passive audience members simulate less than active audience members (or players), as they cannot use production-based representations in actual production. In the same way, simulation is reduced for the audience in monologue compared to interlocutors in dialogue. As prediction is largely driven by simulation, we propose that the monological audience also tends to predict less than contributors in dialogue. And the reduction in simulation is likely to lead to a reduction in alignment, in addition to the effects of not having commentary.

We have argued that alignment is the consequence of commentary and its effects on meta-representation of alignment and subsequent production commands. In monologue, the designer does not have the benefit of such (positive or negative) commentary and so is unable to use it to shape production commands, and the audience is unable to benefit from commands that have been shaped appropriately. The absence of commentary therefore provides an explanation of poor comprehension in Schober and Clark's (1989) overhearers and in Fay et al.'s (2018) route followers in monologue. Monologue is difficult, but people manage. To explain how it is possible, we turn to the mechanisms of monitoring and control in monologue. Chapter 5 culminated in a model of the dialogue control system (Figure 5.5), but this model does not apply to monologue. Instead, we have to return to the intermediate models of production (Figure 5.2) and comprehension (Figure 5.3) and apply them to the designer and audience, respectively.

10.3.4   How the Designer Copes

The designer internally monitors by comparing the utterance representation with the predicted utterance representation, and then externally monitors by comparing the utterance percept (derived from the shared workspace) with the predicted utterance percept (see Figure 5.2). In dialogue, we argued that the internal monitor is relatively unimportant because it cannot be used in dialogue monitoring. But in monologue, the designer can usefully monitor internally as well as externally, and in fact internal monitoring is often more efficient than external monitoring (e.g. Hartsuiker & Kolk, 2001). We therefore expect internal monitoring to be more dominant in monologue than dialogue. The designer can self-correct on the basis of internal monitoring (i.e. altering planning or implementation before behaviour) or external monitoring (i.e. on the basis of utterance itself).

The designer controls the monologue. She is the only one who can contribute to the shared workspace: she makes every decision about what is said and when. That is, she does not distribute control between herself and the (passive) audience. The designer is concerned that the audience understands. Therefore, she wants to meta-represent alignment with the audience, but she is liable to do it badly. When an addressee produces a commentary in dialogue, the speaker has good evidence to meta-represent degree of alignment ('Am I thinking about this in the same way as you?'), and uses the meta-representation to drive the next production command. But without commentary, the designer can do no more than guess whether the audience is aligning.

To be successful in monologue, the designer has to work out what to do by herself. This is difficult, but she has the advantage of not being time-locked to her audience. In other words, she can usually prepare what she wants to say beforehand. That is, she can *compose* her contribution 'off-line' (i.e. planning without accommodating to potential external contributions), and can indeed rehearse it. A skilled designer composes monologues that are very different from contributions to dialogue. Such monologues make use of aspects of language (e.g. words or grammatical constructions) that are often associated with literate culture. They involve routines that are not limited to a particular setting and which are established by cultural conventions, for example the education system or the prescriptions of dictionaries or national academies (see

Chapter 11). A skilled designer has learnt (i.e. internalized) a great deal of such information that she can draw on, and feels (relatively) confident that her audience is likely to understand in the same way and therefore align with her. Our goal is not to understand the nature of monologue, but it is necessary to make it clear how actual monologue contrasts with dialogue.

A central concern for the designer is to shape contributions for the intended audience – something which is known as *audience design* (Clark & Murphy, 1982; Bell, 1984). In dialogue, a contributor of course also shapes contributions, but the 'design' does not reside solely (or even primarily) in the contributor, because contributions are shaped by commentaries from other contributors. In contrast, the designer works out whether a contribution is appropriate for a given audience. One critical skill for designers is to make it as likely as possible that the audience will be able to align with them, and good style guides help designers hone their compositional abilities (e.g. Fowler, 1926; Pinker, 2015). Note that designers are often unaware of their specific audience – a radio broadcaster may speak for a presumed audience interested in politics or football, and a correspondent might record events 'for posterity'.[10]

10.3.5   How the Audience Copes

The audience cannot contribute and therefore does not monitor the monologue or control its progress. Importantly, we referred to the process of comparison in Figure 5.3 as external monitoring in the context of dialogue. But for audiences in monologue, the comparison in Figure 5.3 does not involve monitoring. Instead, it tracks the progress of the monologue in relation to the audience's predictions and enables cognizing – specifically, updating the situation model (and linguistic representations), and using those updates to develop and modify predictions about the upcoming continuation of the monologue. In the context of monologue, we refer to the monitor in Figure 5.3 as a *pseudo-monitor* (i.e. it is the same component but plays a different role). Cognizing is based on the discrepancy between predicted and actual continuations. The discrepancy can be formalized as surprisal (Hale, 2001; see Levy, 2008). We propose that the audience also becomes aware of consistently high discrepancies – that is, realizes when alignment appears difficult and therefore meta-represents low confidence in alignment.

---

[10] Psycholinguistic experiments in dialogue show effects of addressees (e.g. Brennan & Clark, 1996; Isaacs & Clark, 1987), and many of these effects may reflect responses to addressee-specific commentaries. To investigate audience design in monologue, it is of course necessary to rule out any commentaries.

An important difference between comprehension (by a contributor) in dialogue and comprehension (by the audience) in monologue is that it is not possible to respond in monologue. In both dialogue and monologue, the comparison of the predicted and actual utterance feeds back to the planner. In dialogue, the updated planner can be used to instigate a new production command; but in monologue, no such command can be issued. For example, if a dialogue contributor encounters an ambiguity, he can produce a query or other negative commentary – and he has to make decisions about whether, how and when to comment. But if a monologue audience encounters the same ambiguity, all he can do is cognize – that is, work out 'in his head' what the designer is most likely to have intended.

Psycholinguistic experiments focus extensively on resolving ambiguity in monologue. Just as one example, Rayner and Duffy (1986) tracked participants' eye movements as they read sentences such as *He found the coach was too hot to sleep in*, and found that they spent longer reading *coach* (which is locally ambiguous between meaning a vehicle or sports trainer) than the unambiguous word *cabin* when it was substituted for *coach*. Participants could not query the 'author' and so could only cognize. In contrast, an audience member who encountered this sentence in dialogue could listen passively (and wait for subsequent disambiguation) but could also decide to query rapidly (e.g. saying *eh?* soon after hearing *coach*), as occurred in Chapter 8, Example 8.4 (*Forty nine wha:t?*). To understand ambiguity resolution in dialogue, experiments would need to treat whether, how, and when addressees respond (as well as whether they experience comprehension difficulty). Similarly, studies of text comprehension investigate how and when comprehenders draw bridging inferences to link sentences (Haviland & Clark, 1974), but in dialogue contributors can respond, for example by asking whether their interpretation is appropriate. More generally, it is an open question as to whether findings of comprehension difficulty in monologue relate to dialogue or not.

10.4   Conclusion: The Variety of Communication Arrangements

For most of the book, we have focused on minimal dyadic conversation. In this chapter, we have extended our analysis, both to various forms of multi-party conversation and to monologue. In doing this, we have retained all of the apparatus developed for minimal dyadic conversation, such as the shared workspace, the distinction between planner and implementer, the systems analysis and the central concept of alignment. However, the apparatus is used in different ways according to the arrangements. We have also provided an analysis of conversational roles that is appropriate for our systems framework (and which contrasts with traditional analyses).

In Pickering and Garrod (2004), we proposed a 'dialogic continuum' that had highly interactive conversation at one end and monologue at the other. The shared workspace framework also assumes that all forms of dialogue and monologue are related, in different ways. Clearly interlocutors can be more or less interactive, in a way that is at least partly reflected in their conversational roles. In addition, we note that a passive audience listening to a radio debate involves both dialogue and monologue – the debaters are both contributors (to the debate) and designers (with respect to the audience). It is only possible to understand language use in all its complexity if we consider both dialogue and monologue together – though of course our focus in this book is on dialogue.

11 Culture and Language Use

In this chapter, we integrate the shared workspace framework with culture – that is, both cultural institutions (such as conventional activities) and cultural artefacts (i.e. devices that enhance communication). We first integrate our framework for dialogue with the framework for other cooperative joint activities (Chapters 2 and 3), and in particular note that the shared workspace is ideal for incorporating types of linguistic and non-linguistic information. We then consider dialogic activity types (e.g. job interviews, purchasing items in a shop) as a refinement of dialogue games, and their effect on aspects of our framework such as the control, content and prediction of dialogue. In the final part of chapter, we show how the shared workspace framework is augmented by cultural artefacts. We look at the way that illustrations such as complex paintings are integrated with dialogue and text, consider the effects of recordings on communication, and then discuss communication technologies in the context of our framework.

11.1 Dialogue Structures Cooperative Joint Activities

It is hard to imagine cooperative joint activities without some degree of communication. When actors perform a cooperative joint activity such as making furniture, they of course typically use language. The activity therefore involves both non-linguistic and linguistic components, and the actors are 'situated' interlocutors. To explain how this is possible, we must combine the theory of non-linguistic action (Chapters 2 and 3) with the theory of dialogue (Chapters 4–10). Our account of non-linguistic cooperative joint activity was fairly sketchy, in that most of the detailed framework we have developed relates to dialogue. To understand 'situated' dialogue, we need to interpret non-linguistic action in more detail, specifying what action corresponds to a use of language. In outline, such interlocutors put both actions (such as holding a piece of wood in place) and language (such as words) into the shared workspace. They then construct representations that are both linguistic and non-linguistic in nature, and use those representations in the service of alignment, prediction, control and so on. Language allows interlocutors to refine the goals underlying joint activity, so that they can plan a series of joint activities (as when determining an itinerary or indeed in jointly constructing furniture).

In Chapter 2, we introduced cooperative joint activity using an example in which a man and a woman collaboratively constructed furniture. Because this discussion preceded our consideration of dialogue, we ignored the fact that such a joint activity inevitably involves communication, and almost certainly language. Let us assume that the man holds the wood marked with a cross for the woman to drill, and that the man says *drill here*, and the woman replies *OK* and starts drilling (see Clark & Krych, 2004). If so, they treat the action as having four components: the man presenting the wood, the man saying *drill here* in the context of the cross, the woman saying *OK* and the woman drilling.

When we consider the activity without the utterance, we cannot unambiguously 'parse' it into components – the structure of the activity depends on external analysts (as observers). But communicating agents construct meaning by jointly performing the activity, and critically they 'parse' it by the way that they refer to it. So when the man says *drill here*, the act of drilling plus the drill and its target become the components of the joint action. In turn, they become meaningful elements within the shared workspace, and these meaningful elements are interpreted in relation to moves in a dialogue game and in relation to the actors' situation models. The man presents the wood and says *drill here* as two parallel steps (that may take place concurrently), and the woman says *OK* and drills as the next two parallel steps. The four components together constitute an action-seeking game, with the man's components composing the initiation move and the woman's components composing the response move. Both agents construct a situation model that represents the action in terms of its components (with *here* instantiated as the location of the cross).

In Section 6.2.1, we considered another example of furniture-building in which A said *you now need to screw the components together* and B responded by holding up two different screws with a quizzical expression. B's response is a non-linguistic demonstration serving a negative commentary function (corresponding roughly to the utterance *which screw?*). It therefore initiated an embedded information-seeking dialogue game (and is a step that was ordered after A's instruction, even if the two steps overlap). It led to A meta-representing misalignment and (presumably) attempting to complete the embedded game and resolve the misalignment, for example by uttering *the smaller one* or pointing to it.

Now imagine that we are military historians discussing aspects of the Battle of Waterloo over coffee. I place my mug on the table and say *This is Napoleon's cavalry* and point to the sugar bowl, saying *This is Wellington's infantry*. I move the mug in an arc towards the bowl, thereby representing the indirect troop movement. (The use of a mug to refer to cavalry is symbolic, and the use of an arc to represent indirect movement is iconic.) At this point, I take a sip out of my mug before replacing it in position and say *Coffee, please* and you respond by filling the mug with more coffee. Assuming you are following what I am doing, the mug is an object in the shared workspace, but an object that seems to have two functions. First, it is interpreted as a sign referring to Napoleon's cavalry, and second it is a mug – that is, an object that functions as itself. Importantly, the meaningful object is the same in both cases (i.e. it is a mug). But it can be used flexibly – it can have more than one function at the same time, or it can change functions during an interaction.

Note that we have used the term *prop* rather loosely. To be more precise, a prop is a physical object that corresponds to a component of the joint plan and which therefore plays a part in the cooperative joint activity but has no signification in that activity. If you fill my mug as part of a simple coffee-drinking activity (involving or not involving language), the mug is a prop – its only role is as a container of coffee. But in our more complex example, the mug is a sign (standing for Napoleon's cavalry) as well as a prop.[1]

In our more complex example, the mug takes part in two distinct cooperative joint actions. In the military re-enactment, the mug jointly affords reference to *Napoleon's cavalry* and jointly affords either or both actors to move other objects in concert with the mug – for example, moving a spoon forwards 'in support' and a sugar bowl backwards 'in retreat'. In the coffee-drinking activity, it jointly affords being a receptacle for coffee – something that can be proffered in order to have coffee poured into it and drunk out of. And for it to play its two roles, both of us represent both roles. These roles are manifest to both of us – the coffee-drinking role because I proffered the mug to you to fill up and you filled it up, and the re-enactment role because I labelled the mug as Napoleon's cavalry and you accepted the label (as a consequence of your contribution).

Now consider the demonstration in which speaker MB said *And you would go by his office and hear,* 'Well, I can see you Wednesday at three o'clock' (adapted from Clark, 2016, p. 325), and where MB said the underlined expression in a booming voice (and made dramatic gestures). MB put the underlined expression into a workspace shared with his interlocutor. It is an entity (a Piercean sign vehicle) that functions as a (largely) symbolic sign when it is interpreted linguistically, but as an iconic sign when it is interpreted in terms of manner (boomingness). Moreover, the two signs constitute parallel steps – the meaning of the linguistic expression and its iconic interpretation are parallel components to the dialogue plan – and they are implemented concurrently. In other cases, the demonstration fits into an otherwise linguistic

---

[1] Of course, there are components of plans that correspond to events rather than physical objects, and those events need not have signification – for example, pouring coffee as part of the coffee-drinking activity.

sequence, as in *The dictator went* [clenched-fist gesture] *to the crowd* (where the gesture has the linguistic role of a noun phrase argument).

Note that the sound involved in language also has a non-significatory consequence, for example when speaking loudly to a hearing-impaired inter-locutor. The same entity (i.e. physical object) has different joint affordances – that is, it plays different roles in the cooperative joint activity.

The shared workspace framework is ideally suited for this flexibility. Rather than assume the workspace has two types of entities (non-signs and signs), we note that it provides a resource by which the same entities can be either or both, and can also be different types of signs (symbolic or iconic). And it allows the integration of linguistic and non-linguistic contributions to cooperative joint activity. All entities in the shared workspace have a role in the plan – a role which makes reference to their place in the sequence.[2]

The way in which the shared workspace serves as a flexible resource becomes much clearer if we consider slightly more complex examples in which two people are using a physical board (that is manifest to them) to assist organization or problem solving. If two co-workers plan how to tackle a complex task (e.g. building a house extension), then they will add information to the board to facilitate their joint planning. This information can be words (e.g. *bricks needed*, *location of door*, *six hundred*) or sketches (e.g. a floor layout, which might include the location of the door). They can also add information associated with executing the plan, for example ticking off tasks when completed or indicating what is being done (e.g. adding an arrow to the left-hand wall of the floor layout). More generally, the co-workers can add new words or sketches and modify or delete existing ones. At the same time, they each monitor what is happening to the board (both as a result of their own and their partner's activities). The contents of the board are meaningful entities but are not interpreted. For example, they might interpret *location of door* to refer to different doors but the words themselves are the same.

This physical board supports the co-workers planning and building the extension – it is much easier to discuss the extension when they have this resource available. And in the same way, the shared workspace supports planning and implementing the dialogue. The interlocutors share the task of adding words or sketches to the board (and therefore putting the information into the shared workspace), monitoring its contents, and (if appropriate) responding with a new contribution. In Figure 8.1 (repeated from Figure 5.5),

---

[2] Strictly, this means that non-signs have a subscript indicating order. If you say *do you want some coffee?* and I point to my mug, then your utterance has subscript 1 and my mug (as prop) has subscript 2; if you say *here's some coffee* and pour coffee, then the utterance and the action are in parallel, and so have the same subscript.

we see that the interlocutors post contributions via the two thick black arrows, monitor the contents of the shared workspace via the left-facing grey and black arrows and the dotted box, and respond when the planner is used to initiate a new production command. This cyclical process can lead to repeated updates to the shared workspace.

We have explained how dialogue supports cooperative joint activity, in a way that provides structure and meaning to such activity. We now consider how types of activity shape dialogue.

11.2   'Activity Types' as Cooperative Joint Activities

In Chapter 2, we sketched a range of cooperative joint activities, such as playing chess, co-piloting an aircraft or a nurse assisting a surgeon – activities that can be long-lasting and organizationally complex. In contrast, our discussion of dialogue has focused on brief exchanges and their structure rather than on the full interactional setting. In other words, we have concentrated on individual dialogue games, their internal structure and their effects on implementation. But how do such cooperative joint activities constrain dialogue?

We interpret cooperative joint activities in terms of what Levinson (1979) calls *activity types*: 'a fuzzy category whose focal members are goal-defined, socially constituted, bounded, events with *constraints* on participants, setting and so on, but above all on the kinds of allowable contributions' (p. 69). His examples of activity types include teaching, job interviews or football games. They are all cooperative joint activities. As we have just noted, communication is largely essential to cooperative joint activities and we therefore treat them as communicative activity types (see Linell, 2009, pp. 201–211) and focus on their communicative component. Levinson concentrates on activities involving (extended) interaction, as in a complete lesson or interview, or an episode in which a customer purchases a product from a shopkeeper, and we do so too.

Communicative activity types vary on several dimensions (see Clark, 1996, pp. 30–31; Levinson, 1979, pp. 69–70). They differ in scriptedness, from marriage ceremonies in which the participants are required to produce particular utterances at specific moments, to chance meetings. They also differ in formality, for example ranging from some types of interview to gossip sessions. Next, they differ in level of cooperativeness, with interlocutors sometimes agreeing with each other and sometimes arguing, and on governance, with some activity types being egalitarian and some being autocratic. Finally, they vary in the distribution of control – the interlocutors typically share control, but there may be a leader who decides who should speak and when, and this leader may even be an 'external manager' who does not contribute. In a formal interview, the chair dictates the order of contributions by the committee members and candidate, and may also determine content, for example when stating that a line of questioning is inappropriate. In many cases, judges have similar control over courtroom interactions.

11.2.1   Social Norms and Joint Planning

We can typically decompose communicative activity types into parts (which can correspond to different cooperative joint activities). Thus, a wedding may involve a scripted ceremony, a conventionalized but less formal set of speeches, and casual conversations. The actors therefore represent joint plans (and their roles) and represent sub-plans within those plans. Importantly, dialogue games are embedded within larger communicative activity types. Sometimes, the activity has a fairly clear structure with a specific sequence of games (with limits on possible variation). For example, a purchasing episode might include a conventionalized opening, an information-seeking game about a product (as when the customer points and asks *how much?* and the shopkeeper responds *five pounds*), a transaction and a conventionalized closing. In conversations between friends, the types and order of games may be more flexible, but there are still organizational principles – for example, beginning with a greeting, or perhaps asking about family health before focusing on common interests.

Communicative activity types reflect social norms – conventions that provide constraints on forms of dialogue that are acceptable in particular environments. These conventions can be regarded as akin to the rules discussed by Wittgenstein (1953/1958). They are common knowledge and therefore each interlocutor standardly obeys them and assumes (without question) that their partner will too (see Lewis, 1969). Thus, they both represent the social norms and are therefore aligned with respect to those norms (and any misalignment can lead to clashes). The customer can place a product on the counter or the shopkeeper can enter the price into the till, and both participants interpret these behaviours and know what their individual commitments are (what they need to do next). Some of these conventions are instantiated as moves within dialogue games that are manifest to the interlocutors – they know how to play these games and what their individual roles are. In Chapter 6, we treated dialogue games in very general terms, for example distinguishing action-seeking games, information-seeking games, instructing games and so on. But we now interpret games in a much more fine-grained manner, for example distinguishing a polite request to a shopkeeper from an instruction to a child or a military command. Interlocutors represent these conventions about the interaction as part of the fine-grained dialogue game (rather than as monological conventions about how an individual should behave).

Social norms are incorporated into their dialogue plans. So when *B* makes an error, feedback goes back to both *A* and *B*'s joint planners, and they both pay attention to the social norm about how this affects control of the dialogue. In a casual conversation, *A* may tend to overlook errors, and so either *B* self-corrects or the error goes uncorrected (cf. Schegloff et al., 1977). But in a tutorial activity type, *A* may tend to correct *B*'s error. Moreover the activity type affects the content of contributions – for example, *A* might correct a grammatical error in a tutorial but correct only an important factual error in a casual conversation. It is therefore easy to see how the activity type affects the progress of the dialogue (in relation to Figure 5.5).

Another example relates to cross-cultural variation. Fujii (2012) compared American and Japanese task-oriented dialogues and found that Japanese interlocutors were more likely to co-construct multi-clause contributions and to linguistically align than Americans. Most interestingly, they often used the same pronoun to refer to themselves and their partner, suggesting some integration of self and other. Japanese interlocutors appear to use dialogue plans that lead to more closely meshed implementations – indeed, implementations that make the benefits of the shared workspace framework apparent.

Interlocutors can of course be misaligned with respect to the activity type, for reasons that may reflect differences in social norms. For example, *A* may treat a dinner as informal entertainment but *B* may treat it as an interview, because they make different assumptions (e.g. *A* assumes that the recruitment process is limited to a scheduled meeting, but *B* does not). Such misalignment may lead to misalignment of situation models – that is, it may interfere with conversational success.[3]

Clearly, many activity types constrain participants' contributions. In a professional exchange between shopkeeper and customer (in the United Kingdom), both participants' topics are highly restricted. The shopkeeper is conventionally limited to questions such as *Can I help you?*, and the customer is, in turn, conventionally limited to asking whether the shop sells a particular product, where it is on the shelves, or how much it costs; both participants may also make a few generic comments (e.g. about the weather). The shopkeeper then provides little more than answers to these questions or requests for further information (e.g. which brand the customer prefers). Thus, both the content of the utterances and their potential forms are much more restricted in such interactions than in casual conversation.

These conventional restrictions are of course not absolute – interlocutors occasionally violate the conventions (e.g. the shopkeeper complains about her unfaithful partner to the customer). When this happens, it is typically quite

---

[3] Misalignment may be particularly likely in multi-party dialogue (Section 10.2), where there is ample opportunity for different contributors to assume different activity types.

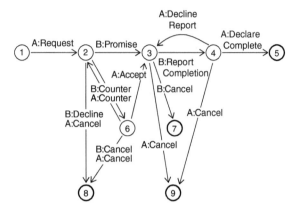

Figure 11.1 A state transition network for conversation.
From Winograd (1987).

apparent to the interlocutors and may disrupt the dialogue.[4] Violations can also, of course, occur at the level of the generic dialogue games (e.g. information-seeking), for example when an addressee fails to respond (or responds in an irrelevant manner) to a direct question.

Many ritualized interchanges (e.g. initiation ceremonies) or those admitting very little variation (e.g. military commands) are even more restricted than exchanges between shopkeepers and customers. They may require participants to utter quite specific forms of words (e.g. *Halt!*, *I agree to honour and obey* . . .). Similarly, auction bidders may be conventionally limited to a few hand signals with specific interpretations (Kuiper, 1996).

In a rather different framework, Winograd (1987) provided an analysis of the effects of activity type (which he calls conversation-for-action) on conversation moves (which he calls speech acts). His analysis uses state transition networks relating to specific forms of interaction such as health professionals reporting on patient treatment. In Figure 11.1, *A*'s request (1–2) allows *B* to make a promise (2–3), make a counter (2–6), or decline (2–8), and so on. After (1–2), *A* can therefore predict *B*'s move. (The heavy circles represent states of completion, which correspond to the completion of a dialogue game.) The possible transitions in a particular exchange reflect the options available to the planner. In sum, these different frameworks all seek to capture the ways in which culture constrains communicative joint activities.

---

[4] This is the rationale for the 'breaching' experiments of Garfinkel (1967), in which the experimenter tried to identify conventions by deliberately violating them.

11.2.2   'Activity Types' Hone Predictions

Prediction (of others) is central to successful joint activity, and therefore anything that makes predictions more accurate is beneficial. When a candidate attends an interview, she predicts that she will take part in a series of information-seeking games (as the information supplier). As the interviewers are likely to ask specific questions (e.g. about motivation, background, or capabilities) at specific points (e.g. after the previous game has been completed), she is able to predict roughly what she is likely to be asked and when. In fact, she regards the activity type and specific game as manifest, and is therefore able to predict what is likely to come next. We therefore assume that she does in fact make such predictions.

   Similarly, when a customer looks at the shelves in a pharmacy, he predicts that the shopkeeper may speak, and, if she does so, that her utterance is likely to be a polite and non-directive question similar to *Can I help you, sir?* The shopkeeper predicts that the customer will respond in one of a small number of ways, including *No thank you* or a contextually relevant question. If the customer says *Do you have . . .?*, then she predicts a noun phrase referring to a pharmaceutical product. In this case, she therefore predicts syntactic form and semantic category but not the specific word. To do this, she combines activity type (purchasing interaction) and setting (pharmacy) to hone her predictions.[5] In fact, activity type plus setting can also constrain to a particular word, as when the customer points to a nail-clipper and says *Is that your only . . .?* These examples also show that activity type plus setting can vary in the degree of constraint. Clearly, if the participants conform to the conventions of the activity type (e.g. talking exclusively about pharmaceutical products), then the utterance will be highly predictable and the interlocutors will tend to make the appropriate predictions.[6] These constraints can be extremely strong; for example when a sergeant-major utters *Left Right Left . . .*, the privates can predict *Right* and its timing with almost complete accuracy. Given the right activity type and setting, the predictability of utterances can be similar to high-Cloze sentences in psycholinguistic experiments (e.g. Kutas & Hillyard, 1984). Cultural constraints therefore enhance prediction and alignment.[7]

---

[5] We refer to the purchasing interaction as the activity type and the pharmacy as the setting, but we could regard a pharmaceutical purchasing interaction as a more fine-grained activity type.

[6] In contrast, friends meeting for dinner may discuss a much wider range of issues (fewer topics are likely to be 'out of bounds'), and so in this respect they may be much less able to predict each other.

[7] As an aside, many experiments 'design out' most aspects of predictability (unless they are specifically studying prediction). To determine whether people prefer 'low attached' sentences (e.g. *The spy saw the cop with the revolver but the cop didn't see him*) or 'high attached' sentences (where *revolver* is replaced with *binoculars*), experimenters typically present participants with equal numbers of 'low attached' and 'high attached' sentences (see Rayner et al.,

Levinson (1979) pointed out that different activity types constrain inferences in different ways. For example, he noted that *It's five past twelve* indicates that a lecture should start if it is uttered by a lecturer, with some listeners present, and the lecture is scheduled to begin by then; as part of a different activity type, the utterance would not permit this inference. In this case, the audience would predict that the lecturer was about to speak and, specifically, to produce some form of words that are consistent with the beginning of a lecture (e.g. *Today I will talk about ...*). The audience can then predict other aspects of what the lecturer will say, most likely in broad terms (e.g. the topic).

Prediction is central to our account, with interlocutors controlling the dialogue by predicting whenever possible, monitoring on the basis of those predictions, and using feedback from the monitor to inform their next move (see Figure 8.1). By honing predictions, activity types become a major component in our framework.

Activity types therefore affect both how interlocutors contribute and what they predict about each other's contributions. By constraining the form of contributions, they help minimize collaborative effort, and help the interlocutors develop the shared workspace in an efficient manner. We now turn to other ways of developing the shared workspace – ones that make use of cultural artefacts.

11.3   Augmenting the Shared Workspace

We identify three ways of augmenting the shared workspace. One is to add information to the (current) state of the shared workspace. The most straightforward example is when communicators use a prop to support communication. For example when *A* says *Do you want some coffee?* and points to a jar of coffee, the shared workspace is augmented from the sign *coffee$_5$* to a (composite) sign that also includes the actual jar (and which can therefore be interpreted differently from the simple sign). Illustrations are a technology that can be used to facilitate this augmentation, as when an interlocutor finds that words are inadequate on their own and therefore sketches a diagram to help explain a difficult concept. Such augmentative technologies enrich the workspace (and relate most directly to focal alignment).

1983). Thus a critic could not claim that any results (e.g. about initial choice of analysis) were due to the frequency of sentence types in the experiment: in this case, the observed preference for 'high attachment' must have some other source (such as the principle of 'minimal attachment'). More generally, rich contexts are an excellent source of predictability, and a very high proportion of experiments in language comprehension eschew rich contexts. It may sometimes be appropriate to 'design out' sources of predictability, but it gives the impression that prediction is not important in language comprehension.

The second way of augmenting the shared workspace is to help people navigate it. When interlocutors discuss a complex visual environment, they sometimes need assistance in attending to the same elements in the same way. Something is salient if people are likely to notice it. Therefore salient entities are likely to attract parallel attention, even if they are not currently in the shared workspace (cf. Schelling, 1960). So augmentation occurs when the context makes an entity salient – for example, an object that stands out from its surroundings because of its striking appearance. Illustrations can also be used in this way – the illustrator can intentionally 'draw the eye' to an object by encircling it or making it flash on a screen. But such navigation can be more extensive – for example, people tend to discuss a cartoon strip in the order intended by the cartoonist. Such augmentative technologies do not primarily serve to enrich the workspace, but rather change the way it develops by helping people navigate it (and relate most directly to global alignment).

The third way of augmenting the shared workspace is to record aspects of it. When an interlocutor sketches a diagram with a pen, it is recorded, and so either interlocutor may be able to return to it. In a similar way, people can return to what they or their partners have written or to recorded speech. Many technologies serve to record linguistic or non-linguistic aspects of communication. They differ in how much they record, how well and for how long. They also differ in the extent to which they facilitate navigation – written words can be accessed by an appropriate eye movement but a recording has to be replayed. Many technologies also allow communication without simultaneity (as in monologue). Recording therefore affects the way in which people use the workspace.

Communicators use a range of technologies that augment the shared workspace. Some technologies relate primarily to its non-linguistic aspects, and include illustrations of various kinds. Others relate to language and include writing and sound recordings. A third group of technologies relate to both linguistic and non-linguistic aspects of the workspace and include both illustrated texts and multi-media technologies. We consider them in turn.

11.3.1   Augmenting the Shared Workspace with Illustrations

Interlocutors can have a detailed discussion about a complex painting of a meaningful scene but could not have a similar discussion of a jumbled-up arrangement of objects. Let us consider *Netherlandish Proverbs* by Bruegel the Elder (Figure 11.2) – a complex painting which contains many embedded scenes that enact proverbs. The painting provides a meaningful contribution to their shared workspace – a contribution that goes well beyond most natural scenes or isolated props. It uses culture to shape the workspace in non-linguistic ways.

Figure 11.2 Bruegel the Elder's *Netherlandish Proverbs*. The man banging his head against the brick wall is near the bottom left of the painting; the man swimming against the tide is towards the top right.

Like all illustrations, the painting is a cultural artefact: it has been designed by an artist in a way that seeks to draw viewers' attention to particular aspects of it. Moreover, the viewers share some background knowledge with the artist. And so when two art enthusiasts jointly look at the painting and discuss it, they can interpret it effectively – that is, they can align on appropriate and rich situation models. They could not do so if they were discussing a random array of objects, or a painting which made little sense to viewers as they did not share enough cultural background with the artist. In our example, the presence of the painting augments the shared workspace because it makes the individual scenes salient. Therefore we argue that the development of the shared workspace is facilitated by non-linguistic cultural artefacts such as this painting.

Illustrations – whether artistic paintings, technical drawings or maps – enrich the shared workspace. When the interlocutors discuss an illustration in front of them, the illustration helps the workspace to develop, because it provides more information than language tends to do on its own, and because the interlocutors both presume that particular details are salient (i.e. to both of them). And they do so in part because they are talking about the painting but in

Figure 11.3 A photograph of an arctic tern (with focus on its subject).

part because the painting has structure. Breughel has carefully organized the painting, and the interlocutors can understand his organization – it is a cultural artefact that is compatible with their culture.

Artefacts do not need to be created from scratch. Photography involves design, even when the subject is natural. For example, a photographer wishing to depict an arctic tern can attempt to isolate the bird by defocusing the background (Figure 11.3). The tern is made salient and so interlocutors can easily discuss its characteristics (e.g. its long beak), but cannot easily discuss the background vegetation. (We therefore treat such photographs as illustrations for present purposes.)

In general, conversations about illustrations therefore have enriched shared workspaces. Two art enthusiasts standing in front of *Netherlandish Proverbs* can refer to any one of the scenes that it depicts, for example the man banging his head against a brick wall. But if they are discussing the same painting while walking in the park, they will typically find it harder to refer to that scene, even if they are both reasonably familiar with the painting – the speaker might not remember the details, or might not be confident that her partner would remember them. And their conversations will be very different – for example, they can point at the relevant scene when it is in front of them but have to describe it otherwise (e.g. Clark & Krych, 2004). In the conversation at the art gallery, aspects of the painting as well as the relevant utterances enter and leave the shared workspace; in the conversation in the park, only the utterances do so.

We have discussed various forms of dialogue that are augmented with non-linguistic material, such as props (e.g. drills and wood). But these props are simple objects that fit into joint activities, including dialogue, for example as part of demonstrations. They do not serve to organize the workspace. In

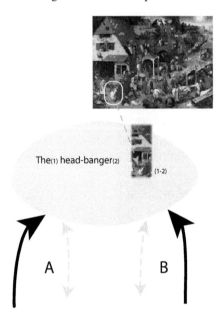

Figure 11.4 The shared workspace augmented by an illustration. *A* and *B* are looking together at *Netherlandish Proverbs*, and *A* refers to a character in the bottom left corner as *the head-banger*. The shared workspace contains the signs for *the* and *head-banger* and the part of the picture depicting the head-banger (which is co-indexed with *the head-banger*). The circle picks out the aspect of visual reality captured in the shared workspace. The dotted arrow provides a way of highlighting that aspect of reality.

contrast, the head-banger (with the brick wall) has a cultural role – Bruegel organized an aspect of his (imagined) world so that it can be appreciated and, importantly, discussed. The painting plays an analogous role to the maze in Garrod and Anderson's (1987) example *You're one along uh huh and one up?* (see Section 4.5) – a culturally constructed object that organizes the conversation, and has different granularities (the box is like the scene, whereas the maze is like the painting).

And so when the enthusiasts discuss the head-banging scene, it enters their shared workspace as a single meaningful component (see Figure 11.4). But if they treat it as a complex scene involving the man and the brick wall, the two components enter the workspace separately (and sequentially). Just as when Garrod and Anderson's (1987) players discussed their positions in the maze (Figure 4.2), the art enthusiasts interpret the linguistic and non-linguistic components of the workspace via their downward grey arrowheads. In doing so, they combine the utterance and the scene. And on the basis of this combination, they can put their next contribution into the workspace via the thick black arrow.

Augmenting the shared workspace of course impacts on the interlocutors' representations, particularly their situation models. When viewing the painting, the enthusiasts have fairly accurate representations of the picture itself (assuming they can see the picture equally well). When they both view the head-banger, they have focally aligned situation models; and if they realize they are both viewing the head-banger, they meta-represent their alignment as well. Of course, our concern is not merely with alignment on the identity of the object but rather with alignment on its interpretation. In this case, the interlocutors might agree that the scene enacts the proverb 'banging one's head against a brick wall'. The fact that they are viewing the painting together helps such alignment, and it does so because the scene is in their shared workspace. In contrast, if the interlocutors discuss the picture in the park (i.e. from memory), their situation models of the picture itself will tend to be less well aligned. That is, they might put partial and potentially incompatible information into the workspace (e.g. if A correctly remembers a detail and B does not). Moreover, if the enthusiasts in the gallery then want to discuss the proverb 'swimming against the tide', they can draw on the saliency (to them) of the relevant scene and attend to it. Here, the organization of the painting (given their knowledge of the artist's technique) allows them to rapidly put this scene into the shared workspace. In the park, the enthusiasts cannot do this, because the painting is not visually available.[8]

Alignment is therefore enhanced by cultural artefacts, and particularly when they are at hand. In fact, our example illustrates how non-linguistic alignment on elements of the scene enhances broader alignment, both with respect to the situation model and with respect to language (in this case, the proverbs). It provides an example of how alignment at one level enhances alignment at other levels (Pickering & Garrod, 2004) – and the fact that the picture is a cultural artefact (and therefore organized appropriately for understanding) means that it enhances alignment particularly well. And the organization of the painting as a whole and the interlocutors' understanding of that organization help them to navigate through its complexity and therefore to develop global alignment.

In terms of the shared workspace, one interlocutor refers to an object at hand (such as the proverbial scene), for example by pointing or using a brief description (e.g. *the head-banger*), via the black arrow. The other can use

---

[8] Two art enthusiasts in the park might have faithful representations of the painting and have a high degree of global alignment in their situation models. To get focal alignment on the head-banger scene, they would (almost certainly) need to refer to it. In such a case, the referring expression would be in the shared workspace but the scene itself would not.

the vertical grey arrow to immediately comprehend or predict the combination of linguistic and non-linguistic information. Such integrated comprehension or prediction is extremely easy, as demonstrated by many experiments using the 'visual world' paradigm (e.g. Altmann & Kamide, 1999; Metzing & Brennan, 2003; Tanenhaus et al., 1995), in which participants comprehend spoken language in the context of pictures relating to the speech (e.g. they look at objects named in the utterance). And effects can be enhanced by culturally defined settings in which objects are appropriately located (see Henderson & Ferreira, 2004). This paradigm is effective in part because the pictures enrich the speech (e.g. the comprehender hears *the guitar* and sees a picture of a particular guitar) and because it makes the intended referents salient.

In related experiments, Richardson and Dale (2005) had speakers describe television shows while looking at pictures of the characters and found that comprehenders looked at the characters in a similar order to the speakers. Comprehenders closely tracked speakers' fixations (following a brief lag), and moreover those who tracked them most closely comprehended them better. In other words, when their shared workspace was more likely to contain the same picture, their situation models were better aligned. Richardson et al. (2007) found similar effects between interlocutors in dialogue. Their interlocutors discussed a structured painting (in their case, *Nature Morte Vivante* by Dali) and there were closer relationships between fixations when the interlocutors had been given the same contextual information (about Dali and the painting) than different contextual information. The shared context helped the interlocutors build up aligned (global) situation models, which caused them to treat similar aspects of the painting as manifest.

In contrast to 'illustrated language', comprehension or prediction of isolated language is harder and much less likely to be accurate or detailed – a description such as *the peasant banging his head* is impoverished in comparison to a description combined with the scene. So the shared workspace framework makes it clear why conversations about illustrations at hand are more likely to lead to strong alignment than conversations about illustrations that are accessed from memory.

The combination of illustration and dialogue leads to a shared workspace that contains different types of sign – ones that are primarily symbolic or primarily iconic.[9] In Figure 11.4, the utterance (*the head-banger*) is symbolic and the co-indexed image is iconic in relation to an actual peasant – that is, it is directly interpretable as its referent through resemblance. But other illustrations are hybrid (i.e. they are partly symbolic and partly iconic). For example, topological diagrams (e.g. a map of the London Underground), engineering

---

[9] We ignore the type of Peircean sign known as an index.

diagrams and instructions for furniture construction are illustrations that are partly symbolic – that is, they are mediated by culture. Note also that one illustration can serve as two types of sign – the image of the head-banger is an iconic sign of a peasant and (together with the wall) symbolizes the meaning of a proverb (getting nowhere). All of these illustrations share the property that they are designed by people so that they can enhance communication – and they do so by augmenting the shared workspace. We return to these issues when discussing multi-media texts in Section 11.3.3.

11.3.2   Augmenting the Shared Workspace with Recordings

Let us return to our example in which two co-workers add information to a whiteboard when they plan their task, and focus on written text. The whiteboard serves to enhance the shared workspace. The text is likely to be part of their shared workspace because they jointly attend to it – and this contrasts with a situation in which two individuals simply read the text on the board independently. Now imagine that one worker has written some text on the board summarizing part of her plan (e.g. for constructing the kitchen). Her partner then comes into the room and reads and understands the text – which is a recording. As he reads the summary, it becomes part of the shared workspace.

In Section 10.3.3, we emphasized that alignment does not require simultaneity. So our individuals have aligned on the summary, even though the writer produces the text minutes or hours before the reader comprehends it. In other words, the designer put the text into an individual workspace which becomes a shared workspace when the audience also attends to it. The text as a whole passes through the shared workspace as a consequence of the designer and the audience attending to it in the same sequence. They do not have to attend to it simultaneously, and indeed the designer might well take much longer to compose (i.e. plan and implement) the text than the audience takes to read it. Note that the individual workspace contains information that has the potential to enter the shared workspace. It has a critical role in recorded text – one that is much more important than it is in dialogue (where the individual workspace is peripheral).

Recorded text is therefore *portable*. It can be produced and comprehended separately – what is produced at a particular time can be comprehended at a different time (and by an audience of unbounded size). It is therefore *temporally portable*, but most recordings can also be moved to a different location, in which case they are *spatially portable*.[10] The recorded text therefore

---

[10] In a sense, telephone conversations are spatially but not temporally portable (they depend on simultaneity).

constitutes a portable workspace – one that passes through a shared workspace when it is interpreted by an audience.

Of course, a particularly important form of recorded text is the printed (or handwritten) document – books, traditional newspapers, letters and so on. By writing a novel, the author puts the text into an individual workspace. Text enters a shared workspace only when someone reads it – which of course may take place long after the novel has been written. Text is in the shared workspace when the reader attends to it, because the writer has attended to it and the text is portable. When the reader moves on, the previous text leaves the shared workspace and is replaced by new text. The reader can sample the shared workspace at his own pace (i.e. preserving the writer's sequence but not preserving timing). If the reader re-samples the previous text (with a regressive eye movement), then the sequence is re-set and the text re-enters the shared workspace. Indeed, the ability to resample is an important benefit of recording. It is likely to facilitate global situation model alignment between reader and author (and may enhance linguistic alignment as well).[11]

Recordings of spoken language also engage the workspace. A podcaster puts a recording into a portable workspace by posting it onto the web, as does a singer by cutting a record. Its contents are in an individual workspace until a listener attends to them, at which point they enter a workspace that is shared between the designer and the audience. The situation is similar when a radio presenter records a programme for subsequent broadcasting. All of these recordings can of course be resampled, just like written language.

In contrast, unrecorded spoken language is ephemeral. The current speech is in the shared workspace, but then it leaves the workspace and the interlocutors' memory for the speech fades rapidly. Of course, the contents are recoded into 'deeper' representations including the situation model. A strong way of interpreting the consequences of ephemerality is the 'now or never' assumption (Christiansen & Chater, 2016) – the comprehender has to process at one level and recode at a deeper level immediately or the information is lost. Recording allows the communicators to partly overcome ephemerality by resampling the recording and thus refreshing the shared workspace.

These examples of recording are monological. Importantly, it is not possible to use recording as part of minimal dyadic conversation, because commentary is time-critical and requires near-simultaneity. But recording is often used in alternating

---

[11] In minimal dyadic conversation, when *A* immediately comments on *B*'s contribution (e.g. *You're one along: Uh huh*), the commentary is on information that is still in the shared workspace. But when *A* queries after a delay (*Earlier, which John did you mean?*), *A* and *B* have to act on *B*'s original contribution (*We saw John on our holiday in London ...*) from memory so that they can work on it together. This process requires memory resources and confidence by both *A* and *B* that they have aligned. In this situation, the earlier information does not re-enter the shared workspace, unlike resampled recordings.

one-way dialogue (Section 10.3.1). In letter-correspondence, the initial writer puts the letter into her individual workspace by posting it, and it enters the shared workspace when it is read. The respondent then puts his answer into his individual workspace, and a cyclic process ensues. The same cycle occurs in written text messages, but more rapidly and with shorter contributions. The operations of the shared workspace framework are largely as described in Section 10.3, but note that recording provides a percept that the designer can use in external monitoring.[12]

Monologue does not have to use recording but in practice it typically does. The lack of commentary makes monologue hard and so designers carefully prepare what they are trying to convey (see Section 10.3.3). Given memory limitations, designers who record their contribution before communicating are likely to be at a considerable advantage. They can also redraft and refine their contributions, often iteratively. In other words, recordings provide an important 'workaround' for monologue. As we have noted, monologue makes use of cultural conventions such as routines that are not limited to a particular setting, and an important reason is that recorded monologue can be re-accessed by the audience or indeed the designer and hence tends to become standardized. Thus the widespread use of recording may itself be likely to lead to language change.[13]

Finally, consider the mechanisms within the communicators when using recordings. When A and B repeatedly text each other, the situation is superficially similar to alternating one-way dialogue. But text messages are 'pre-packaged': A prepares the text on her device before pressing 'send', and during that time the contents of the text are accessible to A but not B. In other words, they are in A's individual workspace. A can therefore use internal monitoring (before typing) or external monitoring (reading what she has written) – but she is aware that B cannot monitor it as well, and her awareness may affect how she designs the message. Most obviously, A might be prepared to put a potentially controversial text into her individual workspace, and then consider whether to delete it before pressing 'send' – before pressing 'send', A does not meta-represent alignment. By contrast, the speaker in alternating one-way dialogue (or any technology in which B can perceive A's contributions as they occur) meta-represents alignment while speaking. Texting may also affect linguistic alignment – because the interlocutors can resample messages, they may be especially likely to reuse each other's expressions.

---

[12] Monitoring requires the ability to cause revision. So when a passive audience member re-reads or replays, he is not doing so in the service of external monitoring. However, such re-reading or replaying can of course facilitate alignment.

[13] It also leads to recordings that specifically support cultural norms, such as dictionaries or legal codes.

11.3.3   Augmenting the Shared Workspace with Communication Technologies

We have pointed out that both illustrations and linguistic recordings can augment the shared workspace. It is therefore possible to combine them. Designers construct monological artefacts such as picture books and illuminated manuscripts. They put the text and the associated illustrations into an individual workspace and these contents enter a shared workspace when an audience attends to them. A consequence is that the designer and audience may achieve alignment. Such alignment may be enriched by linking text and illustration, in a way that constitutes a monological equivalent to the dialogue between art enthusiasts discussing Brueghel's painting.

Recorded text and illustrations need to be organized – for example, diagrams (e.g. Figure 11.4) work better if they are close to the relevant text (e.g. the caption for Figure 11.4). For an entity to enter the shared workspace, it requires parallel attention. Parallel attention is much more likely if the entity is salient, and organization leads to salience.

In minimal dyadic conversation, interlocutors make entities salient by highlighting them to each other and therefore facilitating their entry into the shared workspace. But in recorded communication, it may not be straightforward to make an entity salient. For example, if an illustrated manuscript includes a sentence and a complex illustration, then the reader may fail to attend to the right part of the illustration. The manuscript therefore needs some form of salience marking, such as an arrow, and the same is true for a whiteboard containing several independent fragments of text. Salience marking is obviously related to pointing in dialogue about matters at hand. If an illustration is too cluttered, or there are too many salience markers, then the appropriate entity may not enter the shared workspace and the audience and the designer are likely to misalign.

Communication technologies make careful use of salience marking to attempt to optimize communication. A very simple example is the ping that accompanies A's text message to B. By drawing B's attention to the sign (i.e. the text message), the ping makes it more likely that the message enters the shared workspace.

Much more interestingly, communication technologies are designed to affect the shared workspace by constraining the ways it can be accessed. To communicate effectively, people need to access a small number of pieces of information and be confident that those pieces are also available to their partner. If there is too much information, as in the cluttered whiteboard, it is hard to be confident parallel attention. Many technologies therefore manipulate what can be accessed and hence sampled or resampled by both communicators to ensure that the right information enters the shared workspace.

In Twitter, tweets were limited to 140 characters until 2017 and then 280 characters. As B reads A's tweet, it passes through the shared workspace, like any recording. (The previous two sentences are 140 characters long.) An effect of the length restriction is that the communicators are likely to align on the small number of points mentioned in the tweet – that is, to set up (roughly) aligned focal situation models. Moreover, the tweeter is likely to design the tweet to highlight important information (i.e. make that information salient). The length restriction means that the reader can straightforwardly resample. We propose that the length restriction is an attempt by Twitter to optimize the method of communication (given its purpose of disseminating a certain type of information, via broadcasting to an active audience). The original length was apparently chosen to be compatible with text messages, but presumably its retention was in part due to its popularity. Whether the length restriction and other restrictions (e.g. the mechanisms of retweeting) are actually optimal is not clear.

Twitter allows users to include photographs (or videos) as part of their tweets and so contribute to the shared workspace (i.e. using multi-media). Other communication media are centred around images (that are sometimes annotated with text). An interesting property of some media is that the images themselves are ephemeral. In Snapchat, images are erased after a single viewing and therefore can be resampled only in a single viewing. It is possible that this feature increases the salience of an image: it leads to viewers concentrating on that image during that viewing and hence increasing the likelihood of focal alignment. In contrast, Instagram allows images to persist, but limits the number in a single post – a feature that presumably has a comparable effect to the restriction on tweet length. In summary, it is a design characteristic of communication technologies to manipulate access to the shared workspace and our framework may provide some guidance on the effects of such manipulations.

Another important aspect of communication technologies is to highlight and manipulate conversational roles. In an email, an initiator writes a message to a respondent (or group of respondents) and carbon copies (ccs) to an active audience. The respondent can complete the dialogue game by replying, but it is also possible for an active audience member to comment (or initiate a new game). It also introduces a nuance: if an initiator blind carbon copies (bccs) a message to an audience member, then the initiator and the audience member regard the game as involving two contributors and a non-contributor (who has access to the first move), but the respondent regards the game as involving two contributors only (and therefore bcc'ing prevents conversational role alignment). More generally, email makes conversational roles explicit.

In other technologies, users regularly design the conversational status of other users. In Facebook, users can designate groups of 'friends' as the active audience for a particular interaction. Tweets are standardly public – that is, the tweeter broadcasts to all users who choose to be members of the active audience (typically, no respondent is designated). However, it is possible to write private tweets to a designated respondent and have no audience or overhearers. Communicative media therefore affect conversational roles as well as augment the shared workspace.

More generally, Norman (2013) argued that good engineering designers seek to satisfy affordances – that is, they construct artefacts in ways that facilitate their use. For example, they design doorknobs to fit the hand and place them at the best height to make door-opening easy, and they design remote controls for televisions so that they are user-friendly. In other words, they design artefacts so that they have the appropriate affordances for their characteristic uses. Designers of communication technologies make them appropriate for communication – that is, to support alignment. Alignment is a property of a dyadic system and therefore relates to joint affordances. Thus, a good communication technology has the appropriate joint affordances for interaction.[14]

11.4   Conclusion

By the end of Chapter 9, we had developed our theory of minimal dyadic conversation. In Chapters 10 and 11, we have shown how our theory can be extended – to multi-party dialogue, to monologue, to include culture and technology. Minimal dyadic conversation remains the basic site for language use, but the apparatus that we use (such as the shared workspace, the distinction between planner and implementer, the systems analysis and the central concept of alignment) apply to the full range of communicative situations. And by considering these situations, we can better understand the system itself and its limits.

---

[14] For example, Skype makes use of web cameras that are typically located above the images of interlocutors' faces, and therefore they cannot achieve eye contact – a feature of minimal (face-to-face) dyadic conversation that assists with determining where one's interlocutor is looking. Eye contact assists alignment (Hanna & Brennan, 2007), and Skype (in combination with computer screen manufacture) is not an optimal technology for exploiting alignment. In other words, it does not jointly afford communication as well as it might.

12   Conclusion

People regularly engage in cooperative joint activities with other people, and such activities involve language and communication. The ability to do so is central to human intelligence and sets us apart from other species and indeed most intelligent artificial systems. If we want to understand human intelligence, then we need to begin with dialogue.

In this book we have developed a theory of dialogue in relation to other cooperative joint activities. Our theory is primarily concerned with understanding face-to-face conversation between two interlocutors, but extends to all forms of language use. We regard dialogue as a form of cooperative joint activity in which the interlocutors seek to align on the issue under discussion and bring their partners back into line if necessary. They construct a joint dialogue plan which evolves throughout the interaction and which underlies how they implement their individual contributions.

Our theory covers both the individuals engaged in cooperative joint activities and the system that links them together. It assumes that the individuals are not linked directly but rather through a shared workspace – a workspace that contains the aspects of reality that are relevant to the joint activity. The individuals post their contributions to the workspace and monitor the workspace as a whole – the combination of their own contributions and their partner's contributions, together with the relevant context (see Figure 2.4).

When conversing, each interlocutor uses a dialogue implementer to carry out the dialogue plan. The interlocutors post their linguistic contributions to the shared workspace and perceive, predict, and monitor their joint contributions (see Figure 4.2). In both dialogue and cooperative joint activity more generally, we can see how information flows around the system – from an individual to the workspace, down to one or both individuals, and then up again as required. And the control of the activity is distributed. In dialogue, either interlocutor can direct the progress of the dialogue at any point, for example by producing a negative commentary and eliciting a repair. This process is cyclic and highly interwoven, as we discussed in relation to dialogue control (see Figure 5.5), and draws on interlocutors' tendency to synchronize (see Figure 9.2).

Along with the shared workspace, our central theoretical notion is align-ment – a state that occurs when two individuals represent aspects of the world in the same way as each other. This notion is non-monadic, as it is defined in terms of the relationship between two minds. The successful control of dia-logue depends on alignment – if two interlocutors have misaligned dialogue representations, then their conversation fails. Alignment underlies all inter-action, with interlocutors continuously priming each other's cognitive repre-sentations so that they become more similar to each other. And such alignment occurs at many levels at the same time, with different levels constantly influ-encing each other. Some of these levels are associated with different aspects of language (such as sound, grammar, and meaning), and relate to the dialogue implementer – and such alignment is revealed by tendencies for interlocutors to mirror each other's linguistic choices.

Other levels are associated with the content and structure of the dialogue, and relate to the dialogue planner. Interlocutors construct models of the situation under discussion and aim to align their models. Situation model alignment is the most general way in which individuals understand the world like each other. Such alignment depends on other aspects of alignment that are specific to language (linguistic alignment) or to dialogue (dialogue-game model alignment). Most importantly, interlocutors align their focal situation models – models that correspond to the current issue under discussion. When this happens, they share their current view of the world – a form of shared reality. In addition, they align on dialogue game models – for example, they both realize that they are at a certain point in an information-seeking game and realize their respective roles.

Independent of alignment itself, each interlocutor meta-represents whether the interlocutors are aligned or not. Specifically, an interlocutor meta-represents alignment when she believes that she and her partner have aligned representations, and meta-represents misalignment when she believes that they do not. Meta-representation of alignment plays a major role in our framework. For example, an addressee who meta-represents misalignment of situation models is likely to produce a negative commentary (such as *what?* or a quizzical expression) and does so in order to elicit repair of alignment (though the specific choice of commentary reflects cultural conventions). The speaker then also meta-represents misalignment and plans an appropriate repair (such as a reformulation or expansion), which may lead to realignment and its meta-representation. Meta-representation of alignment is essential to the cyclical control of dialogue.

There is a close relationship between the focal alignment of situation models and the contents of the shared workspace. The shared workspace is a resource in the world that contains entities that individuals can jointly manipulate – that is, entities with joint affordances. The entities therefore have to be in parallel attention (though other entities can be in an individual workspace). So if interlocutors are focally aligned on the representation of an entity, then that entity is in their shared workspace, and vice versa.

Typically but not always, entities in the shared workspace are manifest to both interlocutors – that is, they both realize that they both attend to them. When an entity is manifest, then interlocutors meta-represent focal alignment over the representation of that entity. When an interlocutor has the goal of aligning on the representation of an entity that is not manifest, then she attempts to make it manifest by some device such as pointing to it. If she is successful (e.g. her interlocutor follows the gesture), then she can be confident that it is in the shared workspace and therefore that she is focally aligned with her interlocutor – that is, she meta-represents focal alignment. In successful dialogue, the relevant entities are in the shared workspace, they are manifest, the interlocutors are focally aligned on their representations of those entities, and both meta-represent that they are aligned.

In dialogue, the most important entities are signs, such as words, and the interlocutors use them to support alignment. When a speaker says *Mary* to her partner, she is confident that the word *Mary* is in the shared workspace and moreover that the word *Mary* is manifest. In other words, she believes that her partner heard her correctly (e.g. that he heard *Mary* rather than *Martha*). Importantly, signs are associated with multiple levels of representation and it might be that the speaker meant MARY37, but the addressee interpreted *Mary* as referring to MARY64. If so, the interlocutors are focally aligned on linguistic representations but not on their situation models (and if they realize this, then they do not meta-represent alignment at the level of the situation model). This example illustrates the complexity of the relationship between the shared workspace and alignment with respect to signs. But interlocutors constantly negotiate using commentary, and dialogue typically cycles towards representations that are well aligned.

At any point, the shared workspace is highly limited in scope, because it relates to the focal situation model. But it is dynamic: new entities flow through it as the conversation progresses. A consequence is that interlocutors must use the shared workspace efficiently – they put entities into the workspace when they need to, but keep those entities as simple as possible and do so in a timely fashion.

Our framework is grounded in minimal dyadic conversation. The dialogue system, the process of alignment and the nature of shared workspace are best suited to this basic form of interaction. But the framework also applies to interaction in larger groups, when communicating in a remote or restricted manner, and indeed when engaged in monologue. All language use is dependent on the culture in which it is embedded, and so interlocutors' use of the framework is influenced by social conventions such as who should speak and when, and what each interlocutor is expected to contribute. More generally, our framework allows us to combine dialogue with non-linguistic joint activity – and in fact, we assume that the vast majority of cooperative joint activities are dependent on (and organized by) concurrent language. That is, the components of such activities become clear only in the context of the language that the participants use in performing the activities.

We considered how our framework can help explain the effects of writing, illustrations and communication technology. Perhaps most importantly, we argued that whiteboards and multimedia can present information that corresponds to the information that is in the shared workspace. Users can post signs or other entities to such technologies, and by doing so, they augment the shared workspace. And we believe that technology designers should ask themselves how to augment it best.

Most cooperative joint activities such as dialogue are complex and intricate and they require extensive resources associated with cognition in general and social cognition in particular. In other words, they require intelligence of a particular kind, which we can call interactive intelligence. We speculate that such intelligence is limited to humans, and has to develop in childhood. Cooperative joint activity in animals is highly circumscribed. And researchers in artificial intelligence have great difficulty in developing interactively intelligent dialogue systems. We hope our framework will prove useful in addressing these issues.

Our account has not addressed dialogue that is seriously disrupted because of limitations in one or both interlocutors. For example, Garrod and Clark (1993) found disruption of situation model alignment in seven- to eight-year-olds when they were playing the maze game. Such children persisted with a description scheme (e.g. a path scheme) when their partner had used this scheme and they had not identified their partner's position. The fact that they persisted with their partner's scheme suggests that alignment itself was not impaired. Instead, they had failed to use commentary appropriately to meta-represent alignment or misalignment, and to use such meta-representation to formulate an appropriate contribution (i.e. there is disruption in the dialogue planner and its link to the production command; see Figure 5.5). Older children and adults were twice as likely to introduce a different description scheme when they had been unable to understand their partner's previous use of the scheme. This example illustrates how types of interlocutors can fail to use the shared workspace appropriately.

In a similar way, researchers could apply our account to many types of disrupted dialogue. If one or both interlocutors have serious linguistic impairments (such as aphasia), then clearly they will not tend to 'post' appropriate contributions to the shared workspace. The disruption to dialogue will therefore be a consequence of impaired dialogue implementers. If one interlocutor compensates for the other (e.g. suggesting completions), then the distribution of control is highly asymmetric – and disruption may be minimized.

In other cases, the disruption may relate to meta-representation of alignment. If an interlocutor has an impaired 'theory of mind', then she may not adequately represent her partner's situation model, and may therefore fail to meta-represent alignment or misalignment. Such a failure would in turn lead to inappropriate commentaries and potential confusion for her partner too. Thus various types of impairment can lead to disrupted dialogue, but the source of the disruption can be different.

Finally, human-machine dialogue can also be disrupted. Current communication technologies are typically limited, even though they may have a large database of knowledge to draw on (such as data accessed through the World Wide Web). For example, Alexa and Siri do not provide commentaries when a user asks an ambiguous question. They do not represent dialogue games or meta-represent alignment. The user does not fully compensate for the interactional limitations of such systems. To prevent disruption, the technology would have to incorporate the characteristics of human interlocutors that we have considered in this book.

In conclusion, dialogue is the most remarkable achievement of humankind. It appears so straightforward and effortless for most adults that it may be hard to understand why it requires extensive study and theorizing. But it is complex to understand, because it depends on both the interlocutors themselves and on how they fit into the dialogue system. They are individuals with their own representations of the dialogue, but they interact via a shared view of the world.

References

Aijmer, K. (2014). *Conversational routines in English: Convention and creativity.* New York: Routledge.

Altmann, G. T., & Kamide, Y. (1999). Incremental interpretation at verbs: Restricting the domain of subsequent reference. *Cognition, 73*(3), 247–264.

Altmann, G., & Mirković, J. (2009). Incrementality and prediction in human sentence processing. *Cognitive Science, 33*(4), 583–609.

Anderson, A., Garrod, S. C., & Sanford, A. J. (1983). The accessibility of pronominal antecedents as a function of episode shifts in narrative text. *Quarterly Journal of Experimental Psychology Section A, 35*(3), 427–440.

Arnal, L. H., & Giraud, A. L. (2012). Cortical oscillations and sensory predictions. *Trends in Cognitive Sciences, 16*(7), 390–398.

Arnon, I., & Snider, N. (2010). More than words: Frequency effects for multi-word phrases. *Journal of Memory and Language, 62*(1), 67–82.

Assaneo, M. F., & Poeppel, D. (2018). The coupling between auditory and motor cortices is rate-restricted: Evidence for an intrinsic speech-motor rhythm. *Science Advances, 4(2),* eaao3842.

Austin, J. L. (1962). *How to do things with words.* Oxford: Clarendon Press.

Baddeley, A. (1996). Exploring the central executive. *Quarterly Journal of Experimental Psychology Section A, 49*(1), 5–28.

Bakhtin, M. M. (1981). *The dialogic imagination: Four essays* (M. Holquist, Ed.; C. Emerson & M. Holquist, Trans.). Austin: University of Texas Press.

Bard, E. G., Shillcock, R. C., & Altmann, G. T. (1988). The recognition of words after their acoustic offsets in spontaneous speech: Effects of subsequent context. *Perception & Psychophysics, 44*(5), 395–408.

Bavelas, J. B., Coates, L., & Johnson, T. (2000). Listeners as co-narrators. *Journal of Personality and Social Psychology, 79*(6), 941–52.

Bell, A. (1984). Language style as audience design. *Language in Society, 13*(2), 145–204.

Blakemore, S.-J., Frith, C. D., & Wolpert, D. M. (1999). Spatio-temporal prediction modulates the perception of self-produced stimuli. *Journal of Cognitive Neuroscience, 11*, 551–559.

Bock, J. K. (1986). Syntactic persistence in language production. *Cognitive Psychology, 18*(3), 355–387.

Bock, K., & Levelt, W. J. (1994). Language production: Grammatical encoding. In M. A. Gernsbacher (Eds.), *Handbook of Psycholinguistics* (pp. 945–984). New York: Academic Press.

Bögels, S., & Levinson, S. C. (2017). The brain behind the response: Insights into turn-taking in conversation from neuroimaging. *Research on Language and Social Interaction*, *50*(1), 71–89.

Bögels, S., Magyari, L., & Levinson, S. C. (2015). Neural signatures of response planning occur midway through an incoming question in conversation. *Scientific Reports*, *5*, 12881.

Bolt, N. K., & Loehr, J. D. (2017). The predictability of a partner's actions modulates the sense of joint agency. *Cognition*, *161*, 60–65.

Branigan, H. P., & Pickering, M. J. (2017). An experimental approach to linguistic representation. *Behavioral and Brain Sciences*, *40*, e282.

Branigan, H. P., Pickering, M. J., & Cleland, A. A. (2000). Syntactic co-ordination in dialogue. *Cognition*, *75*(2), B13–B25.

Branigan, H. P., Pickering, M. J., McLean, J. F., & Cleland, A. A. (2007). Syntactic alignment and participant role in dialogue. *Cognition*, *104*(2), 163–197.

Branigan, H. P., Pickering, M. J., Pearson, J., McLean, J. F., & Brown, A. (2011). The role of beliefs in lexical alignment: Evidence from dialogs with humans and computers. *Cognition*, *121*(1), 41–57.

Bratman, M. E. (1992). Shared cooperative activity. *Philosophical Review*, *101*(2), 327–341.

Brennan, S. E., & Clark, H. H. (1996). Conceptual pacts and lexical choice in conversation. *Journal of Experimental Psychology: Learning, Memory, and Cognition*, *22*(6), 1482–1493.

Carbary, K., & Tanenhaus, M.K. (2011) Conceptual pacts, syntactic priming, and referential form. In *Proceedings of the CogSci Workshop on the Production of Referring Expressions: Bridging the Gap Between Computational, Empirical and Theoretical Approaches to Reference (PRE-CogSci 2011)* (pp. 1–6). Amsterdam: Cognitive Science Society.

Chandrasekaran, C., Trubanova, A., Stillittano, S., Caplier, A., & Ghazanfar, A. A. (2009). The natural statistics of audiovisual speech. *PLoS Computational Biology*, *5*(7), e1000436.

Chartrand, T. L., & Bargh, J. A. (1999). The chameleon effect: the perception–behavior link and social interaction. *Journal of Personality and Social Psychology*, *76*(6), 893–910.

Chomsky, N. (1965). *Aspects of a theory of syntax*. Hague: Mouton.

(1981). *Lectures on government and binding: The Pisa lectures*. Dordrecht: Foris.

Chouinard, M. M., & Clark, E. V. (2003). Adult reformulations of child errors as negative evidence. *Journal of Child Language*, *30*(3), 637–669.

Civil Aviation Authority (2015). CAP1421: CAA Annual Report & Accounts 2015/16.

Christiansen, M. H., & Chater, N. (2016). The now-or-never bottleneck: A fundamental constraint on language. *Behavioral and Brain Sciences*, *39*, e62.

Clark, H. H. (1996). *Using language*. Cambridge: Cambridge University Press.

(2016). Depicting as a method of communication. *Psychological Review*, *123*(3), 324–347.

Clark, H. H., & Krych, M. A. (2004). Speaking while monitoring addressees for understanding. *Journal of Memory and Language*, *50*(1), 62–81.

Clark, H. H., & Lucy, P. (1975). Understanding what is meant from what is said: A study in conversationally conveyed requests. *Journal of Verbal Learning and Verbal Behavior*, *14*(1), 56–72.

Clark, H. H., & Marshall, C. R. (1981). Definite knowledge and mutual knowledge. In A. K. Joshi, B. L. Webber, & I. A. Sag (Eds.), *Elements of discourse understanding* (pp. 10–63). Cambridge, UK: Cambridge University Press.

Clark, H. H., & Murphy, G. L. (1982). Audience design in meaning and reference. In *Advances in Psychology* (Vol. 9, pp. 287–299). Amsterdam: North-Holland.

Clark, H. H., & Schaefer, E. F. (1987). Concealing one's meaning from overhearers. *Journal of Memory and Language*, *26*(2), 209–225.

(1989). Contributing to discourse. *Cognitive Science*, *13*(2), 259–294.

Clark, H. H., & Wilkes-Gibbs, D. (1986). Referring as a collaborative process. *Cognition*, *22*(1), 1–39.

Cleland, A. A., & Pickering, M. J. (2003). The use of lexical and syntactic information in language production: Evidence from the priming of noun-phrase structure. *Journal of Memory and Language*, *49*(2), 214–230.

Cohen Priva, U., Edelist, L., & Gleason, E. (2017). Converging to the baseline: Corpus evidence for convergence in speech rate to interlocutor's baseline. *Journal of the Acoustical Society of America*, *141*(5), 2989–2996.

Cowan, N. (1998). *Attention and memory: An integrated framework*. Oxford: Oxford University Press.

Craig, I. (1995). *Blackboard systems*. Ablex Publishing corporation, Norwood, NJ.

Craik, K. J. W. (1967). *The nature of explanation* (Vol. 445). Cambridge: CUP Archive. (Original work published 1943)

Culicover, P. W., & Jackendoff, R. (2005). *Simpler syntax*. Oxford: Oxford University Press.

Cummins, F. (2003). Practice and performance in speech produced synchronously. *Journal of Phonetics*, *31*(2), 139–148.

Danet, B. (1980). Language in the legal process. *Law and Society Review*, 14, 445–564.

Davidson, P. R., & Wolpert, D. M. (2005). Widespread access to predictive models in motor system: A short review. *Journal of Neural Engineering*, *2*, S313–S319.

Dell, G. S. (1986). A spreading-activation theory of retrieval in sentence production. *Psychological Review*, *93*(3), 283–321.

Dell, G. S., & Chang, F. (2014). The P-chain: Relating sentence production and its disorders to comprehension and acquisition. *Philosophical Transactions of the Royal Society, Series B*, *369*, 20120394.

Dijksterhuis, A., & Bargh, J. A. (2001). The perception-behavior expressway: Automatic effects of social perception on social behavior. In *Advances in Experimental Social Psychology* (Vol. 33, pp. 1–40). New York: Academic Press.

Drew, P. (1997). 'Open' class repair initiators in response to sequential sources of troubles in conversation. *Journal of Pragmatics*, *28*(1), 69–101.

Echterhoff, G., Higgins, E. T., & Levine, J. M. (2009). Shared reality: Experiencing commonality with others' inner states about the world. *Perspectives on Psychological Science*, *4*(5), 496–521.

Elman, J. L. (1990). Finding structure in time. *Cognitive Science*, *14*(2), 179–211.

Ericsson, K. A., & Kintsch, W. (1995). Long-term working memory. *Psychological Review*, *102*(2), 211–245.

Evans, G. (1982). *The varieties of reference*. Oxford: Oxford University Press.

Fay, N., Ellison, T. M., Tylén, K., Fusaroli, R., Walker, B., & Garrod, S. (2018). Applying the cultural ratchet to a social artefact: The cumulative cultural evolution of a language game. *Evolution and Human Behavior*, *39*(3), 300–309.

Fay, N., Garrod, S., & Carletta, J. (2000). Group discussion as interactive dialogue or as serial monologue: The influence of group size. *Psychological Science*, *11*(6), 481–486.

Fernández, R., & Ginzburg, J. (2002, August). Non-sentential utterances: Grammar and dialogue dynamics in corpus annotation. In *Proceedings of the 19th International Conference on Computational Linguistics* (Vol. 1, pp. 1–7). Tiapei: Association for Computational Linguistics.

Ferreira, V. S., Kleinman, D., Kraljic, T., & Siu, Y. (2012). Do priming effects in dialogue reflect partner-or task-based expectations? *Psychonomic Bulletin & Review*, *19*(2), 309–316.

Fischer, B., & Glanzer, M. (1986). Short-term storage and the processing of cohesion during reading. *Quarterly Journal of Experimental Psychology*, *38*(3), 431–460.

Flinker, A., Korzeniewska, A., Shestyuk, A. Y., Franaszczuk, P. J., Dronkers, N. F., Knight, R. T., & Crone, N. E. (2015). Redefining the role of Broca's area in speech. *Proceedings of the National Academy of Sciences*, *112*, 2871–2875.

Fodor, J., Bever, A., & Garrett, T. G. (1974). *The psychology of language: An introduction to psycholinguistics and generative grammar.* New York: McGraw-Hill.

Forbus, K.D. (1983). Qualitative reasoning about space and motion. In Gentner, D., & Stevens, A. L. (Eds.). *Mental models* (pp. 53-74). New York: Psychology Press.

Forster, K. (1976). Accessing the mental lexicon. In *New approaches to language mechanisms* (pp. 257–287). Oxford: North-Holland.

Fowler, H. W. (1926). *Modern English usage.* Oxford: Oxford University Press.

Frazier, L. (1987). *Sentence processing: A tutorial review.* In M. Coltheart (Ed.), *Attention and performance 12: The psychology of reading* (pp. 559–586). Hillsdale, NJ: Erlbaum.

Frazier, L., & Rayner, K. (1982). Making and correcting errors during sentence comprehension: Eye movements in the analysis of structurally ambiguous sentences. *Cognitive Psychology*, *14*(2), 178–210.

Fujii, Y. (2012). Differences in situating Self in the place/ba of interaction between the Japanese and American English speakers. *Journal of Pragmatics*, *44*, 636–662.

Fusaroli, R., Bahrami, B., Olsen, K., Roepstorff, A., Rees, G., Frith, C., & Tylén, K. (2012). Coming to terms: Quantifying the benefits of linguistic coordination. *Psychological Science*, *23*(8), 931–939.

Galati, A., & Brennan, S. E. (2010). Attenuating information in spoken communication: For the speaker, or for the addressee? *Journal of Memory and Language*, *62*(1), 35–51.

Gallese, V., & Goldman, A. (1998). Mirror neurons and the simulation theory of mind-reading. *Trends in Cognitive Sciences*, *2*(12), 493–501.

Gallotti, M., & Frith, C. D. (2013). Social cognition in the we-mode. *Trends in Cognitive Sciences*, *17*(4), 160–165.

Galton, F. (1907). Vox populi (The wisdom of crowds). *Nature*, *75*, 450–451.

Gambi, C., & Pickering, M. J. (2016). Predicting and imagining language. *Language, Cognition, and Neuroscience*, *31*(1), 60–72.

Garrod, S., & Anderson, A. (1987). Saying what you mean in dialogue: A study in conceptual and semantic co-ordination. *Cognition*, *27*(2), 181–218.

Garrod, S., & Clark, A. (1993). The development of dialogue co-ordination skills in schoolchildren. *Language and Cognitive Processes, 8*(1), 101–126.

Garrod, S., & Doherty, G. (1994). Conversation, co-ordination and convention: An empirical investigation of how groups establish linguistic conventions. *Cognition, 53*, 181–215.

Garrod, S., & Pickering, M. J. (2004). Why is conversation so easy? *Trends in Cognitive Sciences, 8*, 8–11.

(2015). The use of content and timing to predict turn transitions. *Frontiers in Psychology, 6*, 751.

Garrod, S., Tosi, A., & Pickering, M. J. (2018). Alignment during interaction. In *The Oxford handbook of psycholinguistics* (pp. 1-23). Oxford: Oxford University Press.

Garfinkel, H. (1967). *Studies in ethnomethodology.* Englewood Cliffs, NJ: Prentice Hall.

Gentner, D., & Markman, A. B. (1997). Structure mapping in analogy and similarity. *American Psychologist, 52*, 45–56.

Gentner, D., & Stevens, A. L. (Eds.). (1983). *Mental models.* New York: Psychology Press.

Gernsbacher, M. A. (1994). *Handbook of psycholinguistics.* San Diego, CA: Academic Press.

Gibson, J. J. (1979). *The ecological approach to visual perception.* Boston: Houghton Mifflin.

Ginzburg, J., & Sag, I. (2000). *Interrogative investigations.* Stanford, CA: CSLI.

Giraud, A. L., Kleinschmidt, A., Poeppel, D., Lund, T. E., Frackowiak, R. S., & Laufs, H. (2007). Endogenous cortical rhythms determine cerebral specialization for speech perception and production. *Neuron, 56*, 1127–1134.

Glanzer, M., Dorfman, D., & Kaplan, B. (1981). Short-term storage in the processing of text. *Journal of Verbal Learning and Verbal Behavior, 20*, 656–670.

Glanzer, M., Fischer, B., & Dorfman, D. (1984). Short-term storage in reading. *Journal of Verbal Learning and Verbal Behavior, 23*, 467–486.

Godfrey, J., & Holliman, E. (1993). *Switchboard-1* (Release 2 LDC97S62) [DVD]. Philadelphia: Linguistic Data Consortium.

Goffman, E. (1976). Replies and responses. *Language in Society, 5*, 257–313.

(1981). *Forms of talk.* Philadelphia: University of Pennsylvania Press.

Goldman, A. I. (2006). *Simulating minds: The philosophy, psychology, and neuroscience of mindreading.* Oxford: Oxford University Press.

Gray, J. A., & Wedderburn, A. A. I. (1960). Shorter articles and notes grouping strategies with simultaneous stimuli. *Quarterly Journal of Experimental Psychology, 12*, 180–184.

Grice, H. P. (1957). Meaning. *Philosophical Review, 66*, 377–388.

(1975). Logic and conversation. In P. Cole and J.L. Morgan (eds.) *Syntax and semantics 3: Speech arts*, 41–58. New York: Academic Press.

Gross, J., Hoogenboom, N., Thut, G., Schyns, P., Panzeri, S., Belin, P., & Garrod, S. (2013). Speech rhythms and multiplexed oscillatory sensory coding in the human brain. *PLoS Biology, 11*(12), e1001752.

Grush, R. (2004). The emulation theory of representation: Motor control, imagery, and perception. *Behavioral and Brain Sciences, 27*, 377–435.

Haith, A. M., & Krakauer, J. W. (2013). Model-based and model-free mechanisms of human motor learning. *Advances in Experimental Medicine and Biology, 782*, 1–21.

Hale, J. (2001). A probabilistic Earley parser as a psycholinguistic model. In *Proceedings of the Second Meeting of the North American Chapter of the Association for Computational Linguistics*. Pittsburgh.

Halle, M., & Stevens, K. (1959). Analysis by synthesis. In W. Wathen-Dunn & L. E. Woods (Eds.), *Proceedings of the Seminar on Speech Comprehension and Processing*, USAF Camb.Res.Ctr.2: Paper D7.

Hanna, J. E., & Brennan, S. E. (2007). Speakers' eye gaze disambiguates referring expressions early during face-to-face conversation. *Journal of Memory and Language, 57*(4), 596–615.

Hanna, J. E., Tanenhaus, M. K., & Trueswell, J. C. (2003). The effects of common ground and perspective on domains of referential interpretation. *Journal of Memory and Language, 49*, 43–61.

Hargadon, A. B., & Bechky, B. A. (2006). When collections of creatives become creative collectives: A field study of problem solving at work. *Organization Science, 17*, 484–500.

Hartsuiker, R. J., Bernolet, S., Schoonbaert, S., Speybroeck, S., & Vanderelst, D. (2008). Syntactic priming persists while the lexical boost decays: Evidence from written and spoken dialogue. *Journal of Memory and Language, 58*, 214–238.

Hartsuiker, R. J., & Kolk, H. H. (2001). Error monitoring in speech production: A computational test of the perceptual loop theory. *Cognitive Psychology, 42*(2), 113–157.

Haruno, M., Wolpert, D. M., & Kawato, M. (2001). MOSAIC model for sensorimotor learning and control. *Neural Computation, 13*, 2201–2220.

(2003). Hierarchical MOSAIC for movement generation. *International Congress Series, 1250*, 575–590.

Haviland, S. E., & Clark, H. H. (1974). What's new? Acquiring new information as a process in comprehension. *Journal of Verbal Learning and Verbal Behavior, 13* (5), 512–521.

Heldner, M., & Edlund, J. (2010). Pauses, gaps and overlaps in conversations. *Journal of Phonetics, 38*(4), 555–568.

Henderson, J., & Ferreira, F. (2004). (Eds.) *The interface of language, vision, and action: Eye movements and the visual world*. New York: Psychology Press.

Hesslow, G. (2002). Conscious thought as simulation of behaviour and perception. *Trends in Cognitive Sciences, 6*(6), 242–247.

Hickok, G. (2014). Towards an integrated psycholinguistic, neurolinguistic, sensorimotor framework for speech production. *Language, Cognition, and Neuroscience, 29*, 52–59.

Hickok, G., Houde, J., & Rong, F. (2011). Sensorimotor integration in speech processing: Computational basis and neural organization. *Neuron, 69*, 407–422.

Himberg, T., Hirvenkari, L., Mandel, A., & Hari, R. (2015). Word-by-word entrainment of speech rhythm during joint story building. *Frontiers in Psychology, 6*, 797.

Hommel, B., Müsseler, J., Aschersleben, G., & Prinz, W. (2001). The theory of event coding (TEC): A framework for perception and action planning. *Behavioral and Brain Sciences, 24*, 849–878.

Horton, W. S., & Gerrig, R. J. (2005). Conversational common ground and memory processes in language production. *Discourse Processes, 40,* 1–35.

Horton, W. S., & Keysar, B. (1996). When do speakers take into account common ground? *Cognition, 59,* 91–117.

Hupet, M., & Chantraine, Y. (1992). Changes in repeated references: Collaboration or repetition effects? *Journal of Psycholinguistic Research, 21,* 485–496.

Hurley, S. (2008). The shared circuits model (SCM): How control, mirroring, and simulation can enable imitation, deliberation, and mindreading. *Behavioral and Brain Sciences,* 31(1), 1–22.

Hutchins, E. (1983). Understanding Micronesian navigation. In D. Gentner & A. L. Stevens (Eds.), *Mental models* (pp. 191–226). New York: Psychology Press.

(1995). How a cockpit remembers its speeds. *Cognitive Science, 19,* 265–288.

Indefrey, P. (2011). The spatial and temporal signatures of word production components: A critical update. *Frontiers in Psychology, 2,* 255.

Indefrey, P., & Levelt, W. J. (2004). The spatial and temporal signatures of word production components. *Cognition, 92,* 101–144.

Ireland, M. E., Slatcher, R. B., Eastwick, P. W., Scissors, L. E., Finkel, E. J., & Pennebaker, J. W. (2011). Language style matching predicts relationship initiation and stability. *Psychological Science, 22,* 39–44.

Isaacs, E. A., & Clark, H. H. (1987). References in conversation between experts and novices. *Journal of Experimental Psychology: General,* 116(1), 26–37.

Jackendoff, R. (2002). *Foundations of language: Brain, meaning, grammar, evolution.* New York: Oxford University Press.

(2007). A parallel architecture perspective on language processing. *Brain Research,* 1146, 2–22.

Jaeger, T. F., & Ferreira, V. (2013). Seeking predictions from a predictive framework. *Behavioral and Brain Sciences,* 36(4), 359–360.

Jefferson, G. (1982). On exposed and embedded correction in conversation. *Studium Linguisticum, 14,* 58–68.

Johnson-Laird, P. N. (1983). *Mental models: Towards a cognitive science of language, inference, and consciousness.* Cambridge, MA: Harvard University Press.

Jordan, M., & Rummelhart, D. E. (1992). Forward models: Supervised learning with a distal teacher. *Cognitive Science, 16,* 307–354.

Kail, R. V., & Cavaunaugh, J. C. (2007). *Human development: A life-span view* (5th ed.). Belmont, CA: Wadsworth/Cengage Learning.

Kawato, M., Furukawa, K., & Suzuki, R. (1987). A hierarchical neural-network model for control and learning of voluntary movement. *Biological Cybernetics,* 57(3), 169–185.

Keysar, B., Barr, D. J., Balin, J. A., & Brauner, J. S. (2000). Taking perspective in conversation: The role of mutual knowledge in comprehension. *Psychological Science, 11,* 32–38.

Keysar, B., & Henly, A. S. (2002). Speakers' overestimation of their effectiveness. *Psychological Science, 13,* 207–212.

Klapp, S. T. (1979). Doing two things at once: The role of temporal compatibility. *Memory & Cognition, 7,* 375–381.

Knoblich, G., & Jordan, J. S. (2003). Action coordination in groups and individuals: Learning anticipatory control. *Journal of Experimental Psychology: Learning, Memory, and Cognition, 29,* 1006–1016.

Konopka, A., & Bock, K. (2009). Lexical or syntactic control of sentence formulation? Structural generalizations from idiom production. *Cognitive Psychology*, 58, 68–101.

Kowtko, J. C., Isard, S. D., & Doherty, G. M. (1993). *Conversational games within dialogue*. Human Communication Research Centre Technical Report 31. Edinburgh: University of Edinburgh.

Krauss, R. M., & Glucksberg, S. (1969). The development of communication: Competence as a function of age. *Child Development*, 40, 255–266.

Krauss, R. M., & Weinheimer, S. (1966). Concurrent feedback, confirmation, and the encoding of referents in verbal communication. *Journal of Personality and Social Psychology*, *4*, 343–346.

Kripke, S. A. (1980). *Naming and necessity*. Oxford, UK: Blackwell.

Kuiper, K. (1996). *Smooth talkers: The linguistic performance of auctioneers and sportscasters*. Mahwah, NJ: Erlbaum.

Kuperberg, G. R., & Jaeger, T. F. (2016). What do we mean by prediction in language comprehension? *Language, Cognition, and Neuroscience*, *31*, 32–59.

Kutas, M., & Hillyard, S. A. (1984). Brain potentials during reading reflect word expectancy and semantic association. *Nature*, *307*(5947), 161–163.

Lerner, Y., Honey, C. J., Silbert, L. J., & Hasson, U. (2011). Topographic mapping of a hierarchy of temporal receptive windows using a narrated story. *Journal of Neuroscience*, *31*, 2906–2915.

Lakin, J. L., & Chartrand, T. L. (2003). Using nonconscious behavioral mimicry to create affiliation and rapport. *Psychological Science*, 14(4), 334-339.

Larkin, J. H. (1983). The role of problem representation in physics. In D. Gentner A. L. & Stevens (Eds.), *Mental models* (pp. 75–98). New York: Psychology Press.

Levelt, W. J. (1983). Monitoring and self-repair in speech. *Cognition*, *14*(1), 41–104.
  (1989). *Speaking: From intention to articulation* (Vol. 1). Cambridge, MA: MIT Press.
  (1999). Models of word production. *Trends in Cognitive Sciences*, *3*, 223–232.

Levelt, W. J., Roelofs, A., & Meyer, A. S. (1999). A theory of lexical access in speech production. *Behavioral and Brain Sciences*, *22*, 1–75.

Levin, J. A., & Moore, J. A. (1977). Dialogue-games: Metacommunication structures for natural language interaction. *Cognitive Science*, *1*, 395–420.

Levinson, S. C. (1979). Activity types and language. In P. Drew & J. Heritage (Eds.), *Talk at work: Interaction in institutional settings* (pp. 66–100). Cambridge: Cambridge University Press.
  (2013). Recursion in pragmatics. *Language*, *89*, 149–162.
  (2016). Turn-taking in human communication – origins and implications for language processing. *Trends in Cognitive Sciences*, *20*, 6–14.

Levy, R. (2008). Expectation-based syntactic comprehension. *Cognition*, *106*(3), 1126–1177.

Lewis, D. (1969). *Convention*. Cambridge, MA: Harvard University Press.

Liberman, A. M., & Whalen, D. H. (2000). On the relation of speech to language. *Trends in Cognitive Sciences*, *4*, 187–196.

Lind, A., Hall, L., Breidegard, B., Balkenius, C., & Johansson, P. (2014). Speakers' acceptance of real-time speech exchange indicates that we use auditory feedback to specify the meaning of what we say. *Psychological Science*, *25*, 1198–1205.

Linell, P. (1998). *Approaching dialogue: Talk, interaction and contexts in dialogical perspectives* (Vol. 3). Amsterdam/Philadelphia, John Benjamins.

(2009). *Rethinking language, mind, and world dialogically.* Charlotte, NC: Information Age.

MacDonald, M. C. (2013). How language production shapes language form and comprehension. *Frontiers in Psychology, 4*, 226.

MacDonald, M. C., Pearlmutter, N. J., & Seidenberg, M. S. (1994). The lexical nature of syntactic ambiguity resolution. *Psychological Review, 101*, 676–703.

Mackay, D. G. (1987). *The organization of perception and action: A theory of language and other cognitive skills.* New York: Springer.

MacNeilage, P. F. (1998). The frame/content theory of evolution of speech production. *Behavioral and Brain Sciences, 21*, 499–511.

McCloskey, M. (1983). Naive theories of motion. In D. Gentner & A. L. Stevens (Eds.), *Mental models* (pp. 299–324). New York: Psychology Press.

McNeill, D. (1992). *Hand and mind: What gestures reveal about thought.* Chicago: University of Chicago Press.

Meyer, D. E., & Schvaneveldt, R. W. (1971). Facilitation in recognizing pairs of words: Evidence of a dependence between retrieval operations. *Journal of Experimental Psychology, 90*, 227–234.

Miller, G. A., Galanter, E., & Pribram, K. H. (1960). *Plans and the structure of behavior.* New York: Henry Holt.

Mitterer, H., & Ernestus, M. (2008). The link between speech perception and production is phonological and abstract: Evidence from the shadowing task. *Cognition, 109*, 168–173.

Morgan, J. L. (1973). Sentence fragments and the notion "sentence." In B. B. Kachru, R. B. Lees, Y. Malkiel, A. Pietrangeli, & S. Saporta (Eds.), *Issues in linguistics: Papers in honor of Henry and Renée Kahane* (pp. 719–751). Urbana: University of Illinois Press.

Néda, Z., Ravasz, E., Brechet, Y., Vicsek, T., & Barabási, A. L. (2000). The sound of many hands clapping. *Nature, 403*(6772), 849–850.

Neisser, U. (1954). An experimental distinction between perceptual process and verbal response. *Journal of Experimental Psychology, 47*, 399–402.

Newell, A. (1962). Some problems of basic organization in problem-solving programs (Report No. RAND/RM-3283-PR). Santa Monica, CA: RAND Corporation.

Norman, D. A. (1988). *The psychology of everyday things* (Vol. 5). New York: Basic Books.

Norman, D. (2013). *The design of everyday things* (Rev. and Exp. ed.). New York: Basic Books.

Nozari, N., Dell, G. S., & Schwartz, M. F. (2011). Is comprehension necessary for error detection? A conflict-based account of monitoring in speech production. *Cognitive Psychology, 63*, 1–33.

Onojima, T., Kitajo, K., & Mizuhara, H. (2017). Ongoing slow oscillatory phase modulates speech intelligibility in cooperation with motor cortical activity. *PLoS ONE, 12*(8), e0183146.

Park, H., Ince, R. A., Schyns, P. G., Thut, G., & Gross, J. (2015). Frontal top-down signals increase coupling of auditory low-frequency oscillations to continuous speech in human listeners. *Current Biology, 25*, 1649–1653.

Peacocke, C. (2005). Joint attention: Its nature, reflexivity, and relation to common knowledge. In N. Eilan, C. Hoerl, T. McCormack, & J. Roessler (Eds.), *Joint attention: Communication and other minds: Issues in philosophy and psychology* (pp. 298-331). Oxford: Oxford University Press.

Peirce, C. S (1931–1958). *Collected papers of Charles Sanders Peirce* (8 vols., C. Hartshorne, P. Weiss, & A. Burks, Eds.). Cambridge, MA: Harvard University Press.

Pickering, M. J., & Clark, A. (2014). Getting ahead: Forward models and their place in cognitive architecture. *Trends in Cognitive Sciences, 18*, 451–456.

Pickering, M. J., & Ferreira, V. S. (2008). Structural priming: A critical review. *Psychological Bulletin, 134*, 427–459.

Pickering, M. J., & Garrod, S. (2004). Toward a mechanistic psychology of dialogue. *Behavioral and Brain Sciences, 27*, 169–190.

  (2005). Establishing and using routines during dialogue: Implications for psychology and linguistics. In *Twenty-first century psycholinguistics: Four cornerstones* (pp. 85–102). Mahwah, NJ: Erlbaum.

  (2013). An integrated theory of language production and comprehension. *Behavioral and Brain Sciences, 36*, 329–347.

  (2014). Self-, other-, and joint monitoring using forward models. *Frontiers in Human Neuroscience, 8*, 132.

Pinker, S. (2015). *The sense of style: The thinking person's guide to writing in the 21st century*. New York: Penguin Books.

Poeppel, D., & Monahan, P. J. (2011). Feedforward and feedback in speech perception: Revisiting analysis by synthesis. *Language and Cognitive Processes, 26*, 935–951.

Postma, A. (2000). Detection of errors during speech production: A review of speech monitoring models. *Cognition, 77*, 97–132.

Prinz, W. (1997). Perception and action planning. *European Journal of Cognitive Psychology, 9*, 129–154.

Rayner, K., & Duffy, S. A. (1986). Lexical complexity and fixation times in reading: Effects of word frequency, verb complexity, and lexical ambiguity. *Memory & Cognition, 14*(3), 191–201.

Rayner, K., Carlson, M., & Frazier, L. (1983). The interaction of syntax and semantics during sentence processing: Eye movements in the analysis of semantically biased sentences. *Journal of Verbal Learning and Verbal Bsehavior, 22*(3), 358–374.

Reitter, D., & Moore, J. D. (2014). Alignment and task success in spoken dialogue. *Journal of Memory and Language, 76*, 29–46.

Richardson, D. C., & Dale, R. (2005). Looking to understand: The coupling between speakers' and listeners' eye movements and its relationship to discourse comprehension. *Cognitive Science, 29*(6), 1045–1060.

Richardson, D. C., Dale, R., & Kirkham, N. Z. (2007). The art of conversation is coordination. *Psychological Science, 18*(5), 407–413.

Richardson, M. J., Marsh, K. L., Isenhower, R. W., Goodman, J. R., & Schmidt, R. C. (2007). Rocking together: Dynamics of intentional and unintentional interpersonal coordination. *Human Movement Science, 26*(6), 867–891.

Roediger, H. L., III, & Abel, M. (2015). Collective memory: A new arena of cognitive study. *Trends in Cognitive Sciences, 19*, 359–361.

Rosenweig, M. R., & Postman, L. (1957). Intelligibility as a function of frequency of usage. *Journal of Experimental Psychology, 54*, 412–421.

Sacks, H., & Schegloff, E. A. (1979). Two preferences in the organization of reference to persons in conversation and their interaction. In G. Psathas (Ed.), *Everyday language: Studies in ethnomethodology* (pp. 15–21). New York: Irvington.

Sacks, H., Schegloff, E. A., & Jefferson, G. (1974). A simplest systematics for the organization of turn taking for conversation. *Language, 50*(4), 696–735.

Sagi, E., & Diermeier, D. (2017). Language use and coalition formation in multiparty negotiations. *Cognitive Science, 41*, 259–271.

Sahin, N. T., Pinker, S., Cash, S. S., Schomer, D., & Halgren, E. (2009). Sequential processing of lexical, grammatical, and phonological information within Broca's area. *Science, 326*, 445–449.

Samson, D., Apperly, I. A., Braithwaite, J. J., Andrews, B. J., & Bodley Scott, S. E. (2010). Seeing it their way: Evidence for rapid and involuntary computation of what other people see. *Journal of Experimental Psychology: Human Perception and Performance, 36*, 1255–1266.

Samuel, A. G. (1981). Phonemic restoration: Insights from a new methodology. *Journal of Experimental Psychology: General, 110*, 474–494.

Sanford, A. J., & Garrod, S. (1981). *Understanding written language: Explorations in comprehension beyond the sentence.* Hoboken, NJ: John Wiley.

Schank, R. C., & Abelson, R. (1977). *Scripts, goals, plans, and understanding.* Mahwah, NJ: Erlbaum.

Schegloff, E. A. (1968). Sequencing in conversational openings. *American Anthropologist, 70*, 1075–1095.

  (2000). Overlapping talk and the organization of turn-taking for conversation. *Language in Society, 29*(1), 1–63.

Schegloff, E. A., Jefferson, G., & Sacks, H. (1977). The preference for self-correction in the organization of repair in conversation. *Language, 53*, 361–382.

Schegloff, E. A., & Sacks, H. (1973). Opening up closings. *Semiotica, 8*, 289–327.

Schelling, T. C. (1960). *The strategy of conflict.* Cambridge, MA: Harvard University Press.

Schiffer, S. R. (1972). *Meaning.* Oxford: Clarendon Press.

Schober, M. F., & Brennan, S. E. (2003). Processes of interactive spoken discourse: The role of the partner. In A. C. Graesser, M. A. Gernsbacher, & S. R. Goldman (Eds.), *Handbook of discourse processes* (pp. 123–164). Mahwah, NJ: Erlbaum.

Schober, M. F., & Clark, H. H. (1989). Understanding by addressees and over-hearers. *Cognitive Psychology, 21*, 211–232.

Schriefers, H., Meyer, A. S., & Levelt, W. J. (1990). Exploring the time course of lexical access in language production: Picture-word interference studies. *Journal of Memory and Language, 29*, 86–102.

Schultz, B. G., O'Brien, I., Phillips, N., McFarland, D. H., Titone, D., & Palmer, C. (2016). Speech rates converge in scripted turn-taking conversations. *Applied Psycholinguistics, 37*(5), 1201–1220.

Schweikard, D. P., & Schmid, H. B. (2013). Collective intentionality. In *Stanford encyclopedia of philosophy.* https://plato.stanford.edu/.

Searle, J. R. (1979). Intentionality and the use of language. In A. Margalit (Ed.), *Meaning and use* (pp. 181–197). Dordrecht: Springer.

Searle, J. (1990). Collective intentions and actions. In P. Cohen, J. Morgan, & M.E. Pollack (Eds.), *Intentions in communication*. Cambridge, MA: Bradford Books/ MIT Press.

Sebanz, N., Bekkering, H., & Knoblich, G. (2006). Joint action: Bodies and minds moving together. *Trends in Cognitive Sciences*, 10(2), 70–76.

Seth, V. (1994). *A suitable boy*. New York: Penguin Books.

Shatz, M. (1978). Children's comprehension of their mothers' question-directives. *Journal of Child Language*, 5, 39–46.

Simmons, R., Smith, T., Bernardine Dias, M., Goldberg, D., Hershberger, D., Stentz, A., & Zlot, R. (2002). A layered architecture for coordination of mobile robots. In *Multi-robot systems: From swarms to intelligent automata* (pp. 103–112). Dordrecht: Springer.

Skewes, J. C., Skewes, L., Michael, J., & Konvalinka, I. (2015). Synchronised and complementary coordination mechanisms in an asymmetric joint aiming task. *Experimental Brain Research*, 233, 551–565.

Spreng, R. N., Madore, K. P., & Schacter, D. L. (2018). Better imagined: Neural correlates of the episodic simulation boost to prospective memory performance. *Neuropsychologia*, 113, 22–28.

Stalnaker, R. (1978). Assertion. In P. Cole (Ed.), *Syntax and semantics 9: Pragmatics* (pp. 315–332). New York: Academic Press.

Stivers, T., Enfield, N. J., Brown, P., Englert, C., Hayashi, M., Heinemann, T., . . . Levinson, S. C. (2009). Universals and cultural variation in turn-taking in conversation. *Proceedings of the National Academy of Sciences*, 106, 10587–10592.

Strijkers, K., & Costa, A. (2016). The cortical dynamics of speaking: Present shortcomings and future avenues. *Language, Cognition, and Neuroscience*, 31(4), 484–503.

Strogatz, S. (2002). *Synch: The Emerging Science of Spontaneous Order*. New York: Penguin Books.

Swaab, R. I., Maddux, W. W., & Sinaceur, M. (2011). Early words that work: When and how virtual linguistic mimicry facilitates negotiation outcomes. *Journal of Experimental Social Psychology*, 47, 616–621.

Tanenhaus, M. K., Spivey-Knowlton, M. J., Eberhard, K. M., & Sedivy, J. E. (1995). Integration of visual and linguistic information in spoken language comprehension. *Science*, 268, 632–634.

Tannen, D. (1989). *Talking voices: Repetition, dialogue, and imagery in conversational discourse*. Cambridge, UK: Cambridge University Press.

Taylor, H. A., & Tversky, B. (1996). Perspective in spatial descriptions. *Journal of Memory and Language*, 35, 371–391.

Tomasello, M. (2008). *Origins of human communication*. Cambridge, MA: MIT Press.

Tourville, J. A., & Guenther, F. H. (2011). The DIVA model: A neural theory of speech acquisition and production. *Language and Cognitive Processes*, 26, 952–981.

Traxler, M. J. (2011). *Introduction to psycholinguistics: Understanding language science*. Hoboken, NJ: John Wiley.

Tulving, E. (1983). *Elements of episodic memory*. Oxford: Oxford University Press.

Tuomela, R., & Miller, K. (1988). We-intentions. *Philosophical Studies*, 53, 367–389.

Turnbull, W. (2003). *Language in action: Psychological models of conversation*. New York: Psychology Press.

Van Dijk, T. A., Kintsch, W., & Van Dijk, T. A. (1983). *Strategies of discourse comprehension*. New York: Academic Press.

Van Wassenhove, V., Grant, K. W., & Poeppel, D. (2005). Visual speech speeds up the neural processing of auditory speech. *Proceedings of the National Academy of Sciences, 102*, 1181–1186.

Von Helmholtz, H. (1962). Handbuch der physiologischen Optik (Vol. 1). In J. P. C. Southall (Ed.), *Helmoholtz's treatise on physiological optics*. New York: Dover. (Original work published 1867)

Ward, A., & Litman, D. (2007). Automatically measuring lexical and acoustic/prosodic convergence in tutorial dialog corpora. In *Proceedings of the SLaTE Workshop on Speech and Language Technology in Education, 2007*.

Wilson, M. (2002). Six views of embodied cognition. *Psychonomic Bulletin & Review, 9*, 625–636.

Wilson, M., & Knoblich, G. (2005). The case for motor involvement in perceiving conspecifics. *Psychological Bulletin, 131*(3), 460–473.

Winograd, T. (1987). A language/action perspective on the design of cooperative work. *Human-Computer Interaction, 3*(1), 3–30.

Wittgenstein, L. (1958). *Philosophical investigations* (Vol. 3). Irvine, CA: Macmillan. (Original work published 1953)

Wolpert, D. M. (1997). Computational approaches to motor control. *Trends in Cognitive Sciences, 1*, 209–216.

Wolpert, D. M., Doya, K., & Kawato, M. (2003). A unifying computational framework for motor control and social interaction. *Philosophical Transactions of the Royal Society of London, Series B, 358*, 593–602.

Wolpert, D. M., Diedrichsen, J., & Flanagan, J. R. (2011). Principles of sensorimotor learning. *Nature Reviews Neuroscience, 12*(12), 739–751.

Yngve, V. (1970). *On getting a word in edgewise*. Papers from the sixth regional meeting of the Chicago Linguistic Society (pp. 567–578). Chicago, IL: Chicago.

Yuille, A., & Kersten, D. (2006). Vision as Bayesian inference: Analysis by synthesis? *Trends in Cognitive Sciences*, 10(7), 301–308.

Zion Golumbic, E., Ding, N., Bickel, S., Lakatos, P., Schevon, C.E., McKahn, G., Mehta, A., Poeppel, D. Schroeder, S. (2013). Mechanisms underlying selective neuronal tracking of attended speech at a cocktail party. *Neuron, 77(5)*, 980–91.

Zwaan, R. A., & Radvansky, G. A. (1998). Situation models in language comprehension and memory. *Psychological Bulletin, 123*, 162–185.

Index

For EU product safety concerns, contact us at Calle de José Abascal, 56–1°, 28003 Madrid, Spain or eugpsr@cambridge.org.